Understanding Street Culture

Poverty, Crime, Youth and Cool

Jonathan Ilan

macmillan
education palgrave

First published 2015 by
PALGRAVE

Palgrave in the UK is an imprint of Macmillan Publishers Limited, registered in England, company number 785998, of 4 Crinan Street, London N1 9XW.

Palgrave Macmillan in the US is a division of St Martin's Press LLC, 175 Fifth Avenue, New York, NY 10010.

Palgrave is a global imprint of the above companies and is represented throughout the world.

Palgrave® and Macmillan® are registered trademarks in the United States, the United Kingdom, Europe and other countries.

ISBN 978–1–137–02859–4 hardback
ISBN 978–1–137–02858–7 paperback

This book is printed on paper suitable for recycling and made from fully managed and sustained forest sources. Logging, pulping and manufacturing processes are expected to conform to the environmental regulations of the country of origin.

A catalogue record for this book is available from the British Library.

A catalog record for this book is available from the Library of Congress.

Understanding Street C

Contents

Figures and Boxes

Figures

Boxes

Acknowledgements

This book has been several years in the making. Many of the ideas expressed here had been floating around in my head for the best part of a decade's worth of research, teaching and other scholarly activities. Over this time, I have built a number of significant debts of gratitude to a range of people whose contributions to the writing of this book, or to the thoughts expressed therein, have been invaluable. All errors, omissions etc., of course, remain my own.

Firstly, I would like to thank all of those people who facilitated and supported my PhD research into youth crime, justice and inner-city life in Dublin. This includes the residents of the place I call 'Northstreet', and the young people I call 'The Crew', as well as all the community workers and police officers who participated. I was very fortunate to have the sterling advice and support of Karen Lysaght and Dick Hobbs, whose interventions served to steer me onto the career path I have today. Without engaging firsthand with the realities of street culture and its control, I would never have developed the insight required to write this book.

Secondly, I was very lucky to move from my PhD into intellectually rewarding research led by Colin Scott and Simon Halliday. I learnt a lot from my experience of working with them, and the lessons they taught me, whether explicitly or by example, have served me well since then. Similarly, I'm grateful for the support and interest Ian O'Donnell has shown in my work over the years. I owe a collective debt of gratitude to all of my colleagues at the School of Social Policy, Sociology and Social Research at the University of Kent. By providing an intellectual environment that is challenging yet supportive, curious and open-minded, and critical and engaging, they contributed vastly to the academic position from which this book has been written.

Specifically relating to this book itself, I want to thank all of my colleagues at Kent and beyond who read various chapters and shared their thoughts with me: Kate O'Brien, Ali Fraser, Sveinung Sandberg, Tara Young and Jennifer Fleetwood; Keith Hayward and Chris Shilling for their ever valued advice and support; Vince Miller and Caroline Chatwin for good humouredly putting up with my various complaints about the travails of writing; Phil Carney and

Roger Matthews for always having points to debate. The participants at the Criminology Research Seminar at Sheffield provided great points to consider as well as encouragement at a late phase in the writing, in particular Cormac Behan, Stephen Farrall and Maggie Wykes. I owe a debt to Killian 'Kube' Walsh who provided one of the wonderful photographs that you see in the book and also some sage thoughts.

I was extremely privileged to work with Simon Wheatley who provided a number of stunning photographs that adorn these pages. His approach to photography, to my mind, is inherently ethnographic. His work is both sociological and artistic in the manner in which it chronicles the dissonant experiences of street life and culture.

There are a number of people who have contributed to my appreciation, knowledge and understanding of street expressive practices. Not just the two artists mentioned above, but the AQ and HDD DJing crews that I've worked with over the years who gave me the space to play and learn about a range of different street music genres. Eddie Sheehy's recommendations on music to listen to and films to watch have had a profound impact on the development of my cultural palate as has David Wall's take on visual culture.

Staff past and present at Palgrave Macmillan have been hugely helpful in the completion of this project. In particular, Anna Reeve who initially 'green-lighted' the book and Lloyd Langman and Nicola Cattini who took up the baton of support. Rajeswari Balasubramanian and Partha Goutom at Integra Software Services were extremely helpful in assisting with production. I'm also grateful to the various anonymous reviewers whose thoughts further shaped the finished product. Thanks to all at Maison D'etre where countless pages of this book were written.

Last but not least, I owe a huge debt to my family and friends, too numerous to mention. My mum Helen as well as Tom, my father Yossi and sister Natalie have provided invaluable support and affection. Priya and Thomas merit thanks for their interest, counsel and sanctuary. A special mention is reserved for Trisha whose patience, love, belief in me, passion and editing skills were a constant source of succour and inspiration.

CHAPTER 1

Introduction

London, 2010: three young black men congregated by a low wall have been approached by two police officers. Whilst one officer surveys the men from a step back, her hands tucked into the back of her belt, her colleague is attempting to engage the foremost man who is standing beside a bicycle. There is a university nearby and students mean bikes, perhaps the officers suspect it is stolen. This young man is dressed in a grey Nike tracksuit which tapers in at the ankles, setting off his 'fresh' Nike Air trainers. More noteworthy are his eyes, studiously avoiding the gaze of the apprehending officer and scanning some distant horizon as if searching for people he knows. His face shows an expression of detached amusement. His mouth, which is curled disdainfully at the corners, moves to give monosyllabic answers in a manner that is simultaneously bored and mocking. His two friends and the questioning officer's colleagues have all retreated into themselves, saying and doing little. The young man with the bicycle is performing, not just for those gathered with him, but for anyone else who might see him. The message is clear, he is not engaging with the police and is remaining as defiant as is sensible. He is simultaneously demonstrating his disdain for the authority the police represent and his position as someone who knows how to handle himself on the street.

Casually observed, this brief moment of interaction struck me as having much in common with many others that I had witnessed, both as a researcher of crime and justice in Dublin, Ireland, and as an avid consumer of crime media. Although occurring in London, such performances can be observed on streets and screens throughout the world. From the Favelas of Brazil to scenes from HBO's acclaimed realist drama *The Wire*, the sight of young, poor, urban men negotiating the hostility of police forces and indeed that of their peer groups is a readily identifiable trope. Many questions are raised by this: why the similarities between spaces that are distant from each other spatially, socio-economically and indeed representationally (there are obviously huge differences between 'real' instances of crime and justice and their mediated representations)?

The motivation to write this book emerged from such questions and the idea that such brief moments can teach us much about how inclusion and exclusion are produced and reproduced in everyday life (see Ferrell et al., 2008). It is through events like this, and their underpinning socio-economic dynamics, that young, disadvantaged urban males become criminal and/or criminalized, whilst at the same time providing a template for 'cool' that is ceaselessly harnessed by the global cultural industries.

Underpinning the above event are issues of racial profiling and 'stop and search' powers which disproportionately target young, black men and the underprivileged (Tyler and Wakslak, 2004; Bowling and Phillips, 2003). The vignette similarly raises questions around street crime that, both police statistics and the popular imaginary suggest, is overwhelmingly associated with the urban poor. What is equally important, although all too often left out of consideration, are issues of culture: the ways in which meanings are created and assigned, because it is through such processes that the social structure is lived and produced. Issues of crime, criminalization and cool are inherently cultural: they stem from the ways in which we see the world and act accordingly. These actions beget reactions which themselves impact on the way we see the world. And the spiral continues. Those living within the most socio-economically disadvantaged urban spaces globally can possess world views that prompt particular ways of knowing, being and acting. For those people living in more financially and socially included positions, these ways of being and acting may generate fear and a sense of threat.

This book is centrally concerned with such matters, exploring and developing the concept of 'street culture': the values, dispositions, practices and styles associated with particular sections of disadvantaged urban populations. It seeks to locate this 'street culture' within its social and economic contexts: the globalized world of capital and information flows referred to by some social theorists as 'late' or 'high' modernity (see e.g. Young, 1999; Beck, 1992; Giddens, 1991; Bauman, 2000). Above all, the book is concerned with tracing the intricate ways in which street culture is intertwined with processes of social exclusion and inclusion. Global inequalities in wealth and opportunity profoundly impact on inner-city life throughout the world. Whilst economic, material and existential securities ebb, the mediascape distracts from current predicaments by dangling the trappings of conspicuous consumption tantalizingly close to those who cannot hope to afford them. This is a world where welfarism is in decline, where the state no longer hopes to embrace and include all its citizens and more. It is an era of increased social exclusion, where millions are suspended in a position of 'malign neglect' (see Tonry, 1996) and criminalized where they seek to attain their own version of inclusion.

Street culture is a product of social, economic and cultural exclusion, and yet it is a process of attempting to remain viable, thriving and included within a specific street milieu. More complicated still, as I will argue, is the symbolic power of street culture, which is often understood as authentic, defiant and vital, in other words 'cool'. Thus whilst the urban poor are materially and practically excluded, much of their style is simultaneously admired and emulated by sections of the social mainstream. This becomes a symbolic inclusion which is most often a very poor consolation prize, but on rare occasions offers some exceptional individuals the ability to attain a more concrete sense of inclusion through the cultural industries.

In the opening vignette, one can observe how the young man being questioned is keen to demonstrate that he is more concerned about appearing to be non-cooperative with the police than the consequences that may stem from being viewed as breaking the law. Whether or not he is involved in bike theft is moot, the issue is that he feels he must indicate that he is au fait or at the very least tolerant of such behaviour. He must indicate that he is worthy of respect as a potential street entrepreneur, capable of generating income in a manner that does not compromise his autonomy as a tough, rugged male. Part of this performance is his overt rejection of the police whom he may well distrust and view as hostile, but certainly must publicly regard as such. Any failure to do so may mark him as less worthy of respect and deference within a violent street world in which rates of interpersonal violence and predatory theft are high, and the recourse to the state as protector of property or person is taboo.

Exclusion from the social and economic mainstream necessitates for some the adoption of particular values, concerns and practices, which facilitate survival and a culturally mediated notion of success. For some, the need to perform to strong street cultural standards is constant, for others it is temporarily required to negotiate a journey through a 'tough' part of the city, whilst many more simply adopt street styles and practices as a consumer choice or as a prosthetic element of their cultural practice in their quest to narrate themselves distinctively (see Lury, 1998). The young man in the vignette is dressed in a particular way, adopting a particular posture – all of which contribute to his embodiment of a 'street style' that has no doubt been read by the police officers as a possible indication of involvement with criminality (see Ferrell, 2004). Of course, the assignment of these meanings is highly problematic: a majority of disadvantaged, urban, males have little or no involvement in street crime, and indeed, street styles have been popularized and mass marketed by the youth cultural industries and are not necessarily a clear indication of socio-economic status.

Understanding street culture, I will argue, can illuminate many of contemporary society's issues, problems and trends. With regard to crime, street cultural logics unfold in a range of behaviours from theft and violence, to drug trading and rioting. Moreover, fear of 'the street' (and disadvantaged populations generally) provides a powerful underpinning to processes of criminalization. Questions will be raised around the ways in which vast swathes of the global population are expected to materially support themselves and those dependant on them, against the extent to which 'official', 'recognized' and/or 'legitimate' means of subsistence are available to do so. Engaging with these phenomena provides a means of observing the operation of class, poverty, prejudice, power and exploitation in a world that is arguably more brutal and uncertain than liberal and progressive.

Beyond the 'instrumentality' (practical, utilitarian concerns) of street criminality, the book places an emphasis on understanding street culture's 'expressivity' (emotional, existential and aesthetic concerns). Beyond material subsistence, this provides a paradigm for the realization of a broader set of experiences: dignity, creativity, pleasure to name but a few. The street's art, music, style, sport and dance have come to be widely influential in the mainstream. Thus, the ubiquitous street dance movies, suburban skate parks and appearances by rappers and dancehall artists in pop records belong to another form of cultural exploitation, albeit far less deleterious to the urban poor. As will become clear, across decades and continents, researchers have uncovered similar outlooks, values and attitudes associated with urban socioeconomic marginalization. The aim of this book is to trace how and why this is, weaving together a theoretical frame to understand street culture's significance in contemporary, global terms.

Why study street culture?

The book does this by focusing on some of street culture's most visible manifestations in the realms of criminal lifestyles and urban cool. Despite the term's common, popular use and research identifying street cultures operating in such diverse locations, which include the USA (Anderson, 1999; Bourgois, 1995/2003), UK (Gunter, 2008; Hallsworth and Silverstone, 2009), Ireland (Ilan, 2013), Norway (Sandberg and Pedersen, 2009), Russia (Stephenson, 2001), Brazil (Goldstein, 2003), Jamaica (Gunst, 2003; Stolzoff, 2000), Australia (White and Mason, 2006) and Africa (Institut français de recherche en Afrique, 1997), this is the first book to explore the topic in a more global, conceptual manner. Exploring the links between urban expressivity, urban poverty, crime and criminalization seems to be more of a minority activity than once it was. Drawing such connections is useful where forms of cultural expression (e.g. graffiti, rap and dancehall music) are censured, censored or criminalized and whilst these forms of expression may form part of the everyday life of those individuals who are involved in more serious criminality. Moreover, where street cultural tropes appear so frequently within popular culture and the political imaginary, it becomes germane both to ask why and to analyse the ways in which this occurs.

Some of the issues considered by this book have traditionally been spread between various disciplines: criminology, sociology, anthropology, youth studies, urban studies, human geography, subcultural studies, hip-hop studies and others. And by no means meant as a last word on street culture, this book seeks to provide a single space from which to continue these debates; to set out and theorize what we know; and to raise questions that will be useful as part of future research agendas.

Making sense of street culture

'Culture' is a notoriously difficult word to use accurately. This book thus relies on Raymond Williams' (1986: 87–93) often cited three-part definition, recognizing that the word refers to: the artefacts that humans produce (as various kinds of media, styles and modes of expressivity); the way in which humans make sense of the world and live their lives (through the development of norms, values, definitions, rituals, etc.); and the processes by which things come to be (how phenomena are cultivated). Recognizing that culture is dynamic, mutable and shifting, rather than static, it might nevertheless be argued that there is something fundamental about the experience of social exclusion, however differently the cultures it spawns might manifest. It is important to realize therefore that there are both distinctive street cultures at the local and regional levels and a more universal street culture that exists at the level of ideas and concepts. Debates in social theory have considered precisely this tension between the specific and the general. Much as economic circumstances might change, however, Paul Willis argues that 'the working class *is* the bottom half of... [the] gradient no matter how its atoms move' (1977: 129, emphasis in original). Notions of relativity apply to exclusion and thus whilst the urban poor in the developed world do not suffer many of the same material deprivations as their counterparts in the developing world, they arguably have some commonality in their experiences of marginality. For Charlesworth:

> Styles of being constitute distinct social groups at the deepest level of being. Class is one of those critical mediations of being, and this [his] book tries to show why, across the world, a Pakistani farmer of the Mirpur valley shares

an attitude to perception, experience, persons, objects and belief with a working class person in Rotherham [England] (2000: 17).

In other words, whilst the particular characteristics of being socially, economically and culturally excluded vary hugely over time and between places, states and regions, there is something ultimately similar around the experience of *being* excluded. It is this experience, this state of being, that might be said to be fundamental to street culture. Thus within this book where a variety of terms and phrases are used to describe the population groups associated with it – for example, 'the urban poor', 'disadvantaged city residents', etc. – it is recognized that their experiences will be similar on one level, whilst distinct on another. The goal of this book, therefore, is to identify common orientations and principles as opposed to universal rules.

The diversity of lived experience is a key feature of much of the source material for this book, which consists, in many cases, of detailed ethnographic research conducted by those who have immersed themselves in the communities they study. From 1920s Chicago to near-contemporary Brazil, this approach to producing knowledge has independently identified the common principles discussed later in the chapter. Drawing on the most contemporary perspectives, including those from outside the Anglo-American world, allows this book to offer a more fulsome and comprehensive account of street culture than has previously been attempted. Moreover, the book draws liberally upon media sources which are either forms of street cultural expressivity themselves or treatments of street cultural themes. The breadth of manifestations of street culture, either as a means of ordering life, governing particular actions or interactions, or indeed as an influence on media practice necessitates an expansive and flexible means of thinking about it: a street cultural spectrum.

The remainder of this chapter thus establishes and elaborates on a number of issues that are crucial to this idea. Firstly, I set out what is meant by street culture and how it will be used to understand the various phenomena discussed in this book. I set out what might be termed 'street cultural concerns' which make clear how socio-economic forces manifest in the everyday beliefs, values and behaviours of certain sections of the urban poor. Street culture shares particular principles, styles and aesthetics across continents (Figure 1.1). I will set out the discourses that relate to 'cool' and demonstrate how these relate strongly to the central concerns of street culture. In doing all this, I make the case for understanding street culture in a manner that recognizes its paradoxes: how it is distant and yet proximate to 'mainstream' values, simultaneously feared and valued, avoided and sought out. I furthermore argue that it is important to locate this understanding within a wider consideration of socio-economic principles: globalization,

Figure 1.1 A hip-hop show in Paris, from a visual standpoint alone, could be anywhere in the world. Photo by Simon Wheately

consumerism, neoliberalism, individualization, urbanization, flux and media saturation.

Defining street culture

In the next chapter, approximately 150 years of scholarship, history and public imagination around the lifestyles of the urban poor are considered. It is through building on this legacy that the following more contemporary ideas derive.

Philippe Bourgois, studying the lives of the East Harlem crack dealers, defined street culture as 'a complex and conflictual web of beliefs, symbols, modes of interaction, values and ideologies that have emerged in the opposition to exclusion from mainstream society' (1995/2003: 8). Street culture, he maintains, is a means of realizing self-worth and dignity, facilitating surviving (and at times even thriving) for the multiply-disadvantaged in post-industrial society. Where the urban poor cannot realistically expect much more than subsistence drudgery and humiliating deference, no matter their commitment to work within the mainstream economy, the illicit economy becomes more significant. Moreover, where employment exists primarily within a service sector which values deference, 'polish' and exaggerated manners, Bourgois' participants who had inherited postures, accents and attitudes from a rural Puerto Rican heritage were disadvantaged. By deploying their inherited notions of rugged masculinity – strength, toughness and autonomy – however, they could combine the leisure of street life with the earnings of the drug trade. Here they were advantaged, although the extent to which their culture might be labelled as 'oppositional' merits further discussion later.

Notions of toughness, independence and dignity emerge particularly strongly in a second study that has been fundamental in establishing street culture as a topic of contemporary debate. Elijah Anderson's *Code of the Street* (1999), in extensive ethnographic detail, sets out the 'rules' and norms which underpin violence in a disadvantaged area of Philadelphia. According to this study, 'respect' is a measure of one's standing in the street. It is most frequently earned through the embodiment of a violent potential and/or reputation. Where state apparatuses such as the police are experienced as discriminatory and oppressive, communities cohere around the notion that they are to be viewed as hostile. In such circumstances, interpersonal violence becomes a key means of settling disputes and generating power. Where communities experience exclusion from the state (and indeed where there is no effective state in the first place), parallel economies, welfare and justice systems can emerge as street cultural groups become institutionalized (see Hagedorn, 2008).

Street cultural norms and deference to members of such powerful (often armed) groups can become a form of 'governance from below' (see Lea and Stenson, 2007). For Anderson, street culture is a 'people's culture' (1999: 10), the continuance of pre-modern modes of social configuration and comportment. It can thus be understood as stemming from the exclusion (or ejection) of large swathes of the world's population to varying extents from the modernist project: the formal economy, human rights, dignities and basic protections, technological progress and membership of a stable, functional community. These exclusions, of course, vary widely between the global north and south and indeed within them. Furthermore, individuals are likely to utilize their agency to respond to exclusion in a range of different ways. These are important *caveats* that should be born in mind when attempting to provide a comprehensive and operationalizable definition of street culture in the contemporary world.

'Street culture' is the values, dispositions, practices and styles associated with particular sections of disadvantaged populations. These involve practically negotiating (relative or absolute) material deprivation as well as asserting alternative and/or parallel systems of normativity and expressivity in the face of cultural subordination. The term can be used to refer to a wide variety of practices that are linked to everyday life amongst the urban poor, but it is most vividly expressed by and identified with young men (street femininity will be discussed in detail in Chapter 3). Street cultures have specific historic roots and yet share a number of common characteristics born out of the more ubiquitous effects of exclusion (it is possible thus to speak about both 'street culture' and 'street cultures'). A fusion of tradition and the globalized consumerism which has more than partially displaced it, street culture is a residualized variant of rugged working-class culture in an era of globalized neoliberal economics and political consensus (these concepts are examined in greater detail in Chapter 7). Street culture is the folk culture of the late 20th and early 21st centuries.

Much like mainstream culture, street culture is rife with complexities, contradictions and dissonances. For example, both spirituality and violence can be simultaneously valued. Indeed, street life and cultures are replete with humour, laughter, playfulness, friendships, joys, irreverence, community and collective effervescence, together with misery, oppression, deprivation, competition, conflict, violence, addiction, illness, worry, stress and pain. The extent to which street cultures represent alternatives to, or simply marginalized variants of, mainstream cultures remains open to debate. Nevertheless, street culture often entails a level of suspicion of, and antipathy to, formal mainstream social institutions, particularly where they are associated with coercive practices. It can thus involve a certain level of defiance (see Chapter 8), although care should be taken to avoid romanticizing ways of life which often involve various degrees of exploitation experienced, inflicted or both.

The use of 'street' as the defining prefix is not simply because it is less potentially derogatory than other options, but because the street as a physical and symbolic space is central to understanding this way of life. As will be discussed later, often the small living spaces available to the urban poor mean that surrounding public spaces become central to their social life. Unlike parks, community halls, etc. which may or may not exist in the disadvantaged neighbourhood, streets (paved or otherwise) always will. Moreover, the use of the street prefix conjures notions of informality: as in the 'street food' that may be enjoyed without the rituals and rules of dining. And this informality is significant: street ethnographers are almost always struck by the vibrancy, noise, warmth, closeness and visceral qualities of street life, whilst even the earliest urban sociologists noted that personal relationships are considerably more significant than formal rules in the lifeworlds of the disadvantaged.

Street culture should not be conflated with crime and violence, which may or may not be practised by those who adhere to some level of street cultural orientation. Whilst a strong dedication to street culture can suggest a particular motivation towards committing crime, or at least a tolerance and understanding for those who do participate, the nexus of socio-economic status, cultural orientation and individual behaviour is complex to the extent that it defies simplistic causal explanations. Many of the studies considered in this book reflect the degree to which those who offend often 'drift' between legitimate, semi-legitimate and illegitimate forms of income generation and leisure (Matza, 1964; Bourgois, 1995/2003). Similarly, fragments of street culture may be adopted and exhibited by those who wish to avoid predation in violent areas and coexist with street cultural populations (Anderson, 1999). Moreover, there are those who draw on street culture merely as a symbolizer of 'cool'.

Drawing on the work of Gunter (2008) and Daniel (2012), it is therefore proposed that street culture is best understood in terms of existing as a continuum, spectrum or scale, along which there are a number of degrees of adherence and practice. At the weaker points on the scale, adherents might simply 'hang around' in street spaces and engage in some of the culture's more expressive practices. At the stronger points on the spectrum, individuals might for example use street cultural modes of violence to generate their income. There are a number of loose typologies of relationships that individuals might have to street culture: active or passive adherents either strongly or weakly embedded; those who coexist with street culture in their everyday life whilst identifying themselves against it; those who embody street cultural styles and aesthetics but attempt to eschew the rough behaviours associated with it; those who actively seek to adopt street cultural style as a decontextualized consumer or leisure choice; and those who consume street cultural styles unreflexively.

As is discussed further in Chapter 3, a range of factors, from regional and national context to socio-economic status and age, as well as individual agency, tend to influence both the characteristics and strength of prevailing street cultures at the local level as well as the individual's relationship to it. Furthermore, and as explored further in Chapter 5, it is possible for general youth cultures to be perceived inaccurately as street cultures, as there can be a tendency for young people to transgress and seek autonomy in public spaces, regardless of the styles they choose to adopt. Perhaps this contributes to the wider social anxieties that exist around the conduct of young people (Figure 1.2).

Street culture's existence as an identifiable phenomenon is predicated on the manner in which it is perceived and interpreted by those who hold and exercise power and often associate it with deviance and inferiority. Such meanings are bound up with its associations to crime and criminalization. Elements of street culture, however, have also been harnessed by the cultural industries to market a range of youth cultural products; a most obvious but certainly not sole example being the 'gangsta' tropes popularized by rap music (see Ferrell et al., 2008; Quinn, 2005; Ilan, 2012). As will be demonstrated, this is because street culture is often linked to a variety of vibrant stylistic practices and considered to be vital, authentic, the epitome of 'cool' and saturated with

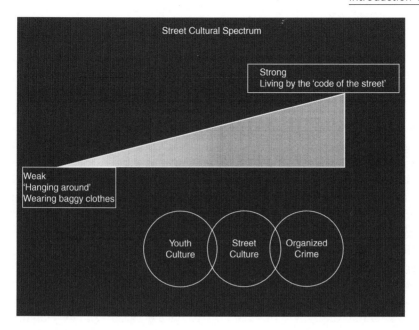

Figure 1.2   The street cultural spectrum

transgressive, 'carnivalesque' pleasures (Presdee, 2000). The commodification of street culture, however, operates in a curious manner, where images of its strongest manifestation are sold as entertainment and accessories to those who sit at the weakest end of its spectrum.

Street culture must be understood as being intertwined with a range of cultural scripts where disadvantaged urban populations produce, consume and repurpose a range of tropes that circulate throughout the popular imaginary (see Box 1.1). Elements and images of it have become separated from their roots in urban poverty and are available to be applied and utilized in a range of different contexts and identities (Harvey, 2005: 166). Teenagers in Europe, for example, can imagine themselves as a marauding American street criminal from the comfort of their homes whilst playing the video game Grand Theft Auto: San Andreas (released by Rockstar Games in 2004). Although those involved in 'organized crime' may draw on the logics of street culture in ordering their world (see e.g. Adler and Adler, 1993; Hobbs, 2013), this must be seen as a somewhat distinct phenomenon.

Whilst street culture is presently most associated with cities in the developed world, there is a need to understand it within a global context. Due to urbanization in the developing world, slum populations are growing far quicker than any other demographic group globally. This growth and the deplorable conditions of poverty and marginality in which so many live are catalogued by Mike Davis in *Planet of Slums* (2006). The need to address standards of living in the 'megaslums' growing in cities such as Lagos, Sao Paolo/Rio de Jainero and Mumbai is one of the most pressing challenges facing 21st-century humanity. Whilst notions of street culture represent a western form of knowledge, not necessarily immediately transposable to the global south (see Connell, 2007), the understandings that these offer may nevertheless provide a point of departure from which to discuss life in areas significantly less studied than the slums of the global north.

In contemporary times, the ever-present and fast-moving media circulates various images and ideas globally, quickening the adoption, adaptation, appropriation and/or rejection of various normative positions and stylistic practices. There are facets of street culture that can be observed to exist globally and others which are particular local variants. There is a large literature, for example, on the topic of street children in the developing world, young people who often must fend for themselves in some of the most impoverished spaces on the planet (Lalor, 1999). Indeed, whilst some of this literature can inform an understanding of contemporary street culture, other sections speak more specifically about matters of service provision and development. Analysing street culture globally can nevertheless illuminate fault lines of inclusion and highlight the universally damaging consequences of social exclusion.

Box 1.1 The flow of street tropes

Tropes, ideas and images flow amongst and between cultures, and this applies equally to 'the street'. An example of such street imaginary flow exists between Jamaica, the USA and UK. During the late 1960s and early-mid 1970s, Jamaican 'rude boys' or street hustlers/criminals were enamoured with the image of the hardened 'shoot first and ask questions later' attitude displayed by gunslingers and gangsters from popular American movies (Gunst, 2003; Stolzoff, 2000). In pop-cultural terms, this manifested in local 'Deejays' (the precursors of rappers) adopting colourful monikers such as 'Dillinger' and 'John Wayne', whilst the Island's earlier Ska music repeatedly referenced these movie themes. Beyond music, however, Jamaica was developing serious issues of street criminality. The rude boy persona (once praised then subsequently critiqued by Jamaican musicians) wove into itself the will to violence of Hollywood gunmen.

The cool and casual way in which brutality could be dispensed would become an enduring trope which Jamaican hardmen would carry with them when operating abroad. Gunst (2003) characterizes the hyper-violent tactics which distinguished Jamaican 'gangs' from their domestic counterparts and allowed them to maintain successful drug enterprises. In doing so,

Jamaican 'yardies' made a lasting impact in US street culture, much as the music brought by Jamaican immigrants to New York contributed to the birth of rap music and revolutionized street cultural style worldwide. The contemporary rude boy would thus go on to be an influential trope in its own right. Part-fictionalized in the lyricism of some contemporary dancehall, the 'bad man' persona of the non-compromising, gun-ready 'don dadda' would become cultural reference points for young street offenders in the UK (Gunter, 2008).

Street cultural concerns

Walter Miller (1958) offered the notion of 'lower-class culture' as an early attempt to describe the traits and dispositions valued within the urban slum. He argued that the young delinquent men he studied exhibited a rugged response to their exclusion, eschewing the middle-class ideals of intellectualism, careerism, life-planning and deferred gratification, valuing instead a separate seven 'focal concerns'. Whilst his study and language are dated, and his notion of fixed distinct criminogenic dispositions is open to criticism, it is nevertheless useful to consider how these concerns resonate with contemporary street culture.

His notion of *trouble* speaks about the ways in which a street cultural orientation can cause individuals to view unfortunate consequences (from injury to imprisonment) as a product of interactions with others: an assured sense of self can mitigate marginalization. The notion of *fate*, an understandable belief in 'luck', which can be used to (ir)rationalize the unfortunate circumstances experienced by many of the urban poor, can also be identified as a trope in contemporary street culture. Superstition, spirituality and religious rituals continue to have a widespread salience, for example, the benediction over babies observed by Bourgois (1995/2003), the growth of spiritualist churches amongst the Brazilian urban poor (Goldstein, 2003), or the lyrical content of particular rap and dancehall songs (Quinn, 2005; Stolzoff, 2000).

Importantly, Miller identified the centrality of *toughness* to inner-city culture: the reverence of physical strength/prowess as well as less tangible forms of bravery and 'heart'. *Smartness* equally continues to be valued, referring here to mental agility, wit and canniness as opposed to formal education which can be viewed as both irrelevant (when there are low opportunities for social mobility) and effeminate. Indeed, in popular speech it is common to distinguish between 'book learning' and 'street smarts': the art of being 'streetwise'. These values, together with *autonomy*, speak to the significance of rugged masculinities within a street cultural context (see Winlow and Hall, 2009; Mullins, 2006; Messerschmidt, 1993). Embodying the potential for violence

and having the nous to work situations to one's advantage mark individuals as worthy of 'respect'. Finally, the valuing of *excitement* persists where the drudgery of low-status labour and a lack of disposable income to avail of commercial leisure opportunities create a need for the manufacture of thrilling pursuits, at times beyond the law (also see Ferrell et al., 2008; Lyng, 1990, 2005; Fenwick and Hayward, 2000; Katz, 1988). Research has advanced and society has changed considerably since Miller's work, and a more updated and expansive notion of street cultural concerns should include the following:

Survival: From urban labour and social welfare in the developed world to small-scale agriculture in the developing world, late-modernity has upset numerous traditional means of subsistence (see Chapter 7). Life in the global ghetto is increasingly defined either by the struggle for survival against the backdrop of street violence, state/commercial oppression or by the lack of food, water and shelter. Survival informs the street cultural orientation of those who join 'gangs' to mitigate the threat from rival or local armed offenders (see e.g. Pitts, 2008; Decker and Van Winkle, 1996). Such pressures increase in the developing world, where the urban poor may need to navigate between more heavily armed street groups and the impunity of unaccountable and brutal police forces (see e.g. Goldstein, 2003). Those living in 'megaslums' often depend on resourcefulness, improvization and the shadow economy to subsist through squatting, scrounging and a range of labour and entrepreneurialism, legal or otherwise (Davis, 2006). The stress of constantly treading the boundaries between life and death is intense.

The Illicit Economy: Casual labour, undeclared street and market trading, the trade in stolen goods and contraband (from drugs to counterfeit), squatting and the provision of various services to friends and family in part constitute economic survival systems. These allow great swathes of the world's population to subsist and earn outside of formal systems of regulation and taxation (see e.g. Venkatesh, 2008; Bourgois, 1995/2003). These are forms of entrepreneurialism that strongly resonate with hegemonic economic ideals (Hobbs, 1998, 2013); indeed, dominant economic interests can profit from the cheap labour that is often created by these processes. The urban poor may need to draw on a range of legitimate, semi-legitimate and illegitimate sources of income. Even in the USA, the world's largest economy, those families which receive both minimum wage income and welfare can find it extremely difficult to subsist (Newman, 1999). References to 'hustling', 'grinding', 'grafting', 'ducking and diving' and other slang terms that denote the combination of hard work, improvization and determination abound within street cultural lexicons.

Respect: Subsistence alone is a mean existence, and street culture has its own mediated notions of achievement: alternative and/or parallel routes to a sense of dignity. By embodying street cultural acumen, respect can be gained in the eyes of the self and others in the immediate vicinity (Anderson, 1999; Sandberg and Pederson, 2009). 'Respect' is linked to survival, where it can signal that an individual is unsuitable to be preyed upon, or indeed should be treated without guile in any trading. It is generally maintained through projecting a potentially violent persona (whether 'wild' or 'measured'), demonstrating entrepreneurial and interactional acumen, as well as through displays of conspicuous consumption. Levels of respect can create street hierarchies and order the ways in which others are exploited and/or feared (Mullins, 2006). It thus must be constantly guarded through the visible defence of one's person and reputation, by demonstrating one's competence and mastery of street cultural life in various different ways (see Chapter 3).

Antipathy to State Authority: Legacies of negative interactions with the state (frequently through policing, but also through a variety of other agencies viewed as neglectful or hostile) have rendered the street world negatively inclined towards it. State institutions are often approached sceptically and cynically by the urban poor with a notion that 'you can't win' without a strong advocate or resorting to corruption, fraud or manipulation. In the legal and formal regulatory vacuum that this creates, interpersonal knowledge and relationships as well as street cultural dispute resolution mechanisms take on great significance. This tends to be reinforced through a relatively strict taboo against speaking to or cooperating with the forces of law and order (see further in Chapter 8).

Collectivism and Community: Whether defined by common locality or a similar outlook, notions of community have always been important in street life where considerable hardship can be more effectively negotiated collectively. Earlier studies of street culture had noted the importance of personal acquaintance and informal relationships in governing interactions. As will be explored later in the book, however, traditional working-class collectivism has been assaulted by neoliberal and consumerist notions of individualism, rendering ties considerably looser and developing the potential for inter-community/collective conflict (see e.g. Scott, 2004; Hall et al., 2008; Ilan, 2012). Nevertheless, issues of inclusion and exclusion remain very important to street culture at a local level and forms of collective practice remain significant, however challenged they may be by instrumental individualism.

Consumerism and Distinction: Contemporary society is underscored by consumerism in disadvantaged areas as much as on the main street (Hall et al., 2008). The varieties practised may, however, differ particularly where classed notions of taste are deployed as a mechanism of othering the urban poor (see Hayward and Yar, 2006; Bourdieu, 1984). Despite street culture's association with poverty, it strongly values conspicuous consumption and 'looking good': from the era when the urban poor would place great stock on 'Sunday best' clothing and presenting well at important occasions to contemporary concerns in western spaces of poverty with consistently sporting branded clothing and expensive jewellery or 'bling'. The impoverished in developing spaces (such as those that exist on the African continent) have similar consumerist desires, although their routes to sating them are considerably more restricted (Nyamnjoh, 2004: 15).

Hedonism and the Visceral: A sense of fatalism born of exclusion from mainstream economic life, coupled with historical roots within visceral cultures, has ensured that the affirmation of life has become a central concern of street culture. This can manifest in numerous different ways: for example, the dark, defiant humour of the Brazilian Favella (Goldstein, 2003), or the vibrant culture of 'block parties' in deprived New York districts during the 1970s and 1980s (Chang, 2005). Presdee (2000) has argued that 'carnival' (once time- and space-limited peoples' celebrations of life) has become an increasingly significant aspect of everyday life, noting how powerful forces variously co-opt and condemn the search for transgressive pleasures. Street cultures often value bodily pleasures, from intoxication to eroticism. Moreover, the living conditions and traditional manual labour of the urban poor have served to render nature and the body a more conspicuous presence in their everyday lives.

Stallybrass and White (1986) have shown how 'high' culture has been constructed as superior. It is connected to notions of 'rationality', formalism, intellectual labour, aesthetic sophistication and an ability to hold oneself above the viscerality of nature and the body. Such traits are associated with wealth and power and therefore considered worthy. Whereas their opposites (aspects of what has been called 'low culture') are associated with the poor and marginalized and therefore to varying extents are viewed as suspect, deviant and transgressive (see also Jenks, 2003). Body-centred, agrarian and working-class traditions as well as the life-affirmative forms of 'folk' cultural expression are increasingly becoming historical in the late-modern era of mechanization, knowledge economies, labour exploitation, global media flows and ubiquitous consumer culture. The body and rhythms of life, however, remain integral to street cultures which often exist in communities with lower than average life expectancies and with fewer routes to participate in the kinds of self-narration that exist within middle-class lifestyles.

Street cool

Street culture's relationship to pop culture and consumerism is mediated by its embodiment of 'cool', a concept that is regularly drawn upon to market and brand a range of products (see Frank, 1998; Pountain and Robins, 2000).

Cool is a rebellious attitude, an expression of a belief that the mainstream mores of your society have no legitimacy and do not apply to you...Cool was once an attitude fostered by rebels and underdogs...today it is becoming the dominant attitude, even (or perhaps especially) among the rich and privileged...(Pountain and Robins, 2000: 23–24).

Where once 'cool' was expressed through the adoption of traditional working-class styles (blue denims, blues/rock music), it is now increasingly associated with street styles, music, aesthetics and attitudes. Traditionally a mark of mastery, casual competence and control, notions of cool have been popularized through media and leisure cultures. The concept is said to have originated in West Africa, transported to the USA through the slave trade and applied by African-Americans to radiate a sense of pride and control, despite experiences of racism and disadvantage (Thompson, 1973; Majors and Billson, 1992). Since James Dean donned his leather jacket to star in *Rebel Without a Cause*, cool has been commodified, not just as a means of capturing the interest of young people eager to distance themselves from their parents, but as the inspiration for mainstream corporate marketers and adult consumers (see Frank, 1998). The style of various youth subcultures can be appropriated and used to vest products with a transgressive edge, marking them as distinct and desirable when compared to competitors (Hebdige, 1979; Ferrell et al., 2008). Cool can thus be a manifestation of what Thornton (1995) called 'subcultural capital' (the extent to which an individual embodies and knows about particular leisure 'scenes').

Cool's association with defiant orientations, shielding emotions, protecting dignity and holding to knowledge-specific forms of taste and style resonate with the concerns and values of street culture. Moreover, as will become clear in Chapter 6, the urban poor are not just disadvantaged competitors in a more universal quest to achieve cool, but can be active producers and definers of it as the originators of a range of now popular stylistic practices in fashion (from low-slung jeans to baseball caps); urban music; art (hip-hop graffiti underpins the now ubiquitous street art movement); dance (break-dancing began as a form of competition between rival New York gangs – see Chang, 2005) and sport (where inner-city streets have produced both sporting stars and informal variants of official games that have become popular in and of themselves). According to fashion authority, Ted Polhemus, it is the authenticity of street cultural products that appeals to consumers seeking something beyond the perceived artifice of many available pop-cultural goods:

The Street is...the bottom line metaphor for all that is presumed to be real and happening in our world today. In the past, 'Western culture' was most at ease and most recognizable within grand interiors. Today, as high culture has given way to popular culture, it is the litmus test of 'street credibility' that is crucial. If it won't cut it on the corner, forget it . . . There is a fundamental irony in this which shouldn't escape us. These no-hopers have none of those things that our society officially decrees to be important (money, prestige, success, fame) and yet they have a monopoly on what we're actually most in need of – The Real. This is the key to The Street's seductive appeal (1994: 6–7).

Indeed, it is common to speak about 'street cred' (or credibility) in reference to being associated with what is authentic or fashionable with young people. This idea has become so hard-wired into popular culture that advertisers can assume an inherent understanding of it. The billboard in Figure 1.3 thus plays on the notion that those in the car-buying demographic would readily like to be associated with street credibility, ironically or in earnest. It thus uses the model designation of the car it advertises, the 'ST' (a widely recognized abbreviation for 'street' in postal addresses), to maximum effect.

To become a commodity, the image of street culture must be stripped away from its harsh lived realities. This is facilitated by what Jeffries (2011) refers to as 'complex cool', the way in which rappers (themselves purveyors of cool) discuss dissonant and contradictory themes in their lyrics: the pains of poverty and the triumphalism of consumerism, their oppression by the institutions of mainstream society and simultaneous claims to mastery

Figure 1.3 A billboard advertisement for the Ford Fiesta 'ST' references the notion of 'street credibility'

of their milieu. The context of street cultural styles, their deeper significance and connections to the histories and local cultures of their producing communities can be readily jettisoned, whilst two-dimensional simulacra remain (images which become more 'true' than that which they are supposed to represent – see Baudrillard, 1983). Consumers can thus become seduced by the 'carnival' of transgression (Presdee, 2000) that street culture appears to offer, without being required to suffer its privations or understand how and why these stylistic practices came to be.

Crime and other aspects of involvement in street culture have their emotional and existential seductions (Katz, 1988; Ferrell et al., 2008), generating a cool persona can arguably be part of this dynamic. Images derived from street cultural sources, meanwhile, offer the possibility to vicariously exhibit some disembodied elements of cool. The postmodern separation of image or product from context is crucial to street culture's commodifiability.

From criminal lifestyles to urban cool

A fulsome understanding of street culture's origins, functions, seductions and appeals, together with a scaled, spectrum-based model of the concept, provides a means of understanding its bearings on the diverse phenomena of criminal lifestyles and the cultivation of 'cool'. Returning to the notion that inclusion and exclusion are drivers of participation in street culture to varying extents, it becomes furthermore important to provide a broader analysis of socio-economic structures. This is what this book offers. The street cultural spectrum explains how street culture variously manifests: as a driver of criminality and expressivity in contexts of urban poverty, or as practices deployed consciously or unconsciously, either to coexist with street cultural adherents or as a means of signifying 'cool' that can be bought and sold out of context. The spectrum's qualities can be explained through an analysis of neoliberal globalization which has placed particular pressures on the urban poor, stripped away many routes towards meaningful inclusion, bolstered the significance of the consumer culture and contributed to a politics of exclusion and criminalization. Moreover, street culture's presence can be viewed at the level of the 'micro' (i.e. individual decisions, personal motivations and embodied emotions). These abstract arguments are concretized and fleshed out throughout the book.

Chapter 2 focuses on the ways in which street culture has historically been, and is currently understood. By adopting an approximately chronological approach to this, it allows for a concurrent exploration of socio-economic conditions and cultural developments. The chapter continues to discuss a number of key debates that are active within the study of street cultures, criminal lifestyles and urban cool. Ultimately, the chapter establishes how street culture has tended to be understood and in doing so provides a more detailed platform to establish the need for the arguments that this book offers. A more pointed analysis of the role of demographics, specifically class, gender, race and age in the development and practice of street cultures, is offered in Chapter 3. It reflects on the decline of industrial labour in the developed world and the difficulties this has raised for traditional classed and gendered identities. Here too, the role played by racism in shaping the existence of specific street cultures is analysed. The chapter proceeds to consider theoretical positions which explain some of the contradictions within street culture and the role that individual choice, emotionality and agency plays in locating individuals along its spectrum of adoption.

Chapter 4 discusses the role of space and gangs in the understanding of street culture. Whilst it is relatively straightforward to associate street cultures with particular ghettos, slums, townships or barrios, there is a need to consider the complicated ways in which contemporary socio-economic and technological developments have altered spatiality. The need to move beyond what otherwise seems to be 'common sense' understandings is then emphasized by a consideration of 'gang discourse' which has arguably created a very rigid way of understanding street culture, driving assumptions that do not necessarily bear on reality. It is argued that the street cultural approach offered by this book provides a more accurate and flexible means of understanding the 'gang' phenomenon. This is followed by two chapters that are primarily concerned with the book's foci: Chapter 5 considers key aspects of criminal lifestyles: space, economic and violent criminality, whilst Chapter 6 discusses key elements of street stylistic expressivity: art, fashion, music and sports. These two collections of activities – the 'criminal' and the 'stylistic' – cannot be seen as wholly separate. Crime can be expressive, whilst style can be criminal (Ferrell and Ilan, 2013). Understanding the street culture that is so visible and at times problematic requires this manner of broad understanding.

As mentioned, processes of neoliberal globalization have both driven the prevalence and shape of street culture whilst also contributing to the ubiquity of the consumer culture which draws so heavily on its tropes and images. Chapter 7 specifically addresses these issues, providing a detailed and specific examination of the political-economic developments which have linked wage slavery in the developing world to conspicuous consumption in the developed. It furthermore examines the global flows of people, goods, images, desires and ideas which underpin a global variety of street cultures, crime and expressivity, as well as more mainstream desires and aspirations. Finally, Chapter 8 focuses on issues of social control and resistance in a world where the possibilities for transformational politics have largely been sidelined.

Street culture, it will be argued, is not a form of 'resistance', but rather a posture of defiance where it believes, much like the 'mainstream', in the importance of gaining and displaying wealth. Indeed, the 'criminalizing gaze' and 'fear of the street' exhibited by many governing forces is argued to be a key marker of street culture's 'difference' as opposed to any fundamental difference in values.

Finally, it is argued that street culture often interacts with processes of governance to ultimately reproduce and exacerbate exclusion, which in turn feeds back into the underpinnings of street culture. Breaking this cycle will arguably call for something more than the 'business as usual' of standard criminal justice practice. Of course, this book's consideration of street culture must begin somewhere, and thus proceeds to an examination of how the concept came to be developed and the lives of the urban poor understood in the scholarly and popular imaginations.

CHAPTER 2

Understanding Urban Poverty, Culture and Crime

Introduction

The previous chapter's definition and discussion of street culture has only been possible due to decades of academic study on the links between poverty, culture and crime in the main part, and a thinner volume of research into the links between class, lifestyle and cool which began to emerge from the 1960s onwards. This research, arriving alongside the maturation of the social sciences, provided sociological explanations of the factors underlying social problems, which otherwise had too easily been dismissed as the product of defective ethical or personal development. Equally, the expansion of the mass media meant that a wider range of tastes would become catered for, which left increasing space for material that addressed public fascination with life 'on the wrong side of the tracks', and ultimately dovetailed with the growth of a 'youth market' hungry for products which at least approximated a sense of the 'authentic' (see Box 2.1). To ground and contextualize the material that follows in subsequent chapters, it is important to first locate it within the rich scholarly tradition that is described in the next section.

This chapter thus first examines the emergence of the notion of street culture from over 100 years of academic research and popular fascination. This enriches the definition of the concept offered in the previous chapter. It furthermore places it within its historical and socio-economic context and identifies the background to some of the debates which continue to take place amongst contemporary social scientists and public commentators. Ultimately, much of the literature to date has been grounded within its states and times of origin. It remains useful to place these within a wider narrative whereupon the reasons for many of the similarities in findings across time and space become clear. This harmony not only justifies the approach taken by this book but begs questions as to what overarching phenomena explain this.

The chapter proceeds to consider a number of live debates. In taking a position in relation to them, I advance the overall argument of the book: that street culture is best understood through its meaning and significance within lived lives. In this way, it is best conceptualized as a spectrum running from stronger to weaker variants that ultimately provides a similar scheme for understanding the world, but which orders life very differently depending on levels of enculturation within particular contexts. As opposed to viewing street culture as 'pathological' or inherently problematic, its similarities to the values of neoliberal capitalism will be highlighted. The chapter alights on theoretical perspectives that convincingly explain the ways in which individuals respond to their material conditions and levels of socio-cultural inclusion to invoke street culture to varying levels and in varying contexts. The chapter thus engages widely with the question of how the lives of the urban poor have been, and might most usefully be understood, setting a foundation for material that is to follow later in the book.

Studying street culture: Past

The links between urban poverty, crime and culture have intrigued researchers, journalists, novelists and photographers in the developed world since at least the mid-19th century. Although these authors generally did not use the term 'street culture', it can be argued that this is what they were referring to. In England, the pioneering research contained in Friedrich Engel's *The Condition of the Working Class in England* (1891/2009) highlighted the desperate conditions in which so many industrial labourers and their families lived. The journalism of Henry Mayhew and fiction of Charles Dickens both illustrated these conditions and furthermore examined a range of behaviours from the criminal to what now might be referred to as the 'anti-social' (Hobbs, 2001). The pickpocketing gang in Dickens' *Oliver Twist* provided a popular imaginary of an underground world with its own rituals, logics and hierarchy, where the cunning of Fagin and the strength of Bill Sykes afforded them the power to exploit others in their pursuit of illicit profit. At the same time, the developing medium of photography allowed images of the urban poor to be captured with greater dynamism and immediacy (Seabourne, 2011).

Much as the more included were fascinated with the lives of the urban poor, they often felt threatened by their behaviour. This applied particularly to groups of young working-class men who were frequently perceived as participating in waves of 'new' and dramatic forms of street crime (Pearson, 1984). Similarly in US cities such as New York, a plethora of youth street cultural groups existed during these times, which invoked the concern and condemnation of the included (Gilfoyle, 2004).

More academically, substantive analyses of urban poverty and its links to distinctive lifestyles (and at times criminal behaviours) emerged from the Chicago School in and beyond the early 20th century. One of the first 'professional' schools of sociology, the influence of anthropology, journalism and divinities on their work is evidenced by its attentiveness to everyday life and subjectivity as well as concern for their participants' living conditions (see Bulmer, 1984). Classic works by Zorbaugh (1925) and Anderson (1927) highlighted the distinctive social worlds of the 'slum' and 'hobos' respectively, drawing their connections to wider socio-economic dynamics. The Chicago School's early canon also includes Thrasher's pioneering study of 'gangs' (1927), which provided an academic basis for nearly nine decades of continued research on the topic. Such studies were examples of an early ethnographic tradition: the researcher's immersion in the culture and way of life of participants in order to understand their social world. They understood thus that urban poverty can be linked to manners of relating and subsisting that seem distinct from those that dominate society.

Indeed, in *The City* (1925), Park and Burgess offer an account of the tensions between traditional modes of relating (through 'primary' relations of personal acquaintance) and the modern systems of impersonal bureaucracy, laws and regulations which order urban life under conditions of capitalism. For these authors, Chicago's slum dwellers ordered their lives and interactions through local ties, networks of acquaintance, kinship and friendship and were bound to come into conflict with the 'mainstream' regulating systems which serve the more powerful (ibid.: 23–35). The importance of informality and interpersonal forms of regulation in street life and culture were already apparent, as were the tensions that can exist between 'the street' and the forces of control and criminal justice. Later Chicago works on the connections between urban poverty and street crime included a greater reliance on statistics. Shaw and McKay's seminal *Juvenile Delinquency and Urban Areas* (1942) espoused a theory of 'social disorganization'. This essentially argued that areas which experience waves of immigration and transient populations cannot as effectively form social institutions or transmit norms to young people.

This notion was challenged by Whyte's classic *Street Corner Society* (1943). This ethnography of a Boston slum identified two youth groups and two adult groups who exemplified distinct cultural orientations. On the one hand, the Corner Boys displayed an array of cultural values and behaviours which derived from the rugged masculine culture that many of the slum residents brought with them from impoverished rural Italy. They emphasized notions of respect and reciprocity within their peer group. Their status within it took precedence over their relationship to the institutions and rules of dominant (middle-class) American culture that could lead to greater inclusion in mainstream socio-economic life. This youth group had links to the adult street world of racketeering. Although similar in background to the Corner Boys, the College Boys exhibited values and behaviours much more in tune with those of middle-class America: they emphasized individualistic notions of education and careerism. These young men were upwardly mobile and had links to the adult world of local politics. Crucially, Whyte demonstrated that there was a high degree of social organization in the slum, it was simply that one variant of this structure was animated by a culture and operated according to values that differed from those of the 'mainstream'. Without using the term, Whyte had, in effect, identified a street culture.

His work would prove particularly influential, where Albert Cohen (1955) drew heavily on it in developing his 'subcultural' theory of delinquency. Merton (1938) had theorized that impoverished individuals engaged in crime because they shared the 'American Dream' goals of material wealth, but lacked the means to achieve them legitimately. Cohen, however, recognized that a significant proportion of youth crime did not produce any financial advantage. So-called 'negativistic' behaviours such as vandalism and violence for its own sake required an alternative explanation. Cohen argued thus that disadvantaged young men formed distinctive delinquent subcultures as a result of a reactive 'status frustration' that stems from their failure to live up to middle-class behavioural expectations. Non-utilitarian acts of crime were understood in this way to be an expression of frustration and the performance of a subcultural identity.

The notion that such subcultures were formed in reaction to the middle-class was challenged by Walter Miller (1958). He argued that the law-breaking young people he studied operated according to the 'focal concerns' of a 'lower-class' culture, independent and distinct from that of the included mainstream. Although not yet referred to as such, these authors were effectively debating about the nature and roots of a street culture, distinct from that of the mainstream. Even at this stage, criminologists Matza and Sykes (1961) challenged the notion that delinquent cultures were significantly different from the 'subterranean values' (or buried, present but less acknowledged elements) of mainstream culture: excitement seeking and the simultaneous celebration of leisure and consumption. As will become clear in Chapter 8, many of these debates continue to persist.

During the 1960s, new ethnographies and theories contributed to understandings of the links between urban poverty and street culture. Suttles' *The Social Order of the Slum* (1968) discussed 'street life' in Chicago. The working-class population possessed small living spaces. With privacy in short supply (particularly where families were large) and scant free space, the street became a key space of socializing and socialization, particularly for young men (ibid.: 73–83). The study also emphasized the role of personal acquaintance and ties, private knowledge, rumours and gossip in establishing a sense of normativity at a local street level. The importance of informality and personal knowledge to this notion of 'slum' morality contributed to difficulties in trusting the formal institutions of the state, solidifying local networks and culture in exclusion from the 'mainstream'. Indeed, this legacy continues to be visible in the antipathy that many disadvantaged present to their police forces (see Chapter 8).

The complexity, richness and variety in forms of street life and working-class culture were also explored by Ulf Hannerz (1969). In a Washington DC ghetto he studied 'mainstreamers', 'swingers', 'street families' and 'streetcorner men' who to varying extents embodied cultural orientations that might be seen as 'respectable' (in tune to dominant cultural norms) or 'undesirable' ('rough', more concerned with hedonism and street respect). These cultures were seen to coexist (see also Pryce, 1986). A 'ghetto-specific' morality was seen to act as a repertoire that residents could variously draw on to smoothly relate to their neighbours and to negotiate the constraints that poverty placed on their opportunities to thrive (on this latter point, see also Liebow, 1967). As will be argued in the next chapter, the contemporary proliferation of street culture owes something to the alteration of this balanced coexistence in the era of deindustrialization.

Given the plentiful manual employment available in the post-war decades and with parallel forms of study developing in the UK (Parker, 1974; Mays, 1964), it is possible to conceptualize understandings of inner-city life in this era as reflecting on a multifaceted 'working-class culture'. The lives of slum residents featured sharply defined gender roles of female domain over the domestic space, a masculine culture which often placed primacy of notions of autonomy and leisure, and a male youth culture which could often involve offending behaviours. Labour market opportunities, however, supported transitions to 'respectability' and allowed this orientation to flourish alongside the rough. Questions around how race operated to create social exclusion in America also came to the fore. Meanwhile, studies in the sociology of deviance, such as Howard Becker's *Outsiders* (1973), were arguing that deviance is not an inherent quality, but it is attributed to particular behaviours and scenes (operating according to their own rules and logics) by more powerful groups.

This sociological tradition was picked up in the UK by the Birmingham School of Contemporary Cultural Studies who in the 1970s produced works which explored the relationships between social class, flamboyant consumerism, style, youthful expression and deviance (see Hebdige, 1979; Hall and Jefferson, 1976). The group argued that colourful youth subcultures such as the 'skins', 'mods' and 'punks' negotiated their position to the social structure and dominant culture through cultivating their own variants of urban cool (and, at times, also criminal lifestyles). In this sense, echoing Downes (1966), subcultures were conceptualized as providing a 'solution' to the predicament of class disadvantage (although a 'magical' resistance that never succeeds in disturbing the social structure). Nevertheless, visible subcultures were seen as providing fodder for the culture industries interested in marketing the 'next big thing' to young people (Hebdige, 1979). Moreover, subcultures provided a lightning rod for wider social anxieties around class and youth, where 'moral panic' could attach to relatively less-serious instances of law breaking (Cohen, 1972).

Interestingly, moreover, in asking 'why working-class kids get working-class jobs?', Willis (1977) discovered the operation of two distinct cultures within the working-class school and community he studied in northern England. The *lads* that he saw defying the discipline of school, valuing instead the heady laughs and defiant, ruggedly masculine culture of their peer group, naturally gravitated to the same low- to semi-skilled factory work that their fathers undertook. They had little but scorn for the *ear 'oles* whose efforts within education and adherence to their teachers' behavioural expectations marked their culture as more attuned to that of middle-class inclusion (even if they did not attain it). These questions around the reproduction of disadvantage are particularly original and interesting. Indeed, street culture can be understood as a key mechanism by which disadvantage is reproduced where it orientates individuals against behaviours that might ultimately benefit them (e.g. securing an education, cooperating when confronted with the forces of law and order). Contemporary matters relating to this idea are discussed further in Chapter 8.

It is little surprise that the work of the Birmingham School had taken a 'cultural turn', seeking its source material in the way young people dressed, the music they listened to, their leisure activities and the films they preferred. Their work had followed more than two decades of youth cultural explosion in the developed world where rising prosperity amongst nearly all classes had vested young people with increased spending power which markets had emerged to harness (see France, 2007). In this context, the blues and rock 'n' roll music which emerged from the southern USA and developed with the northward migration of its black citizens had transformed mainstream music tastes (see Ramsey, 2003). The Civil Rights movement gaining pace in 'blues country' evidenced, however, that black people continued to face considerable discrimination both under the law and within the mainstream popular consensus. Black 'folk' music, from jazz to blues within this imaginary, was largely seen to be transgressive (Springhall, 1998), undoubtedly lending it a great degree of currency amongst white young people keen to establish themselves as different to their parents in terms of norms as well as values. Meanwhile, in former colonies such as Jamaica, new-found independence was inspiring musical and stylistic innovations that would spread through immigration (see e.g. Bradley, 2001). Significantly, the labour requirements which necessitated the influx of immigrants were part and parcel of the post-war economic and social settlement. This had seen, within the developed world, an unprecedented equalization of levels of wealth, coupled with the growth of state-provided social welfare (Hobsbawm, 1994), a high point in the history of social inclusion.

As the 1970s advanced and concluded, this post-war social contract began to unravel in favour of more individualistic, neoliberal economics and governance (see Harvey, 2005; Young, 1999). Job security and availability began declining with the onset of deindustrialization, whilst support for state welfarism similarly decreased. These processes were to have a particularly pronounced effect on American inner-cities (Bluestone and Harrison, 1982). Within this socio-economic context, 'street gangs' were becoming understood as vehicles through which economic opportunity, social solidarity and subcultural inclusion might be attained within the most excluded and impoverished urban communities (e.g. Hagedorn and Macon, 1988; Vigil, 1988; Moore, 1978). Indeed, a number of scholars identified the degree to which the street gang might be thought of as channelling economically rational instincts through an alternative system of shadow enterprise (Padilla, 1992; Sanchez-Jankowski, 1991). This notion of the gang as enterprise raises questions around the extent to which the street institutions that form amongst the urban disadvantaged share the ultimate values of the mainstream. Particular gang scholars also explored the extent to which specific forms of street literacy, folklore, style and expressivity existed amongst their research participants (Conquergood, 1994a; see also Phillips, 2009; Brotherton and Barrios, 2004).

Disadvantaged urban youth enacted various forms of expressivity that could become incorporated into the brutal and violent world of gang life. An early example can be found in the documentary footage of flamboyant dress and demeanour of the New York City gangs featured in Gary Weis' documentary film *80 Blocks from Tiffany's* (1979). As gang battles increasingly took second place to the vibrant music and break-dancing scenes that had been organically emerging in that city, 'hip-hop' became the period's most potent cultural legacy, which, as will be discussed, had a significant impact on the culture industries. Such cultural developments themselves formed the subject of a thread of productive hip-hop scholarship (see e.g. Perkins, 1996; Rose, 1994). By this stage, and indeed continuing into the future, 'the street' had been established in itself as a subject of popular culture (see Box 2.1). Further significant strands of research focused on the drug trade (e.g. Jacobs, 1999; Williams, 1990) and indeed wider issues of poverty and everyday life amongst the American urban disadvantaged.

It was from this wider body of work that the work of Bourgois (1995/2003) and Anderson (1999) emerged and with them emerged the contemporary academic use of the term 'street culture'. To recall, Bourgois articulated the concept as a set of oppositional values and dispositions, whereas Anderson concentrated on the existence of a 'street code': a normative system by which violence is deployed and 'respect' as a status currency is won and lost. Clearly thus, contemporary uses of the term 'street culture' draw on a long history that is built on academic studies of life in areas of urban disadvantage. Considering the changing nature of both slum communities and the wider economic, social and cultural climate in which they sit allows contemporary scholars to determine what is specific to particular eras and what is common to experiences of exclusion. Indeed, contemporary scholars are furthermore equipped with a range of updated methodological tools, theoretical concepts and academic infrastructures to engage in debates that have been ongoing for over 150 years. The manner in which this is occurring is set out in the following section.

Box 2.1 'The street' in popular culture

Street cultural themes abound in various forms of popular culture. Inevitably, this has involved an amount of appropriation, exploitation and stereotyping. In the last 60 years or so, with the 'massification' of the media, there have been not only greater opportunities for this to take place, but also a greater appetite for cultural products which capture something of the authenticity (or at least the drama and immediacy) of street worlds. The following is a very selective sweep of some key moments in this recent history.

West Side Story, a piece of Broadway musical theatre first staged in 1957 and written and composed by Arthur Laurents, Leonard Bernstein and Stephen Sondheim, essentially rehearsed the classic *Romeo and Juliet* narrative in the context of rivalry between two ethnic street gangs in 1940s/1950s New York. Whilst the popularity of the show is evidenced by its enduring legacy, the notion of tough gang members engaging in choreographed dance is an absurdity that has proven fertile ground for parody.

A Clockwork Orange, a dystopian novel by Anthony Burgess, was published in 1962 (and later became the 1971 cult film directed by Stanley Kubrick). It centres on a central character Alex and his friends who essentially constitute a street gang, dressing and speaking in a very distinct manner, and dispense violence (often simply for the 'pleasure' it gives them) against rival groups and members of the public. It also reflects on the thin line that can exist between breaking and enforcing the law.

In the Ghetto, the 1969 recording by Elvis Presley, appropriator of black music par excellence, mournfully depicts the privations of a life born of poverty. Comparisons can be drawn to 'Little Ghetto Boy' (1972, Atco

Records) by black soul singer Danny Hathaway whose own origins in a Chicago public housing project arguably imbue his song with a specially significant poignancy.

The Warriors (1979, dir: Walter Hill) is a cult chase film which is animated by its large cast of young men (and some women) who play a plethora of flamboyantly dressed street gangs. The titular gang, falsely accused of murdering a leader intent on unifying the city's sparring groups, must flee to their home turf with New York's entire gang population in pursuit. The endurance of this classic is observable in its more recent incarnation as a video game and in numerous samples within hip-hop music and beyond.

The Message, the 1982 song by Grandmaster Flash and the Furious Five, and its accompanying video was one of the earliest and most popular forays by rap/hip-hop music into the realm of social commentary. The song depicts the material and emotional pressures of life within the American ghetto with its attendant poverty and crime.

Boyz n the Hood, written and directed by John Singleton and released in 1991, is a critically acclaimed film that tells the story of young men growing up in a crime-blighted suburb of Los Angeles. Significantly, beyond depicting the guns, drugs and gang-banging, the film highlights the humanity of its characters: their hopes, dreams, struggles and resignations.

The Streets, a UK urban music outfit led by poet-musician Mike Skinner, takes as its name the source of the ultimate inspiration for their musical style. Drawing on various subgenres of urban music, their debut album *Original Pirate Material* (2002, Locked On Records) won critical acclaim. With much evocation, atmospheric as well as lyrical, its various songs arguably capture the pleasures and pains of the lifestyles associated with Britain's urban club music scenes.

City of God is a Brazilian film that centres on growing up and criminal networks in a favela that shares a name with the title. Directed by Fernando Meirelles and Kátia Lund and an adaptation of a novel by Paulo Lins, it achieved worldwide release in 2003. The film exposed a wider northern audience to the issues of poverty and crime that exist within the developing world.

Understanding street culture: Present

Issues of urban poverty, culture, crime and expressivity continue to interest scholars, some of whom deploy the term 'street culture' whilst others examine issues pertinent to it without doing so. There are a range of approaches that are deployed and various positions taken around links between exclusion, culture, crime (and indeed cool), and these are examined in turn. Engaging in the exercise not only provides an overview of contemporary literature on these matters, but it provides the space to engage with these arguments, demonstrating how this book relates to contemporary, live debates.

Quantitative researchers have sought to 'test' Anderson's 'Code of the Street' thesis, running sophisticated statistical tests on large-scale datasets (Nowacki, 2012; Stewart and Simon, 2010; Stewart et al., 2006; Brezina et al., 2004). Analyses have rendered conclusions which can resemble mathematical formulae (see Silverman, 2004). Without extensively entering into method-ological debates that have been thoroughly tackled elsewhere (see Young, 2011; Ferrell, et al., 2008), these studies generally confirm Anderson's thesis but do not capture the immediacy, energy, nuance and humanity that attach to experiences (often violent and exploitation-rife) of social exclusion. Tables, charts, numbers and formulae can obscure as much as they explain, partic-ularly where lived experiences of elements of street culture can be so varied and contradictory. As will become clear in the next chapter, an appreciation of an individual's internal world of emotionality and reactivity is particularly useful in explaining why particular people behave in ways that are more street culturally potent within particular contexts.

Another strand of street cultural research has focused on narratives, the sto-ries that offenders tell about themselves. Accounting for their participation in robbery, offenders have spoken about the street cultural concerns motivating their behaviour, including the promise of 'fast cash' to facilitate consumerism and partying, the desire to avoid the drudgery of available work and the maintenance of a rugged masculine persona (see e.g. Shover and Honaker, 2009; Jacobs and Wright, 1999). Individuals have equally narrated the 'code of the streets' to explain their participation in violence (Brookman et al., 2011). Within the study of prisoners, focus has been placed on how the incarcerated narrate the rules of their world: the 'convict code' (Irwin and Cressey, 1962). It has subsequently been argued in the US context, however, that such is the crossover between prison and the street, that the two codes have become so deeply intertwined that they are ultimately indistinguishable (Miller, 2001a). Narratives alone can at times provide an incomplete picture, being as they are, post-facto and subject to the storyteller's construction of self (Brookman et al., 2011). They are useful where used to examine how the narrator hopes to present her/himself. Thus, those who hope to appear street culturally com-petent draw on street cultural tropes, established notions of how a person should look and behave to thrive in the street world.

Street tropes are arguably becoming increasingly homogenous in a global-ized world where 'gangsta' imagery circulates with ubiquitous US rap music (Hagedorn, 2008). Disadvantaged Danish youth in detention centres, for example, speak about learning to be a 'gangster' as part of their accultura-tion process (Bengtsson, 2012). Narratives in this way also provide a sense of the social world: what is valued and denigrated, where individual narrators are positioned in relation to this and where they wish to position themselves (see Presser, 2009). Sandberg (2010), for example, has explored the extent to which Swedish drug dealers use both street and conventional narratives intertextually (together) to articulate a sense that whilst they may be somewhat more ready to become violent than 'average' citizens, they would do so only in defence of what most in society would agree is important, for example family. Thus the tropes, language and values of street culture compete for articulation with less extreme and more conventional stories, phrases and concerns, representing one of the ways in which street culture occurs on the basis of a scaled spectrum.

Narratives of adhering to strong variants of street culture may reflect the particular material circumstances of the narrator, or a justification for their use of violence, or an attempt to seem more 'tough' than they are. Equally, narratives of adhering to a weak variant of street culture may signal that the narrator is attempting to articulate a sense that they are 'streetwise', to conjure a sense of cool, or that they are trying to downplay their criminality and appear more 'respectable'. The point is that narratives can indicate the shape of the social structure operating around the storyteller and their act of narration within that is a form of social action. Although they are unlikely to articulate it as such, this notion permeates various forms of urban music whose lyricism often grapples with issues pertinent to ghetto living and the code of the street (see e.g. Kubrin, 2005).

Notions of the 'street code' have not been without criticism. Loic Wacquant (2002) has argued that it is somewhat over-prescriptive; failing to account for the agency and nuance that exists when socio-economic forces are manifested through cultural dispositions and individual behaviour. Thus, attempts to understand street culture should not be satisfied with reductive constructions of the code alone. Street culture involves far more than a simple need to maintain respect through violently responding to perceived personal slights, and indeed can at times mean less. Recently, there has been a move to understand street culture in Bourdieuian terms, recognizing that 'the street' operates as a field of human practice and that various traits, conditions and connections can provide advantages to individuals within it. These might simultaneously disadvantage them within mainstream social and economic fields. Street cultural competence can thus be understood in terms of existing as a 'street capital' (see Fraser, 2013; Ilan, 2013; Sandberg and Pedersen, 2009; Sandberg, 2008a, 2008b). Whilst this concept will be explored in greater depth in the next chapter, suffice it to say for now that it provides scope for better understanding why various individuals participate in street culture to various extents and in particular contexts. It addresses issues of pre-conscious 'habitus' or way of being (Bourdieu, 1977), where street competence can be embodied in a physicality that is difficult for 'wannabes' to imitate, and furthermore in patterns of automatic reaction that can involve violence (Winlow and Hall, 2009). It addresses issues of decision-making, however implicit or conscious.

This book attempts to understand street culture in a manner that is 'appreciative': cognisant of the lived logic that informs criminality (see Matza, 1964). It draws on the ethnographic tradition that has, and continues to be, a vital resource when making sense of the social worlds of the excluded. Winlow's *Badfellas* (2001) demonstrates how criminal street cultures in the north of England are heavily steeped in the logic of the working-class masculinities that revolved around his fieldsite's past heavy industries (see also Nayak, 2006). Deindustrialization, by negating the material value of rugged working-class masculinities has had a key role in the proliferation of street culture in the global north. Ostensibly, welfarist housing policies have also played a role, with MacDonald and Shildrick (2007) demonstrating how street cultural leisure careers are forged in areas of poor housing and employment in the north of England. Although material conditions vary within and between global regions, processes of meaning-making and behavioural response give relatable concrete forms to the more abstract notion of structural inequality.

For scholars such as David Harvey (2005), the processes of neoliberal economics impact on a range of issues pertinent to street culture. They have seen the stripping away of decently paid, low-skilled jobs in the developed world whilst elevating the culture of consumerism, creating both a push and pull effect in terms of criminal motivations (Young, 1999). More than this, the decline of organized labour accompanying this (combined with the end of the Cold War) have contributed to a decline in transformational politics, weakening the left significantly, and leaving the current politico-economic orthodoxy effectively unchallenged. As will be argued in the following chapter, an individualistic street culture is to some extent the successor to declining working-class and agrarian solidarity. Neoliberal economics, furthermore, entail the reduction in welfare and public services, exacerbating levels of inequality and exclusion. They tend also to be accompanied by neo-conservative crime control policies (Harvey, 2005) which responsiblize the poor for their reaction to their structural disadvantage and seek to punish them to the maximum extent. It should also be noted, and elaboration will be provided in Chapter 7, that this has been accompanied by a process of neo-colonialism that renders the developed world a source of cheap labour and resources, exacerbating issues of urban poverty within them.

This book argues that understanding the spatial dimensions of street culture should go beyond the western inner-city itself, and a growing body of literature is exploring the additional pressures faced by those who live in the global south, where the boundaries between institutionalized armed groups, slum communities, politics, violent police forces and militias can blur (see e.g. Hagedorn, 2008; Winton, 2004; Dowdney, 2003, 2005). In Jamaica, for example, the crime groups in 'garrison communities' can serve as a hub for global flows of cash, drugs and consumer goods. The latter are distributed throughout the community in elaborate 'treats', which in part cements support for the gangs (Gunst, 2003). Garrison gangs, moreover, have acted as supporters and enforcers for the political parties that arm them, challenging their labelling as exclusively an institution of the 'criminal other' (ibid.). A similar fusion of gang and political violence operating in Haiti is vividly illustrated in Leth and Loncarevic's documentary film *Ghosts of Cite de Soleil* (2006). As will become clear throughout the book, adopting a more expansive global approach to issues of street culture tells more than a story of floating and fusing styles and traditions. It indicates the extent to which understandings of particular crime issues within the developed world are conceptually limited by geographic myopia, sometimes mistaking what happens within a single region or country as indicative of a general truth that is not necessarily observable in southern contexts.

An appreciative and expansive understanding of street culture can furthermore address the myths of poverty's pathologies. There is a pernicious discourse that blames the urban poor for sustaining their own condition: 'if only they went to school/got a job/had fewer children/stopped using drugs/stayed out of jail, then they would have a better life'. Like so many clichés and stereotypes, such statements reduce complex problems and historic legacies to a seemingly straightforward logic which overlooks the structural barriers to upward mobility. The concept of a self-propagating 'culture of poverty' gave way to approaches which 'other' the poor in different ways (Young, 2007: 24). On the left, a 'liberal othering' asserts that the contemporary culture of the urban poor is a result of 'deficiency': a lack of the materials and opportunities which allows for mainstream values to hold sway; whereas on the right the suggestion is that an emergent 'underclass' hold a set of inherently destructive values. The proponents of this latter theory (e.g. Murray, 1990) assert (with questionable logic) that welfarist principles erode the value of work and discipline and thus encourage disorder, promiscuity and crime amongst the disadvantaged. Not only is this position ahistorical, lacking in a wider consideration of social, economic and cultural change, but taken to its logical policy conclusions would merely generate further exclusion, itself the fuel of street culture. Instead, I advocate for an understanding of the ways in which street culture reproduces itself and the disadvantage of those who strongly adhere to it. In this way, understanding the roots of the culture offers a conceptual approach that might ultimately better serve the cause of addressing it.

The book thus seeks to recognize an ultimate sameness between street and mainstream cultures. Street culture's key difference lies in the fact that it entails attempting to flourish within a lifeworld that is distinctly subordinate to the lifeworld of the included. Its adherents do not have the same kinds of access to material and existential fulfilment, where even what it means to be successful and fulfilled is defined by the powerful. Whilst this might be seen as resonating with Mertonian notions of strain, it cannot be easily inferred that street culture operates under a separate set of rules to the mainstream. As Sumner (1994) points out, it has become difficult to identify a category of deviant rules or behaviours when mainstream rules are highly contingent, selectively enforced, often contradictory and hypocritical and subject to the operation of power.

Hyper-included high-end bankers and traders practise a rugged masculinity and engage at times in aggressive harm-causing entrepreneurialism in pursuit of conspicuous consumption (see Goodley, 2012; Lewis, 1989). Apart from the status of its participants and the opportunities and strategies available to them, how does this differ from street cultural practice? Whilst the harm, violence and brutality of street culture must always be recognized, it is important to remember the 'symbolic violence' (Bourdieu and Thompson, 1991) and harms (environmental destruction, exploitation of the powerless and death-inducing wars, see Hillyard and Tombs, 2004) arising from the operation of 'mainstream' culture. Street culture is doubtlessly related more directly to violence and brutality than mainstream cultures in terms of the day-to-day experiences and sensibilities of its adherents, yet both cultures have their links. Moreover, as will be explored in Chapter 8, there has been a historical tendency to criminalize street culture and the disadvantaged. Rather than dismissing street cultural values and behaviours as symptoms of social disorganization, 'mindlessness', wanton brutality, vulgarity or 'sheer criminality', it is more useful to understand the functions that they serve within street life and indeed the appeal of their imagery to consumers who occupy included positions within society.

To that end, questions furthermore arise around the extent to which street culture should be viewed as 'oppositional'. Although they do not use the term 'street culture', Hall et al. (2008) argue that it should not be viewed as a form of resistance as it is underpinned by the narcissism and individuality of the ubiquitous, mainstream consumer culture. They challenge the notion that street offending is meaningful beyond its facilitation of desired consumerist lifestyles. Whilst this second notion is not without potential counter-arguments, it powerfully illustrates parallels between voracious earner-consumers on both sides of the law. Drawing on Nightingale's (1993) ethnography of street cultural youth, Hayward (2004) argues that 'ghetto fabulous' styles, that is the hyper-consumption of the urban poor, represent an over-identification with mainstream culture. Where individuals are excluded from meaningful inclusion in society they voraciously participate in such elements that are open to them. The marginalized poor play a key role in supporting the economic mainstream, by variously providing cheap labour, necessary markets or both (Young, 2007). Participating in street culture, however, ultimately serves to reproduce their status and subordination, arguably a form of acquiescence to the status quo. Moreover, much as street cultural participants may try to consume, they are open to do so in the 'wrong' ways, marking themselves as gauche 'flawed consumers', with bad taste and/or insufficient means (Hayward and Yar, 2006; Bauman, 2004), rendering their exclusion all the more conspicuous.

The tendency of subcultural theory to view both criminal acts and cool lifestyles as somehow connected to processes of resistance requires unravelling in the case of a street culture that bears so much resemblance to the mainstream hegemon. The conduct of strong street cultural adherents, nevertheless, clearly chafes at the behavioural expectations and values of the included mainstream. What exactly constitutes 'resistance' remains a contentious topic (see Hollander and Einwohner, 2004). It is particularly useful therefore to revisit it, alongside the notion of 'opposition' to explore what it is that street culture represents in contemporary times: is it a form of post-transformational, inchoate politics? Is it apolitical, aggressive self-assertion? Could it be something of both: a form of ultimately self-defeating but meaningful defiance? Chapter 8 examines such questions in detail, demonstrating how moderate to strong street cultures foster behaviours which offer meaningful (although often transient) sensations of power and create avenues for an alternative sense of inclusion. Ultimately, an argument can thus be made for understanding street culture as a form of 'parallel' as opposed to 'oppositional' values. This position poses challenges to those that would brand street culture as a form of almost quasi-revolutionary action, meritorious of lionization.

This distance from unquestioningly assuming the existence of 'resistance' resonates with developments in the more 'lifestyle' arena of subcultural theory, which is often associated with examining 'cool' practices. In particular, scholars associated with 'club cultures' and 'post-subcultural theory' have critiqued some of the Birmingham School's assertions, pointing out that subcultures rarely exist as clearly bounded entities unconsciously playing with their class identity, but as amorphous groupings of those who are more instrumentality interested in securing 'good times' (see e.g. Muggleton and Weinzierl, 2003). Whilst earlier subcultural theory had viewed authentic youth movements as supplying the raw materials for the creation of consumer products, rendering the original sources passé and devitalized (Hebdige, 1979), it has become necessary instead to view creativity and commerciality as mutually dependant in a late-modernity of rapid communication and omni-marketization. Indeed, street cultural artistes are often reflexively conscious of the steps that are required to render their products commercially successful and are happy to undertake them, to the extent that mainstream success becomes the articulated goal of underground subcultures (see e.g. Ilan, 2012). The position set out in this book therefore challenges the notion that street cultural expression is an entirely authentic form of cultural production harnessed by the mainstream industries, but instead a phenomenon that has infiltrated many mainstream media production structures and strategies, whilst itself often a product of mainstream commercial concerns.

Finally, the approach to understanding street culture offered here owes a considerable debt to cultural criminology (see Ferrell et al., 2008) which advocates an attentiveness to the role played by meaning in matters of crime, control and indeed wider matters of transgression, popularity and protest. It is this perspective, for example, that has stressed the importance of recognizing the emotional dynamics of transgression – that is, for some doing what is said to 'be wrong' can generate pleasurable and agreeable sensations. Cultural criminology has similarly discussed the role of 'carnival' in everyday life (see Presdee, 2000): the way in which the leisure industries often draw heavily on the notion of inverted morality to lend an indulgent and adventurous tone to its products. Indeed, cultural criminology's notion of the commodification of crime and the marketization of transgression have done much to explore how and why images of criminality are so ubiquitous, not just in forms of popular culture from films to novels, but in advertising, music, fashion and even tourism. Arguably, street expressivity is a unique variant of this wider phenomenon, as it has had such an influence on the very architecture of mainstream media production and thus merits its own consideration (which will be provided in Chapter 6).

Conclusion

From Victorian London to 21st-century Latin America, the connections between urban deprivation, culture, crime and expressivity have long captivated social researchers and theorists. More than this, media producers and consumers have displayed a strong appetite for both factual and fictional accounts of life 'in the streets'. What is most surprising about this extensive and varied body of material are the similar themes that flow through it. This chapter has set out what these are as a means of supporting the definition and understanding of street culture offered at the start of the book. More than this, by grounding, setting out and responding to current debates relating to these matters, I begin to give greater shape to this book's particular perspective: its considerations of matters of street crime and expressivity side by side, in a manner that is more contemporary and global than previous efforts, and recognizing that street culture is not so different from the mainstream cultures from which it is excluded from.

Having set out the historical development of understandings of street culture, in the context of changing socio-economic structures, consumerist practices and public debates, it becomes possible to identify the role of demographic-structural factors (class, gender, age and ethnicity) in the shaping of community cultures and individual practices. These matters are considered in detail in the next chapter.

CHAPTER 3

Demography and Development: Class, Gender and Ethnicity

Introduction

This chapter explores the demographic and structural factors underpinning street culture. This is a fraught terrain where inevitably questions of structure butt against those of agency. To what extent do our backgrounds shape our beliefs and ultimately our behaviours? Why is it that some of the urban poor become involved in street crime, whilst others do not? Issues of structure should furthermore be considered with history in mind. Why has street culture emerged as the force that it is today? How does it relate to the working-class and agrarian cultures that preceded it? Why is it most visibly embodied by young men, and how do women make sense of their identities within street contexts? These are the questions that this chapter will address by examining various research findings and theoretical positions.

Specific attention will be paid to accounts of life in the disadvantaged western inner-city before, during and after deindustrialisation. Traditional working-class cultures arguably reached their peak where supported by an abundance of relatively well-paid manual employment. These economic conditions provided a material basis for the cultural imperatives of rugged masculinity and class/neighbourhood solidarity. The social, economic and cultural rationale of these traditional cultures unravelled, however, with the advance of neoliberal globalization. Street cultures can be understood as emerging from their ashes. Structural and cultural explanations of an individual's life course, however, must be understood as partial. Individual choice (however structurally bounded) and situated performances (however culturally mediated) have clear roles to play.

Whilst considering the contemporary complexity of life within the disadvantaged inner-city, this chapter focuses on how classed identities, gender roles and performances, conceptions of youth and maturity as well as ethnicity and experiences of exclusion manifest in cultural orientation. The chapter moves on to consider how other scholars have addressed the balance between structure and agency in the world of the street and returns to the notion of the street cultural spectrum introduced in earlier chapters. The chapter offers some thoughts on how the balance might be best conceptualized. Ultimately, it is demonstrated that the spectrum-based understanding of the culture allows for the flexibility and nuance to understand why it emerges on the one extreme as a series of norms and concerns with life-and-death importance, whilst at the other as a mere lifestyle choice. This, in turn, allows questions of inclusion and exclusion to be better understood in the context of macro socio-economic structures, meso-level questions of culture and micro-level questions of individual 'choice' and emotionality.

Urban poverty and social class in transition

The previous chapter discussed how scholars have explored the cultures and ways of life particular to various western urban slums. Notably, a lot of their work identified a range of relatively stable and durable institutions which ordered the lives of their participant groups: communities (spatial and/or ethnic), social clubs and trade unions, mass employers, pubs, markets, cornershops, churches, extensive kinship networks and youth friendship groups. From the 1950s, steadily available, decently paid employment played an important role in cementing such institutions, economically supporting the social and cultural composition of the urban working-class. This did not occur in a homogenous manner, however, where hierarchies of labour, tenure and respectability created 'family' and 'street' values (Hannerz, 1969) and 'established' and 'outsider' identities (Elias and Scotson, 1994). Indeed, such categories were mobilized by various residents to understand and explain the changing ethnic composition of their communities, often with a certain amount of hostility (Foster, 1990; Suttles, 1968).

Despite changing neighbourhood characteristics, traditional working-class cultures for a time provided a sense of identity and inclusion for many of those ensconced within them. The purchasing power of the working-class man's 'family wage' and the respect that accompanied his hard, physical work vested him with a sense of mastery, autonomy and place in the community. This was echoed by the achievements of his wife in the domestic sphere who supposedly gained her gendered sense of esteem from child rearing and keeping house to particular standards.

With social mobility less emphasized and a culturally mediated level of comfortable consumption available to the working-class family (depending on wider political, social and economic factors), a sense of continuity, stability and order could exist. In contrast to middle-class notions of careerism and professional identity, work (particularly low status) was often viewed as an instrumental means to earn and spend (see e.g. Gillespie et al., 1992). Thus whilst employment within particularly iconic industries could be a badge of identity (see Winlow, 2001), for others material subsistence remained at the forefront. Where individuals and families lacked means, certain low-level property criminality was understood as representing a legitimate coping strategy, particularly where undertaken within the boundaries of wider community norms. These operated through mechanisms of mutual acquaintance and would usually demand the overall display of 'fair play' and respect. Similarly, there are many reports of families and neighbours supporting each other through difficult circumstances (see e.g. Ilan, 2011). With that said, there can be a tendency to nostalgically recall a 'golden era' of working-class community and collectivity that obscures an essential concern for individual and factional interests. Overall, however, this should not be seen as voiding the existence of more substantial institutions, political participation, defined life trajectories and secure class identity than those that exist today (see Savage, 2000).

Even during periods of relative prosperity amongst the western working-classes more generally, there were signs that material factors, such as the availability of reasonably well-paid and stable employment had considerable bearing on local cultures. A lack of opportunity to secure such could give rise to what might be viewed as a 'proto-street culture'. The 'corner men' studied by Liebow (1967), lacking the ready means to support a family, could most effectively project the appearance of a successful (although 'rougher') masculinity through their participation in street life. Rather than board the van that passed through their neighbourhood to offer sporadic casual employment (providing insufficient income or stability to establish themselves as respectable heads of household), they passed their days partaking in banter, booze and boasts at the corner. This allowed them to feel a sense of mastery of their milieu, constructing themselves as able exploiters of earning opportunities and available women, rather than unemployed workers at the mercy of a foreman's daily labour requirements. The structural conditions experienced by these men did not allow for autonomy to be expressed within the bounds of employment. By contrast, traditional industrial employment, as Willis (1977) demonstrated, offered scope for men to 'foot drag' and subvert their subordination to management through surreptitious mockery.

Furthermore, distinct working-class youth cultures with different gradations of 'respectability' could be identified. Jenkins (1983), for example, distinguished between the street-based delinquency of the rougher 'lads' he studied, the structured club-based leisure of conformist 'ordinary citizens' and the drifting 'kids' whose preferences were in between. Street spaces were particularly important to those young men who sought independence and autonomy. They tended to reject the supervision of youth and sports clubs, whilst a lack of means often ruled out commercial leisure opportunities. Rather, mischief, low-level violence, petty theft and minor vandalism were used to pass time and generate 'fun' (see Corrigan, 1979; Gill, 1977). Willis (1977), however, demonstrated that the young 'lads' he studied misbehaving in school and engaging in acts of petty delinquency would go on to work in similar industrial jobs to their fathers. Life stages were thus particularly important within traditional working-class cultures, where kinship and contact networks would facilitate the transition from early school-leaving to working life. The juvenile law-breaking that preoccupied mid-20th-century criminologists was often simply thus: youthful, where a relatively predictable mature life in work, family and community awaited. Indeed, petty youth offending can often be understood as an attempt to accelerate beyond bio-legal realities and enjoy what are (youthfully) understood to be the 'advantages' of adult life: earning, intoxication and self-determination. As was noted in earlier times:

> Young people have an unhappy knack of imitating the least desirable features of adult behaviour when they are anxious to convince the world and themselves that they are really grown up (Mays, 1964: 102).

Studies, more recently, have chronicled the effects of late-capitalism on the economic, social and cultural order of the disadvantaged inner-city. For William Julius Wilson (1996) there was a dissolution of the traditional, institutional inner-city community in the USA. The decline of manufacturing employment and trade unionism, accompanied by the growth of opportunities in the service and information economy had led to a significant dearth in decently paid employment for its residents. Available decently paid employment required educational qualifications which the lower sections of the urban working-class had traditionally deemed superfluous and inappropriate. Available service work tended to be poorly paid and insecure, to some not worth the privations that would accompany their exit from the (retreating) social security system (see also Newman, 1999). Furthermore:

> The strongly held US cultural and economic belief that the son will do at least as well as the father in the labor market does not apply to many young inner-city males (Wilson, 1996: 30).

The demographic consequences of these economic changes were vast, concentrating poor, ethnic minority, younger and older people within increasingly depopulated and economically moribund ghettos. These developments created the conditions under which the market in illegal drugs could flourish as the illegitimate economy began to occupy a proportion of the vacuum left by the decline of its legitimate counterpart. With drug markets come various assorted forms of crime and violence. Where Wilson identifies the development of a 'ghetto-related culture' as a response to the failure of mainstream institutions to sustain the livelihoods and traditional normative structures of such areas (1996: 55), he is in effect describing the conditions that gave rise to street culture's dominance within them. Where a number of his research participants spoke of the difficulties of financially subsisting and avoiding predatory crime, their need to variously adopt street culture became acute. To put this another way, the traditional principle that one did not steal from one's neighbours (however strongly this applied in reality) reverted to a need to be watchful of them.

Overall, it can thus be argued that street culture's emergence as a dominant force was in part connected to the demise of traditional working-class generational dynamics, where an adult life of 'respect' awaited a great number of young people even if they 'misbehaved' in their youth. The ability of traditional working-class normativity to support this, and ultimately allow 'rough' and 'respectable' cultures to coexist, relied heavily on the aforementioned social/cultural institutions. These too were eroding alongside their economic material base (see also Hobbs, 2013; Hall et al., 2008). In a sense, thus, street culture would become prominent because it became associated with remaining economic and affirmative opportunities, whilst traditional, 'respectable' working-class culture lost many of the conditions which sustained it. Mullins (2006: 13) rightly points out that street culture tends to be strongly practised only by fringe elements of the disadvantaged community. Their neighbours, however, tend to be versed in it to varying extents, at the very least to ensure that they can coexist with its adherents whose influence arguably grew. There was an increasing need thus for many to perform comfortably within, at least, its weaker-to-moderate modes, and for at least some of the time.

Wilson's reflections on the fraying of traditional ghetto norms tended to focus most firmly on safety, work ethic (which he observed had not diminished, but adapted to the lack of suitable employment opportunities) and the family. Important British works have focused on another component of the late-capitalist order. For Hall et al. (2008) the homogenizing and individualizing forces of the consumer culture, coupled with deindustrialization, have ground down the bulk of the traditional northern English working-class community into narcissistic individuals competing for consumerist distinction. This has particular implications for crime where theft and drug sales finance spending on designer clothing, jewellery and expensive nights out.

The working-class cultural model of respect deriving from the performance of demanding labour in exchange for a living wage is to varying extents seceded by a street cultural model where respect accompanies the ability to exhibit violent potential and/or conspicuous consumption. Such novel forms of respect generation may only be partial.

The internal hierarchy of disadvantaged communities shifts, and where elements of the poorest within them might be feared, respected and/or criticized for their anti-social and violent ways, they can be simultaneously ridiculed and scorned for their lack of consumer acumen (Ilan, 2011, 2013). For example, the 'Aldi bashers' in Hall et al.'s work are named after an inexpensive supermarket chain and are viewed by the consumer-offenders that form the focus of this study as an inferior group who do not apply sufficient taste and resources to their consumption. The transition from production- to consumption-based economies, experienced by much of the developed world, has meant that the lower working-class are no longer criticized for being 'flawed producers' but for being 'flawed consumers' (Hayward and Yar, 2006; Bauman, 2004). As will become clear in Chapter 8, however, Victorian era concerns around the moral character of the 'undeserving' poor persist. Thus when the urban poor conspicuously consume they are open to be perceived as doubly deviant by members of the included classes (Young, 2007): not just poor (and possibly criminal and violent) but wasting their money on fripperies.

Grand narratives around class and social transition, whilst inevitably utilized in academic analysis, must be treated with caution. Space must be left for counterfactuals, nuance and local variations. Traditional working-class culture did not represent a utopian set of norms that maintained a sense of safety for all (certain forms of violence flourished within them). The traditional working-class has similarly not been wiped out with its more upwardly mobile members swept into the middle-classes as some might suggest (Savage, 2000). Rather, what was once academically imagined to be a rather straightforward stratification of society is understood to be substantially more complex. Scholarly understandings of street culture should reflect this. Street culture comes to inform a wider group of experiences where marginalization has become increasingly pronounced in the cities of the developed world (Wacquant, 2008), global flows connect distant archipelagos of disadvantage (see Chapter 7) and markets increasingly sell deracinated images of inner-city criminality (see Chapter 6).

Street life: A man's world?

Understanding the gendered nature of street culture is vital. It is strongly masculinist, intertwining with violence and the will to deploy it, stratifying the street world in a manner that disadvantages women (Miller, 2001b). Poverty can tend to render gender roles more essential and delineated than those observable within the included classes. Nevertheless, individuals respond to these structured conditions with agency, variously conforming to, deviating from or exaggerating idealized notions of masculinity and femininity. Indeed, a number of street cultural archetypes combine aspects of both. The manicured pimp in the mould of Iceberg Slim (see Slim, 2009; Quinn, 2000) preens over his appearance and emotionally blackmails the women he exploits as prostitutes, whilst remaining ready to deploy vicious violence against them. The 'bad girl' may combine an adherence to a feminine aesthetic with the physical and psychic strength to respond forcefully to any perceived slight or unwanted advance (although such women are not as common as myth might suggest; see Young, 2009; Miller, 2001b). Both genders must nevertheless be understood as operating within relatively tight bounds of 'gender accountability' (West and Zimmerman, 1987) on the street, no matter how innovatively they respond to them. Understanding how this has historically developed through various modes of disadvantage contributes to a deeper understanding of contemporary street cultural dynamics.

Whilst patriarchal hegemony was, and continues to be, almost ubiquitous, particular forms of working-class variants developed during the industrial period of western development. Vividly illustrated by Barron Mays (1964) in his account of working-class life in 1950s Liverpool, the man's accepted authority left him free to allocate his family wage between the household, administered by his wife, and his own spending on leisure in the local pub. Their male children were exempted from household chores and could enjoy the freedom of the street, whilst their female children were expected to labour in the domestic sphere. Accounts of historical working-class masculinities frequently refer to the use of violence, either to establish a 'pecking order' amongst young men or to settle disputes between adults. In Dublin, for example, contemporary street violence is contrasted to the historical 'straightener' or fair fist fight which is recalled as concluding with the shaking of hands and the purchasing of drinks (Ilan, 2011). Whilst men could generate status through their earning and physical distinction, women were more negatively held to account over issues of sexual purity.

In Parker's 'View from the Boys' (1974) his study participants were keen to ensure that the girls they would marry had maintained such sexual respectability. Of course, double standards applied. Men had a particular dominance of their local street and leisure spaces whilst female dominion was domestic (although historical accounts of boisterous women occupying street spaces problematizes the notion that 'bedroom' culture dominated the lives of young working-class females; see McRobbie, 1978). Female indices of esteem were nevertheless generally restricted to their ability to keep home, raise children and maintain sexual purity/fidelity and their attractiveness to men.

As will become clear, it is arguable that despite some shift in the precise expectations of women, contemporary street cultures continue to place them in a difficult and subordinated position. Bourgois' work (1995/2003) demonstrates how Puerto Rican agrarian cultures contained strongly delineated gender roles which continued to impact on the values and behavioural expectations of his participants now living in New York. In other words, traditional gender roles continued to have a bearing on street cultural notions of gender.

For Bourgois, however, the contemporary street world can also be understood as challenging certain traditional gender roles. The economic opportunities presented by the drug trade, he argues, present possibilities for female emancipation. But this notion is problematized by a range of other studies. Within the crack trade, for example, women are often consigned to lower status and lower paid roles, at times coexisting with sex work (see Maher and Curtis, 1992). The display of violent potential orders interactions on the street to the extent that women may seek to perform a more masculinist 'tough' role. Such logics, similarly, can explain the cultivation of an image that draws on male rather than female styles of dress and comportment which are noted amongst certain female street offenders (Grundetjern and Sandberg, 2012; Miller, 2001). This strategy, in other words, calls for women to be more like men in order to operate within street culture.

The violence of the street world forces women to make complex and loaded decisions around even trivial seeming matters such as dress and demeanour. Jodi Miller (2008) writes about the harrowing balancing act that many young females in the US inner-city must perform daily. Dress too provocatively and they might be viewed as sexually promiscuous and therefore 'down' for sex acts that are in fact multiple-perpetrator rape. Dress too 'square' and they are open to be viewed as lacking in street cultural acumen and therefore an easy target for sexual violence. Those women who join street 'gangs', the ultimate street cultural institutions, may gain a particularly advantageous position. They may not be expected to engage in serious offending to the same extent as their male counterparts but nevertheless become shielded from the predation of males outside the gang (Miller, 2001). They remain, however, vulnerable to the possibility of being raped by males in rival gangs as a savage challenge to their male colleagues. They also might be sexually assaulted by their male gang compatriots but more typically and at the very least they must condone or participate in sexist talk and attitudes. Toughness and criminal acumen (what I will later discuss in terms of 'street capital') have value in contemporary street life to the extent that although they are generally thought of as masculine traits, they may also be useful for women to deploy.

Arguably, popular imaginaries of street femininities are dominated by images of inner-city women concerned more than anything else with their sexual desirability in the eyes of men, enhanced through dressing revealingly and embodying overt sensuality. This probably owes some debt to the ubiquitous media presence of 'hip-hop honeys' (see also Stephens and Phillips, 2003), women whose careers and/or aspirations are tied to appearing in urban music videos. Judgement is often passed on the perceived lack of 'respectability' exhibited by women in street life, viewing them as overly vulgar and lacking in decorum (see Hernandez, 2009). Such imaginaries are contaminated by the same kinds of moral emotions that underpin 'othering' discourses around teenage pregnancy and the perceived excessive fertility and lasciviousness of 'underclass' women. Understanding the complex nature of street femininities allows for a rejection of such caricatures.

Whilst a certain logic might suggest that street cultures prematurely and excessively sexualize young women through valorizing ostensibly 'adult' behaviours and rugged masculinities (which street femininities might be viewed as serving), this does not tell the full story. There are tensions here between structure and agency and between a variety of gender roles that women might deploy (or be forced into). Certainly there can be upsetting levels of abuse, sexual violence and coercion at play. Deploying an exaggeratedly sensual female persona may invite such unwanted consequences but may also be (consciously or otherwise) deployed to heighten levels of consumerist distinction and to signal the occupation of higher status within feminine street hierarchies. Appearing particularly sexualized could signal that women are sufficiently 'respected' to safely carry such a persona in a dangerous environment, either through their own toughness or the violence they have access to procure through their social, familial, or romantic networks. Indeed, carefully judged displays of sensuality may secure advantageous romantic connections. There are of course many complicated issues relating to sex work which space precludes this book from analysing in any detail.

Traditional feminine tropes of 'care' both about one's own appearance and the welfare of others can produce feminine capital on the street as well as in wider milieus (see Skeggs, 1997). The cultivation of a 'less threatening' feminine persona can facilitate certain roles within the drug economy, connected to storing drugs and/or money, or 'copping' drugs for middle-class men afraid to approach male dealers on the street (Maher, 2000). Moreover, the cultivation of sensuality provides sex working women within the street world with opportunities to 'vic' male clients (take money without providing sexual services; see ibid.). Once again, however, such activities take place within environments often regulated by masculine violence and subject to the masculine gaze. Women in the drug trade may find the cultivation of a less street, more respectable persona important. In this way they can maintain their standing in the eyes of their family and peers and obscure the visibility of their illegal activities (see Fleetwood, 2014). Equally, other women's involvement in their local street culture may entail considerably less risk of sexual violence and be undertaken to access the heady thrills and fun times that intoxication and leisure in public spaces might offer (see O'Brien, forthcoming). Ultimately, much as levels of manifested violence differ between varieties of street culture, so too does the level of risk faced by women. Nevertheless, their more universal experiences of disadvantage within the street milieu result in their particularly complex location within street culture.

Street masculinities on the other hand are arguably more straightforward where they order the more violent aspects of street culture. In the absence of those working-class institutions and routes to acceptable livelihood described earlier, for many of those in urban poverty there is but a shard of masculine value remaining to fight for: an ephemeral and disembedded notion of respect. As such it can be difficult for men strongly embedded in street culture to publicly condone sleights against them or to dismiss the opportunity to increase their wealth or status through publically robbing, disadvantaging or humiliating someone else.

Christopher Mullins (2006) vividly sets out how such values throw up hierarchies, whereby those who can muster little respect are viewed as 'punks' who must submit to the instruction and domination of more respected male peers. Effeminizing language (e.g. bitch, pussy) is deployed as a form of gender accountability to denigrate those men alleged to be falling short of absolutist, stark and essentialist constructions of appropriate gender performance. Men thus accumulate 'juice' (power, or 'street capital') through appropriately reacting to the levels of deference afforded to them, the treatment of the women they are associated with and the levels of violent potential exhibited by others. Connell (1995) uses the notion of 'protest masculinity' to understand contemporary working-class cultures of toughness. For her, the relative powerlessness experienced by the working-class male throughout his early life-course, and his experiences of lacking power within contemporary socio-economic configurations causes him to over identify with seemingly 'powerful' aspects of masculinity: physical strength and psychic toughness. Indeed, and following on from Connell's work, Messerschmidt (1993, 1997) views crime as one of the arenas in which disadvantaged men can 'do' masculinity (where the legitimate arenas of earning a decent wage and supporting a family are beyond ready reach).

Here once again questions of internal class divisions and individual agency come to the fore. Winlow and Hall (2006) demonstrate, for example, how white working-class men in the north of England have settled into lives sweetened by participation in the consumer culture and funded through work in the service-orientated 'call centre' industry. Whilst thus steeped in what might be viewed as the effeminizing environment of placating clients and dressing well, these young men on weekend nights enter into a carnival of bravado, violence and masculine display on their city high streets. They drink to excess, search for sexual conquest and the adrenaline rush of a fight to take part in or observe. Steve Roberts (2013), on the other hand, speaks of attenuated forms of masculinity that exist amongst working-class men working in retail and participating in domestic chores. The existence of such varied kinds of masculinity is linked to the existence of varied material/economic circumstances, but also different conceptions of what it is to be a man (see Box 3.1).

Individuals can have the opportunity to perform to non-street- or weaker street-orientated forms of masculinity where immediate community standards afford a space to do so. Even within the stricter confines of street masculinity, individuals may opt to draw on different facets of maleness, variously deploying generosity, good humoured largesse, merciful understanding, stern orders, intimidating severity or brutal violence. Examples that come to mind include Ray the drug boss from Bourgois' *In Search of Respect* (1995/2002) who in one recounted incident buys beers and chats naturally with his workers and the anthropologist before becoming annoyed and breaking up the bonhomie when he is forced into an embarrassing situation. Unpredictability coupled with violent potential is a powerful means of generating 'street capital'. Two-dimensional understandings of 'street codes' that infer inelastic rules for the deployment of violence are no substitute for a nuanced reading of individual strategies and situated moments. These matters will be explored in greater detail later in this chapter.

Much as socio-economic change may have led to a 'material' crisis of masculinity (in terms of man's relative economic dominance) it has not led to an 'ideological' crisis, where the male-centred view of the world remains dominant (Hearn, 1999). Street life is not an exception to this rule. The precarious position of women within violent street worlds is driven in part by a hyper-masculinity which views sexual conquest as a mark of prestige. Street masculinities might be viewed as an exaggerated variant of hegemonic masculinity, the dominant ideal of what it is to be a man, rather than an oppositional form (see Connell and Messerschmidt, 2005). Similar might be said about street femininities which variously call for displays of respectability or sensuality, idealizations that owe much to the masculine gaze. Echoing the focus of this book, the above analysis of gender in street life is disproportionately related to matters of crime and it must be recognized that these principles operate in wider areas of social life. To mention the book's second focus, issues of gender weigh heavily in certain aspects of inner-city expressivity. Scholars of urban music, for example, have noted the levels of misogyny and linguistic violence deployed within it, together with less prevalent exemplars of empowered female sexuality (see e.g. Stolzoff, 2000; Rose, 1994). Strong embodiments of idealized gender provide street culture with particular appeal to young people who may find it a useful resource with which to perform identity work as they grow. Gendered action is central to how street culture becomes urban cool, but so too are issues of race and ethnicity, whose role in processes of social inclusion and exclusion must also be considered.

Box 3.1   Reel men: Street masculinities in *The Wire*

Cinema and television can at times reveal more nuanced accounts of street masculinities than even some academic studies (whilst of course they can also provide little more than clumsy stereotypes). *The Wire*, HBO's critically acclaimed realist drama on crime, policing and society in Baltimore City, USA is a particularly good example of a piece of media that explores the many varieties of masculinity that exist in contemporary conditions of urban poverty: from religious figures who represent 'decent' concerns and aspirations, to drug dealers at various points within an institutionalized street hierarchy. Indeed, the show's portrayal of race and gender has generated academic interest itself (see e.g. Waldron and Chambers, 2012). Below is an account of a number of the TV show's characters and the aspects of street masculinity that they most typically embody:

Avon Barksdale, one of the programme's drug kingpins, embodies an unbridled 'rough' masculinity. Emphasizing the criminal elements of his economic activities, he responds violently to challenges and sees his future tied to an ability to continue to operate with high degrees of street capital.

Stringer Bell, by contrast, is Avon's business partner and attempts to cultivate 'respectability', donning suits and hoping to shift his illicit profits into 'legitimate' business. A particularly interesting aspect of the TV show is the manner in which it demonstrates the power of money (however gained) to garner influence within the worlds of building development and politics. Does he possess a level of cultural capital that will allow him to realize success within the mainstream economic realm?

Cutty, a drug gang lieutenant who returns to 'the game' after spending time in prison, finds that he no longer possesses the ability to engage in the requisite levels of violence and instead wants to leave crime to coach teen boxing. When put to Avon that Cutty was once 'a man', the boss disagrees: 'he a man today'. By carrying a particular history and level of street capital, the non-criminally inclined can still be considered as performing an appropriate form of masculinity.

Marlo Stanfield, a relatively new drug gang leader, rivals Avon and Stringer and surprises all with his tenacity and belligerence. Bold decision-making and a willingness to abandon convention and tradition are arguably components of contemporary hegemonic masculinity and allow young, upwardly mobile individuals to perturb their more established rivals in the street sphere.

Bubbles, physically weakened by his drug addiction, is portrayed as both pathetic and canny. Imbued with a sense of ethics, these can nevertheless be subordinated by a constant need for money. Whilst rich in the kinds of street capital which facilitate survival, he arguably lacks that which is required for generating 'respect'.

Omar, an openly gay robber of drug dealers, arguably embodies some significantly contradictory forms of masculinity. Simultaneously derided and feared, his violent capacities and quick intellect render him capable of provoking entire drug dealing networks whilst nevertheless retaining a lucrative illicit and equivocally ethical business.

These characters tend to be portrayed as capable of reacting differently in different contexts, responding according to their specific habitus and readings of their situations. This is the kind of nuanced understanding of street cultural behaviours that is arguably the most revealing.

'Ain't it Black?' Ethnicity and race

Such are the links between street culture and wider structures of colonialization (historical and new; overt and economic) that it is often inaccurately conflated with 'black culture'. This is highly problematic. Where 'ethnicity' speaks to the nature of peoples' backgrounds and cultures, 'race' speaks broadly to physical characteristics. Power relations create patterns of dominance and disadvantage against particular groups to the extent that it is not always useful to separate the notions (Grosfoguel, 2004). It is very difficult to speak meaningfully to a notion of 'black culture', where the 'black' racial moniker refers to a range of ethnicities and cultures. Racism, however, has a considerable bearing on the development of street cultures. Ethnic/racial power relations manifest both in terms of exclusion and oppression, but also in instances of assimilation, hybridization and co-option. The noted socio-economic exclusion of 'Black Atlantic' populations (see Gilroy, 1993) and their cultural productivity have arguably forefronted their associations with street culture in the public imaginary. Street cultures, however, exist in societies that have traditionally been predominantly mono-ethnically white (e.g. Ireland; see Ilan, 2011). Moreover questions of race are often entangled with those of class (e.g. within the USA, Wilson, 1996). Further complications are added by the global reach, co-option and adaptation of black American street cultural tropes, and the fact that these are a product of various hybridities themselves (see Chang, 2005; Gilroy, 1993). A more expansive understanding of the role of race/ethnicity in the formation of street cultures is required.

Population movement and ethnic difference have been central to the development of street culture (see further in Chapter 7). Early studies of the urban disadvantaged were attentive to the role of migration and immigration in shaping experiences of city life. For Shaw and McKay (1942), immigration flows destabilized experiences of neighbourhood residence and interrupted the formation of coherent communities. For scholars such as Whyte (1943), intersectionalities of ethnicity, class and gender could explain why some of the slum residents he studied demonstrated adherence to a culture that owed more to the mores of the Italian working-class than those of the American middle-class. The fragments of rural Puerto Rican culture observed amongst the crack dealers studied by Bourgois (1995/2002) provide a more contemporary example, as does the proposition that African-American street cultures express elements of rural, southern US cultures of 'honour' (e.g. Butterfield, 1995). This is not a matter of inherently problematic and pathological cultures being carried by migrant populations, but rather how aspects of cultures of origin become manifest in responses to exclusion.

Earlier accounts of inner-city gang violence spoke about the role of ethnic/racial difference in demarcating membership and rivalry (see e.g. Suttles, 1968). Equally however, as illustrated by Wild (2003), working-class communities could operate as proverbial 'melting pots' where friendships developed across ethnic lines. The hybridities facilitated by this process gave rise to some of the most exciting and influential developments in street expressivity. Rap and hip-hop emerged from the interplay of American, Jamaican and Puerto Rican genres and styles in New York's South Bronx (Chang, 2005), whilst British youth cultural movements owed much to interactions between the white working-classes and the newly arrived and second-generation immigrants from the West Indies (Hebdige, 1977/2005; Hall and Jefferson, 1976). Even matters as seemingly 'light' as music preference, however, can reveal the operation of corrosive social forces. Jamaican dancehall in Britain, for example, provided a haven and free forum for black young people who experienced overt racism on a day-to-day basis (Henry, 2006). Wacquant (2008) demonstrates moreover that patterns of ethnic/racial segregation and cohabitation vary between Europe and the USA, but that othered races are ubiquitously disadvantaged.

Beyond the more 'cultural' issues of expressivity, matters of race and ethnicity significantly impact on crime and justice, key processes by which social exclusion is maintained and reproduced (see further, Chapter 8). Sampson and Wilson (1995) demonstrate that 'race' as a variable in itself does not indicate any particular propensity to commit crime, but that poverty, residence within a disadvantaged area and family dissolution (all linked to the increased likelihood of being identified as an offender) are disproportionately experienced by black inner-city Americans. These authors note that poor people of colour are more likely to live in concentrations of disadvantage than their white equivalents, allowing greater opportunities for the formation of ghetto-specific cultures. Black men are less likely to be viewed favourably by prospective employers (see Wilson, 1996). They experience greater alienation in terms of their interactions with agents of the mainstream state (particularly the police; see Brunson and Miller, 2006). Furthermore, they are more likely to live close to others with similar experiences who can provide solidarity through a shared street cultural understanding. It is racism not race that underpins the development of street culture.

Within certain developing countries, 'shadism' – the idealization of lighter over darker skin (see e.g. Stolzoff, 2000)—explains, for example, the disproportionate ghettoization of populations of African descent within South American cities (see e.g. Goldstein, 2003). Colonialism's shadow continues to fall, not just across the developing world, but in the developed, where racial/ethnic minorities are subject to laws which they are rarely involved in shaping and which target them disproportionately (see Staples, 1975). As starkly put by Dorothy Roberts in relation to the US experience: 'On any given day, nearly one third of black men in their twenties are under the supervision of the criminal justice system – either behind bars, on probation or on parole' (2004: 1272). This is a staggering figure which explains to some extent the need for a culture that bridges the violent world of the prison with life on the outside. Mass experiences of imprisonment within, for example, African American communities, further attack labour market opportunities and levels of civic and political engagement (ibid.). In other words, widespread experiences of prison and punishment exacerbate the exclusion already felt my some of the most disadvantaged communities, contributing to local cultures which exist in alienation from mainstream social institutions and behavioural norms.

It is wrong to assume that this phenomena is wrapped up in the 'exception' of American over-incarceration, where similar processes (albeit on a lesser scale) operate in continental Europe and the UK towards particular immigrant populations (see e.g. Wacquant, 1999; Tonry, 1997). In Australia ethnic relations are complex, but nevertheless some similar patterns can be viewed between what is observable there and the international context: both Aboriginal and immigrant young people can be associated with 'gangs' in the public imaginary (see e.g. White, 2008, 2009). This speaks to poor public understandings of street culture and also the particularly excluded position of Aboriginal young people who feel that the peer associations they make (at times through

Figure 3.1 Street cultural practices at the weaker end of the spectrum are barely distinguishable from youth cultural practice in general. Photo by Simon Wheately

their disproportionate experiences of state care) take on an almost familial character, given a lack of potential to otherwise form connections to mainstream Australian society (White, 2009). Clearly, there is considerable global variation in the ways that race/ethnicity link to street culture. Where it has connections to wider processes of socio-economic exclusion, however, it will often intersect with class, gender and various other structural factors to play a role in the existence and character of particular street cultures.

Structure, individuality and the street cultural spectrum

Street culture becomes a means for those disadvantaged by configurations of class, gender and race/ethnicity to deal with the material deprivations and cultural subjugation that result from their position. Rather than 'causing' street culture in a 'linear' manner, these intersectionalities of structural disadvantage are refracted through individual agency, community characteristics and relationships to mainstream norms and forms of presentation. Hence the 'spectrum' of weak to strong embeddedness in, and dedication to street culture referred to in the previous chapter. Street culture at the strong extreme of the scale orders a struggle for survival, whereas at the weak end it becomes fodder for the cultivation of cool, and in the middle it offers opportunities for excitement and income and creates hierarchies of less deadly import (see Figure 3.1).

Theoretically, one challenge is to understand how characteristics that underpin socio-economic exclusion, with the poverty and criminalization that accompany it, can be simultaneously linked to desirable characteristics that are emulated by particular members of the powerful included. Bev Skeggs (2004) offers an understanding of the ways in which states of 'self' are classed and classified. Simply put, she argues that personhood, much like commodities, is subject to systems of 'value' and 'exchange'. The value that is attributed to various classed, gendered and raced states of being is determined and 'inscribed' by power relations. The powerful included have the ability to have their dominant characteristics understood as the most worthy and valuable, whereas the states of being associated with the excluded are viewed as dangerous and unworthy. This does not preclude the excluded from understanding their own characteristics and ways of being differently. For the included, however, such states of danger and transgression also represent a source of fascination and appeal (see also Jenks, 2003). For the excluded, their own states of being have little 'exchange value' (unless couched in the attitudes and symbols of respectability), but when harnessed by the included they can become valuable:

> The contemporary reinscription of the working-class as the site of culture and characteristics means that they have an exchange-value, as some of their dispositions are being re-converted into temporary cultural dispositions (such as 'cool') that can be tried on and used as a resource for the formation and propertizing of the 'new' middle-class self … different inscriptions generate different boundaries between what is recoupable and what is not; so the one body may carry the 'benefit scrounger' along with the 'naughty criminal' (Skeggs, 2004: 22–23).

Skeggs explains that issues of gender and race have a strong bearing on how value is inscribed onto the excluded self. Thus whilst black cultures of disadvantage are frequently a source of 'cool' and stylistic appropriation, the same cannot always be said for equivalent white cultures, whether 'chav' in the UK (Hayward and Yar, 2006) or 'white trash' in the USA (Hartigan, 1997), which beyond irony value seem to have much less cultural resonance.

Sections of the excluded attempt to highlight their value and worth through embracing 'respectability' (traditionally, middle-class notions of propriety, self-improvement and careerism). Without social mobility or decently paid employment available, however, this is unlikely to yield material benefits. The increasingly viable strategy becomes to embrace what proves to have value in the world of the street, even to valorize it. Where political narratives around the value of labour and the structural nature of poverty are greatly diminished, this affirmative (yet stigmatizing) street cultural approach to exclusion resonates stronger. These alternative paths to 'worth' – one shared with the powerful included and the other distinct to the excluded – are not mutually exclusive and can be simultaneously pursued. Different values and performances can be displayed depending on the audience, hence individuals may vary their position on the spectrum depending on context. The particularities of global regions, national states and local communities dictate the levels of material resources available to the urban poor and the levels of violence which threaten them. This too shapes the overall character of local street cultures which may appear more or less 'extreme'.

The second challenge involves understanding how individuals, based on their structured identity, personal histories and particular orientations, come to occupy various positions on the street cultural spectrum. This is a classic question of structure versus agency, reflecting on the extent to which social conditions and individual choice variously pattern human behaviour. Field, capital and habitus, concepts associated with Pierre Bourdieu (1977, 1986, 1990), are being increasingly utilized in the field of street culture to understand such tensions. For Bourdieu, social life can be conceptualized as a number of different 'fields' or arenas in which individuals accumulate and expend different kinds of 'capitals' or resources to attain status and advantage. These forms of capital are economic (money/material resources), cultural (knowledge, learning, capacities, states of being), social (the product of networks and associations) and symbolic (relations to accepted/dominant forms of power) (see Skeggs, 2004: 16–17). Fields have traditionally been conceptualized as 'orthodox', that is, mainstream and legitimate: a person's place in society or the official economy, or one's progress within a particular career. Anderson, however, has commented that

> [T]he savoir faire of the street world – knowing how to deal coolly with people, how to move, look, act and dress – is a form of capital, not a form middle class people would respect, but capital that can nonetheless be cashed in (1999: 134).

Sveinung Sandberg (2008a, 2008b) and Willy Pedersen (Sandberg and Pedersen, 2009) have thus argued that there is a case for understanding this as 'street capital'. To do so, the street must be conceptualized as a field in itself, but one that is 'heterodox' or in opposition to dominant conceptions of worth, value and legitimacy. In other words, those ways of being that advantage a person in the world of the street will tend to devalue their position in mainstream fields, thus significantly limiting their overall value (see Sandberg, 2008b: 157). To put this in concrete terms, if a person possessess a tough demeanour that hints of violent potential, this can serve them well in terms of the drug economy but could significantly impede their progress in the mainstream jobs market. Street capital can have cultural and social forms and can be converted to economic capital (see Ilan, 2013). It cannot, however, be converted into classic symbolic capital and indeed prevents its potential accumulation, that is, inhibits the ability to display 'respectability'.

'Habitus' refers to dispositions, habits and instincts that form in a person over time. It is a key concept to bridge agency with structure, as these embodied characteristics are the mechanism by which configurations of class, gender, culture and ethnicity manifest at an individual level. Famously, Bourdieu described it as 'a feel for the game' (1998: 25), the ways in which individuals instinctively and pre-consciously interpret and respond to that which happens around them. It channels past experiences into current ways of being. Thus the convicts studied by Caputo-Levine (2012) wear a 'yard' or 'screw' face, combining a facial expression of aggressive indifference and a willingness to escalate confrontation that can be read from their stance and body language. The habitus of the violent men studied by Winlow and Hall (2009) is such that they respond to challenges with force as a response to past memories of humiliation. The challenges that have been faced by individuals are written into the way they orientate themselves towards the future. Fraser (2013), moreover, calls for a specific understanding of 'street habitus': the patterned dispositions and embodied characteristics that stem from, and facilitate street cultural life.

When speaking about 'individual agency' and considering whether those who are deeply embedded within street culture are exercising 'rational choice', it is crucial to realize that decisions are often made on the basis of this structured habitus, not merely a set of cognitive calculations. Capital accumulation and expenditure are usually not weighed up explicitly in a person's mind but form part of a 'practical rationality', an implicit underpinning logic (Grundetjern and Sandberg, 2012; Bourdieu, 1990). In other words, social structures bind and influence the choices made by individuals who are free agents only within this framework. Adhering to, and enacting various degrees of street culture proper can thus be understood as a pre-conscious strategy to make the most of the opportunities for material gain, pleasure and worth that individuals *feel* are realistically available to them. Habitus and cultural capital are embodied, they cannot easily be 'tried on'. Thus those who genuinely experience exclusion may practice street culture and those who merely sport some of its symbols and styles are easily identified as 'fake'.

Knowledge of street styles and the cultural products associated with them may allow a person to accumulate 'subcultural capital' (Thornton, 1995) within particular scenes, appearing to be more savvy and 'on trend' than others. Being a well-regarded urban tastemaker, however, requires a different set of qualities than those most useful for moving safely within a slum. Within the arena of cool, weak street cultural identities are much more likely to be *performed* or deployed consciously and reflexively, and have little more than a rhetorical connection to crime and violence (see Ilan, 2012). As Chapter 6 details, this is an option that the consumer culture makes available to a broad market. The strong street cultural values and behaviours that are a response to harsh conditions of exclusion are more likely to be pre-consciously *practiced*. The underclass discourses explored in the previous chapter that seek to represent the poor as victims of their own bad choices are thus disingenuous.

Given that rational decision-making processes are rarely at play within individual moments of crime (or for that matter, embodied cool) (see Hayward, 2007), it becomes especially important to consider the role of emotionality. For Jack Katz (1988) issues of structure form the 'background' to particular moments of action which have emotions in their 'foreground'. In other words, whilst structures place people in particular social and cultural contexts, and their agency provides them with certain powers to choose their response, frequently it is emotional dynamics rather than rational choice that underpin the outcome of a situated moment. Rage is quelled, thrills are generated and power is conjured in a range of behaviours which may make little sense to an observer 'rationally' appraising a situation: for example, the theft, joyriding and burning out of a car; or assaulting an individual with many tough male relatives in his family.

Scholars such as Silverman (2004) who attempt to mathematically calculate the operation of street culture could conclude that there is individual status to be gained through both of these expressive crimes. Whilst the risk of detection and punishment might add to the excitement of joyriding, risking the retaliation of an individual's street network in the case of the second example might not be seen as a street culturally astute action. Gains that may be made in terms of being viewed as having 'heart', 'balls' (note masculinist language) or the will to violence could be countered by perceptions of hot headedness. In other words, a failure to demonstrate appropriate judgement might mark an individual as less deserving of respect in other contexts and thus deepen their exposure to the risk of violence on those occasions. The point to note is that decisions made 'in the heat of the moment' are viscerally satisfying and even when street culturally advantageous, are not necessarily the product of rationality but of emotional logics. This notion resonates well with the concept of habitus, which effectively describes a process by which individuals draw on their history and position to 'feel' for the appropriate response to a situation. In contrast to the supposedly rationalistic world of official laws and justice processes, street culture's reliance on primary, personal acquaintances is a space in which emotionality might be openly recognized as the basis of a particular interaction/reaction.

Interestingly, Katz (1988) was also attentive to the 'ways of the badass' and noted that the adoption of street cultural styles is, much like emotionality, an embodied process. He recognized that holding oneself in a powerful posture is tied to feeling a particular sense of mastery over one's immediate environment and those in it. Whether slouching, leaning or strolling to exaggeratingly signal one's state of calm; standing with shoulders set and legs wide apart to communicate strength and impassability; or adopting the simultaneous-crouch-and-look-down that was characteristic of the Chicano gang Katz used as an example; physical expressivity is both part of an individual's habitus and linked to their emotional sense of self within particular space. In a similar sense, 'cool' is tied to notions of mastery and manipulating one's own emotionality. Cool is arguably thus equally embodied, providing a visceral sense of satisfaction and relative superiority through the outward display of a muted emotionality.

For Hayward (2004), furthermore, the culture of western capitalism is tied up with the emotional dynamics of consumerism: impulsivity and the attainment of immediate gratification (which the lower classes have traditionally been critiqued for embodying), to the extent that these are mainstream rather than 'subterranean' states of being (see also Matza and Sykes, 1961). For this author, certain expressive crimes can be understood as part of the search for emotional pleasure and existential affirmation that for included populations is achieved through participation in the consumer culture. Thus, as will be explored in greater detail in Chapter 5, expressive crimes such as vandalism and joyriding become in effect the 'extreme sports' of disadvantaged urban youth, who lack the financial resources to generate the same emotional states by other means. The consumer culture has furthermore created within included populations a desire to sport the trappings of cool.

Conclusion

Class, gender, race/ethnicity, age, nationality and various factors in combination inherently colour not only an individual's circumstances, capacities and opportunities, but the ways in which they come to define and capitalize on them. Positions are taken on the street cultural spectrum based on structural exclusion as well as individual and communal readings of it. In everyday life, individuals will enact and react to exclusion in various ways, and this in turn results in behaviours and states of being that the included might judge to be dangerous, desirable or a combination of both.

The street cultural spectrum remains a useful conceptual tool to understand the variety of street cultural behaviours, which on the weak end might be consciously deployed to cultivate a sense of 'cool', whilst at the strong end these become the unconscious, contingent modes of interpretation and reaction that give rise to criminal and/or predatory behaviours. Located both within a historically conscious and geographically aware analysis of meso-level (group-level) cultural concerns and a critical analysis of macro socio-economic structures, this individual-level consideration of being and behaviour arguably provides a relatively complete schema by which to understand street culture. Ultimately, moreover, there are specific spatial factors that come into play in such matters and these are considered in detail in the next chapter.

CHAPTER 4

Space, Territory and Gangs

Introduction

This chapter explores the important relationships that exist between street culture and space. The notion of the 'disadvantaged area' – a spatial concept – is central to how street culture tends to be understood; but there are a number of nuances within this broader notion that require unpacking. Central also to public imaginaries of street culture's relationship with space is the concept of 'territory': the notion that areas of urban poverty are divided up between competing street cultural institutions (e.g. 'gangs') who attempt to exercise some manner of control over it, whether symbolically, physically or politically. There are complex spatial processes at play within contemporary spaces of deprivation, however, that render such general presumptions problematic. Instead, it will be argued that a more nuanced understanding of street cultural spaces and institutions is required in late-modernity. Focusing here on the micro-space of cities, neighbourhoods and communities, this chapter can be read alongside Chapter 7 on globalization, which provides more of a macro-spatial context.

The chapter traces the tensions that exist between the spatial qualities of ghettoization (containment) and flow (liquidity), which variously order the lives of the urban poor through restricting their abilities to either cross boundaries or settle securely. It highlights the role of differently constituted forms of social inclusion and exclusion, as well as the varied presence of the state within these processes. The chapter charts various ways in which scholars have understood the relationship between poverty and city space. Particular focus is placed on the 'new' forms of spatial practice linked to new media technologies as well as the increasing pace of urbanization, gentrification and commodification of city space. Where the spatial practices of street cultural institutions are considered, it will be argued that a more useful street cultural discourse should replace outdated and politically loaded 'gang' terminology. Obfuscating a lot more than it clarifies, the word will be shown to serve the cause of populist politics more than in-depth understanding. Ultimately, thus, the chapter provides a more contemporary and comprehensive set of analytical terms to speak to forms of street cultural practice, both spatial and collective/institutional.

In various cities globally, the socio-economic status of particular neighbourhoods tends to be written into the nature of their spaces: the size of the houses, the quality (and very existence) of road materials and street furniture, their cleanliness and aesthetic character. Even devoid of people, city spaces themselves say something about those who use them. Abstract maps indeed can also reveal much about the status of an area through indicating the spacing and scale of buildings, or by failing to recognize the existence of sizeable settlements of the urban poor. City dwellers come to instinctively understand those spaces that are the domain of the included as well as those that are marked by concentrations of poverty and exclusion: often the zones where street culture flourishes. Reflecting on the notion of habitus, how individuals internalize the effects of social structure (see Fraser, 2013), it can be useful to consider how different people read the nature of the space around them and adjust their behaviour accordingly: do people feel at home and at ease? Or intimidated and out of sorts?

Socio-spatial exclusion in the ghetto *firma*

Traditionally, various kinds of city space have tended to be conceptualized as solid, definitely bounded entities. This is no more apparent than in the Chicago School's classic division of its city into concentric rings. Hagedorn (2007: 17) indeed notes that such was their progressive nature that they tended to vest these spaces with a quality that borders on agency: a power to act and influence. The members of the Chicago School could thus view the 'zones of transition' or least stable, most impoverished areas of the city as contributing to the motivation to commit crime, as opposed to the ethnic status of their inhabitants. The notion that space should be understood as a significant dimension of the poverty–culture–crime nexus would prove influential. As the idea of these spaces fostering 'social disorganization' lost favour, scholars instead began to see patterns in the ways that various disadvantaged communities occupied and used slum spaces (see e.g. Suttles, 1968). Within relatively fixed spatial boundaries populations could be seen to ebb and flow, variously altering the economic fortunes, ethnic composition and configurations of community that existed. For Cloward and Ohlin (1960), these neighbourhood characteristics could determine the illicit opportunities available to young people growing up within them. In effect, this constituted an early formation of the argument that the nature of local spaces, criminal networks and neighbourhood norms shape qualities of particular niche street cultures.

There is a certain logic to the 'naturalism' of the early Chicago School understandings of the development of impoverished areas. Convenience and lack of means could certainly explain why working-class communities lived in cramped accommodation in close proximity to the factories, railroads, tanning and meat processing plants which sustained them. As decades progressed, however, greater attention was paid to the roles of political economy, commercial and housing policies in the creation and reproduction of slum areas. In the latter regard, the example of the British welfare state became particularly noteworthy, where it was active in clearing slums and housing the urban poor in newly built accommodation in suburbs and garden cities (see Young, and Wilmott, 1957/2012). This was not a purely benign process where it placed great strains on familial bonds and the close-knit community cohesion that had developed over time (see Robins and Cohen, 1978; Parker, 1974).

Owen Gill (1977) furthermore demonstrated the extent to which housing allocation could concentrate residents with the greatest number of social and economic difficulties within a small space, creating addresses that were particularly disorderly and stigmatizing. State intervention in the spatial conditions of the urban working-class is often formed in the absence of any nuanced consideration of how such communities live (Haylett, 2003). For a pioneering David Harvey (1973/2009), the development of cities replete with social, economic and spatial inequalities is a facet of capitalist society, a process facilitated by various modes of municipal governance. As the social and economic consequences of globalization and neoliberalism unfolded, various scholars articulated a sense that global cities were becoming increasingly polarized: 'dual cities' that offered divergent and mutually exclusive experiences to the rich and poor (Mollenkopf and Castells, 1991; Marcuse, 1989). As noted already, it is these socio-economic developments that can be used to explain contemporary forms of street cultural manifestation, and in part this has been due to their patterning of the urban spatial environment.

The links between space, experienced deprivation and cultures of exclusion, for Loic Wacquant (2008), should be appropriately grounded in a socio-spatial analysis:

> To forget that urban space is a *historical and political construction* in the strong sense of the term is to risk (mis)taking for 'neighbourhood effects' what is nothing more than the spatial retranslation of economic and social differences (2008: 9, emphasis in original).

In other words, when analysing the role of the disadvantaged community in shaping forms of street culture, it is important to see past explanations like Sampson et al.'s (1997) examination of the role of 'collective efficacy' in effectively pacifying local populations. Whether or not and why communities are associated with violent crime should not come down to a question of whether or not they are effectively helping themselves. Rather, Wacquant advocates understanding the fact that disadvantaged communities occupy a particular position, and fulfil particular functions, variously within different kinds of states. Such communities can represent a source of flexible, cheap and disposable labour. Indeed, they might remain as a discarded residue of an era in which such a function was required, now 'warehoused' by increasingly stringent discourses and regulations surrounding welfare and increasingly coercive criminal justice.

In addition, despite 'flaws' in the consumerist practices of the disadvantaged, their role in markets for consumer goods, private rented accommodation and a variety of other products and services should not be forgotten (Ilan, 2011; Davis, 2006; Bauman, 2004). There is profit to be made from servicing the poor. Wacquant's (2008) notion of 'advanced marginality' is a means to understand the varieties of socio-spatial exclusion within the west (and arguably further afield). It explains both the racially homogenous 'hyperghettos' of the USA and the racially heterogeneous (though immigrant dominated) urban peripheries of France as stemming from the advance of neoliberal late capitalism. For him, varying qualities and quantities of state interaction with such communities (through policing and social programmes) play a role in shaping particular forms of advanced marginality, but the phenomenon has three common features, examined in more detail below.

The first factor to consider is the concentration of disadvantage. Wacquant here shares concerns with Wilson (1996). They show that the story of the US inner-city is one of middle-class flight and the residulization of the most deprived sections of the black population within spaces that show the scars of economic and municipal neglect. Vacant lots, burnt and boarded-up buildings and shops bear testament to spaces and populations that have been relegated to a particularly low level of social and economic inclusion. Wilson (ibid.) notes how official housing and municipal policy has tended to further disadvantage such areas and their residents. As previously noted within the UK context, state housing provision can indeed serve to concentrate disadvantage. Within the developing world, on the other hand, where the state is not such a significant presence in the housing sector, Davis (2006) discusses how 'megaslums' tend to be built on squatted land, lacking basic amenities, often close to areas of industrial hazard and distant from sources of employment. Official recognition becomes something of a mixed blessing, as whilst some amenities might be provided and some residents might gain more secure tenure, the speculators and profiteers move in to take advantage of the ground work put in by those who lack the means to retain their housing there. Though differing in levels of material scarcity and in terms of social and physical infrastructure, both models of 'ghettoization' serve to concentrate poverty and its accompanying privations and problems within particular spaces. These themselves become the mark and crucible for the perpetuation of disadvantage and the practice of street culture.

A second relevant issue cited by Wacquant is the way in which stigma can accumulate within particular spaces. As well illustrated by Garbin and Millington (2012) in their study of La Courneuve, a deprived *banlieu* on the outskirts of Paris, living in particular areas can mark individual residents with a particular stigma in the eyes of the wider population. In their example, slum residence often becomes automatically associated in the popular imaginary with problems of unemployment, crime and urban disorder. Residing in particular parts of the city, indeed, renders it more difficult for individuals to attain employment (see e.g. Wilson, 1996). Participants in my study of inner-city Dublin, for example, reported that they supplied a relative's address when applying for jobs, knowing that revealing their true area of residence might have deterred employers from giving them a chance (Ilan, 2011). They also reported, corresponding with Wacquant's analysis (2008: 30), difficulties in securing basic financial services such as bank loans and insurance. Indeed, David Sibley (1995) argues that divisions are erected within the imaginary of the included to impose a sense of spatial order on the world; people seen as dangerous, impure and polluting in Mary Douglas' (1966) sense become associated with impure spaces (particular areas of the city) and identities (e.g. through underclass discourse). In such a manner, the consequences of poverty and exclusion exist within a cyclical, iterative dynamic by which they also become their causes. Of course, and as will be explored further down, those who reside within spaces of deprivation remain capable of interpreting their areas in a different manner.

The ghettos of the 20th and 21st centuries tend to differ from their historical counterparts in that they are not 'walled in'. Instead, the dual process of politically framing the poor as inherently problematic and criminalizing their behaviours can serve to maintain effective spatial boundaries (Waquant, 2008: 34). It is for these reasons that matters of criminalization and containment (the third component of Wacquant's analysis) retain relevance. Research has demonstrated the extent to which disadvantaged populations tend to view their police forces as oppressive (see e.g. Brunson and Miller, 2006; Sharp and Atherton, 2007). Such is the disproportionate attention lavished by the justice system on disadvantaged urban areas that the prison can become a de facto orbiting element of their spatial make-up. Indeed, when reading the *Justice Atlas of Corrections*, compiled by the Justice Mapping Project NGO (www.justiceatlas.org), it becomes clear that the distribution of poverty and incarceration is such that within many deprived areas a great number of individuals will not be residing in their homes (or that of their families) but in prison cells. To contextualize this, the Spatial Information Design Lab (2009) has demonstrated the disparities that exist in terms of spending on imprisonment versus education on a block-by-block basis in New Orleans. Investment thus can tend to be directed at containing rather than alleviating this kind of concentrated disadvantage. Given strong spatial connections which thus bind the prison to the slum, it is no surprise to see street cultures travelling along these lines. The practices and styles of the street and prison blend. This is exemplified by the gangs studied by Moore (1978) which provide a system of protection and belonging that facilitates a street cultural life on both sides of the bars, as well as the influence that prison dress has on street style (see Ash, 2009 and Chapter 6, this volume).

'Representing': Alternative experiences of socio-spatial disadvantage

This elaboration of Wacquant's analysis of socio-spatial exclusion is not the final word on the matter. Keith Hayward's (2004) work on the lived processes of crime and consumerism in the city highlights the importance of exploring how various kinds of urban space are experienced. He notes how the straight lines and definitive designations of 'official' plans of, and for the city are rarely replicated in the messy realm of human experience. This notion resonates with the agency of disadvantaged groups to understand their own environment differently from how it is experienced by the included. Thus, for outsiders who experience the disadvantaged area as a space of danger, this is not always the case for its own residents. Some may well experience it so, depending often on local climates of violence and their own street capital, but in various areas of deprivation both historically and in contemporary times, the dilapidated urban environment can be home: a space of familiarity, safety and indeed pride. Thus, for the lads in Parker's study of Liverpool 'once you're in the Block you're laughing' (1974: 39), the community defended its residents from outside challenges or incursions.

Indeed, Jane Jacobs had noted that the street facing nature of life in the 'classic' slum provided a source of constant vigilance by residents and therefore a certain amount of safety for those who walked its streets. The disadvantaged Glaswegian youth studied by Fraser (2013) in their vernacular state that they *are* 'Langview' (their district of residence) as opposed to being from there. Local pride and affiliation saturates street cultural expression: classic NY graffiti artists often included the number of their street alongside their tag; the names of garrison slum communities pepper Jamaican dancehall music; in rap music and videos local spaces, neighbourhood friends, typical scenes and distinctive landmarks feature heavily as lyrical and visual themes (Forman, 2002). The US street cultural term 'representing' (one's area) is recognizable to many English speakers across social groups as a succinct representation of the strong relationship between disadvantaged populations and their physical and social environment.

For Hayward (2004), urban spaces that are generally viewed as deprived and high crime can simultaneously be used and experienced by the excluded in an alternative manner. In this way, abandoned factories can become graffiti galleries; parks meant for child's play can become the site of impromptu bar- beques; street corners become party spaces where intoxicants are consumed, music is played and celebration can coexist (or even momentarily trump) an otherwise pervading misery. The street space can thus be the restaurant, nightclub, department store (and tragically also the sewer system, homes and day-care centres) for the urban poor. Particular street cultural areas can come to take on particular symbolic value, especially where they are associated with particular forms of commercially successful street cultural expression. Quinn (2005) for example, demonstrates how on foot of the rap group NWA's iconic album/song 'Straight Outta Compton' this entire sub-city of Los Angeles became synonymous with strong variants of street culture. Residence of this district would thus be held up by its other rappers hoping to gain a greater share of the mainstream market. The ways in which the disadvantaged city is experienced by its residents are not limited to their impact on modes of street cultural expression, but extend to influence the forms of street cultural insti- tutions and behaviour that might take root within them. The presence of the state within them becomes particularly important in this regard.

As noted by Hagedorn (2008), those areas in the developing world that are largely neglected by the state, for example, the garrisons of Jamaica or the favelas of Brazil, tend to be serviced by 'grass roots' street cultural institutions. These act simultaneously as illegal enterprises in drugs and/or weaponry, informal militia and ad hoc social welfare and basic infrastructure providers. The police cannot enter these areas without significant force and they become essentially 'defensible spaces' (2008: 14) for the cultivation of criminal net- works and markets. These institutions partially fill voids in the economic and social fabric of communities that mainstream forms of order maintenance, employment and municipal maintenance neglect. These communities in turn can provide recruits, acceptance, customers, protection and camouflage to such institutions.

In less extreme terms, a similar dynamic can exist in cities across the devel- oped world. The patterns of material neglect and aggressive policing that characterize the relationship between many communities of disadvantage and

Figure 4.1   An East London housing estate demonstrates both the remarkable support (subsidized public housing) and exclusion (neglect and the concentration of social problems) that is supplied to those on low incomes in the UK. Photo by Simon Wheatley

the states which house them render street cultural institutions more viable as they manage host communities through fear and favours, safe in the knowledge that cooperating with the authorities is taboo. The partial and varying nature of state oppression/neglect in western jurisdictions, however, tends to mirror the more limited embeddedness of street cultural institutions within them (Figure 4.1). This, in part, might account for the differences Wacquant (2008) finds between American and French spaces of deprivation and their difference from spaces in the developing world.

Street cultural space in flux

Street culture has traditionally been associated with the solid city, as I have noted in previous work:

> Solidity refers to a sense of cohesion within particular groups and communities, a connection between geographical spaces and stable sources of industrial employment, and a reification of locality as a marker of place and identification...In the solid city, the locality is the prime location for the performance of work and leisure: simultaneously constituted or distinct, legal or otherwise. Thus Willis's (1977) working-class kids find their working-class jobs geographically proximate to their fathers' shop floors and the 'lads' observed by Paul Corrigan (1979) are confined by limited financial resources to 'hanging around' their local street spaces. In such a manner, the neighbourhood can be a constraining force limiting the opportunities for economic and social realization, narrowing horizons, compounding and reproducing exclusion...(Ilan, 2013: 5–6).

This kind of socio-spatial containment continues to hold relevance for many disadvantaged populations as evident, for example, from studies of young people in post-industrial Britain who are strongly embedded in local street cultural networks and have limited possibilities of experiencing wider geographic, social and economic realities (Fraser, 2013; Reynolds, 2013; MacDonald et al., 2005). This accords with the 'dual city' thesis that was earlier discussed. There does exist, however, a more complex form of socio-spatial exclusion based on what has been conceptualized as the more 'liquid' forms of space that exist in late-modernity (see Young, 2007; Bauman, 2000). The pace of urban and technological change associated with the socio-economic characteristics of this era open up new spaces, disperse older ones and connect people, images and ideas instantaneously. Moreover, whilst cultural geography has been creative in its engagement with wider and more sophisticated notions of space, other disciplines (notably, criminology) have not always been equivalently attentive (see Hayward, 2012). The material below presents some of the more complex ways in which street culture and space need to be understood within the context of late-modernity.

The scale and scope of urban transformation should be considered when attempting to use classic explanations of space. Drawing on Mooney and Danson (1997) amongst others, Jock Young (2007: 31–32) argues against the dual cities thesis:

> The late modern city is one of blurred boundaries, it was the Fordist city of modernity which had a segregated structure, a division of labour of specialised areas, a Chicago of concentric rings. Now the lines blur: gentrification occurs in the inner city – deviance occurs in the suburbs.

Informing this notion is the flow that occurs where poor domestic workers maintain the manicured spaces of the privileged and where digital media and communications constantly underpin a bi-directional flow of images which acquaints the occupiers of one kind of space with the residents of the other. Furthermore, the role played by the urban real estate market in post-industrial economies has markedly altered the social composition of various parts of the city. Famously, processes of gentrification have transformed former slumlands and industrial spaces across western metropolises into desirable apartments, lofts and townhouses, often proximate to key city centre areas (see Smith, 1996). In these contexts, the urban poor initially tend to coexist with bohemian creative cultures and subsequently middle-class and elite consumers before they are eventually displaced, with nothing but shards and traces of their street culture remaining variously in markets, food stalls and art installations contrived for more salubrious tastes and wallets.

Moreover, it becomes clear from Smith's later work (2002) that this popularly understood notion of gentrification is particularly western-centric, but that the same socio-economic principles underpinning it inform a great deal of urban transformation in the developing world (see also Davis: 2006). In previous works, I have noted how these notions of property lead regeneration place strain on community identities, spatial practices and street cultural tendencies (Ilan, 2011, 2013). Where the boundaries between spaces of deprivation and wealth are more fluid and porous and populations flow between them, this necessitates a reconsideration of the relationship between street culture and space.

One consequence of these radical spatial transformations is the displacement of populations and communities. Processes of spatial migration and the existence of precarious residence thus also should be considered. The poor are particularly disadvantaged here, often unable to exercise agency within private markets and increasingly denuded public housing provision and unable to assert ownership of 'squatted' or quasi-legal settlements. Moreover, the overarching neoliberal social and economic principles which have reordered the city have simultaneously transfigured patterns of employment and attitudes to social welfare (see e.g. Bauman, 2000), which have had significant effects on tendencies in national residence. Flows of population, economic capital and images of consumerism have manifested in the neo-colonial patterns of manufacturing wage slavery in the developing world and immigration into the developed.

As millions seek out a better life in the west, these neoliberal economic policies tend to go hand-in-hand with a neo-conservatism (see Harvey, 2005) that underpins the use of criminal and quasi-criminal regulations to control the behaviour of immigrants (see Aas, 2007). As will become clear in Chapter 7, global flows have become increasingly significant for understanding street culture. On a micro-spatial level, however, population flows and tough popular and legal reactions to immigration have left vast populations less secure in their immediate residential status. Brotherton and Barrios (2011), for example, have demonstrated the extent to which Dominicans in the USA face the risk of deportation and can thus exist in the flux of spatial migrations between areas of deprivation in both countries. This kind of insecure tenure is no more apparent than in the experiences of street children in the developing world whose micro-geographies are defined by extreme fluidity (see Van Blerk, 2005). It is significantly less likely that individuals would build an affinity with, or sense of control over space that they very tenuously occupy.

Furthermore, I have shown how particularly disadvantaged young people native to Dublin city, due to the vicissitudes of public housing policies, private markets and the operation of the care system, are excluded from their local community and are frequently forced to move around (Ilan, 2013). They use their tough street cultural acumen not to defend their space of residence (in which they have little stake and over which they have little control) but to travel the city in search of materially and/or existentially affirming experiences. Their experiences of spatial 'flow' in the metropolitan city must be contrasted to the young men in post-industrial Britain who are constrained and trammelled within their local areas from which the opportunities for mobility ebb. Thus whilst debates take place around the role of new media technologies in facilitating mobility in real space (see Skelton and Gough, 2013), power continues to exercise considerable bearing on spatial practices.

Street space has a rhetorical power beyond its physical boundaries with the 'ghetto', 'hood', 'manor' (and other terms for disadvantaged spaces) taking on a signifying quality. It thus exists as a form of discursive space. Notions of 'ghettoness' become popular shorthand to refer to street culture in everyday parlance, for example, 'a ghetto ting dis' (in UK slang derived from Jamaican Patois) or 'I had to get ghetto' (in US slang referring to the assertion of street capital). This phenomenon is no more apparent than in the case of urban music. As extensively catalogued by Rivke Jaffe (2012), the 'ghetto' tends to be associated with the 'soul' and suffering of marginalized (particularly black) populations, imbuing the music which references it with the transgressive 'otherness' important for its commodification, but also serving as an identifying trope for a range of disadvantaged communities. '[The ghetto] can serve as a site for the production of transgressive, cosmopolitan "immobile subjects", connecting marginalized groups across borders' (Jaffe, 2012: 675). As such, the mournful tones of Donny Hathaway in the 1960s and the defiant snarl of Baby Cham in the 2000s narrate shared experiences of street life though separated by decades and seas. Moreover, as demonstrated, for example, by Van Hellemont (2012), online blogs can be utilized by youth groups in Belgium to lay claim to 'gangness' by referencing the street culturally potent space of the Bronx in New York and connecting it to their city of Brussels. References to 'Bronxelles' (ibid.: 170) demonstrate how notions of 'ghettoness' can be detached from their spatial moorings and used to articulate identity within other disadvantaged areas.

Finally, it is important in contemporary times to consider the salience of virtual space, cyber communities and information flow. The ever-growing phenomenon of digital life and culture renders it increasingly important to note how virtual spaces have opened up, variously interrupting, maintaining, altering and complicating patterns of social life (see Hayward, 2012; Miller, 2011). This too has consequences for variants of street culture. Beyond specialist 'communities' (if we can always call them this) of street-style enthusiasts who communicate through a plethora of boards, blogs and websites, there are 'strong' street cultural practitioners whose criminality bleeds between real and virtual spaces. Ultimately, the use of virtual spaces tends to be characterized by the 'liquid': the hybridizing of previously distinct genres and tropes; the increasing difficulty of distinguishing between real-life crime and its mediated representation, the role of images of criminality in the commercial success of various products as well as the role of commercially successful digital services in opening up new spaces for the performance of criminality (see also Yar, 2012; Ferrell et al., 2008). Below I consider two examples of these significantly more widespread phenomena:

Getting up online: 'Style Wars', the evocative documentary of early hip-hop culture (Silver and Chalfant, 1983), observed the classic New York City graffiti writers of the 1970s/1980s congregated around a particular bench, comparing sketchbooks and watching graffitied subway trains roll by (an early analogue example of 'information flow'!) As graffiti culture permeated the world and digital technology advanced, the bench and trains have been replaced by a range of websites, hosting a global community of writers posting photos and accounts of their work online. The competitive 'economy of prestige' that assigns places on the graffiti hierarchy according to aesthetic vision, painting skill and daring (see MacDonald, 2001) operates within a global milieu calling for further skills in media production, self-promotion and new media mastery. This together with the burgeoning industry in graffiti products (paints, nozzles, inks, etc.) marketed and for sale online are part and parcel of the sub (or street) cultural businesses and careers that thrive under these conditions (Snyder, 2009). Ultimately, websites such as '12oz Prophet' and 'ArtCrimes' represent prime examples of genre hybridity: part virtual gathering space and global graffiti wall, part repository of knowledge and lore and part platform for 'legitimate' entrepreneurialism – promoting gallery shows and the sale of paraphernalia. The demands of local visibly diminish for writers who can paint in more obscure spaces and still be sure that their work can be viewed by a global audience; the existence of virtual space impacts on the practice of writing in 'real' space.

Online repping and Twitter beefs: The themes of street cultural supremacy, rivalry and conflict have long featured in the sphere of street cultural expressivity, where the name-checking of particular factions crops up frequently in urban music, graffiti, pirate radio and other media (see further in Chapter 6). Significantly, this phenomenon has been remediated in the digital age where it is considerably easier for street-based productions and forms of expressivity to be directly accessed by outsiders and rivals. One example of this has been the proliferation of 'hood videos' in which British young people who profess membership in various criminally associated 'crews' post home-made music videos to YouTube (see Ilan, 2012). Alongside communication in the open fora constituted by social media sites such as Facebook and Twitter, this material has been used as a form of intelligence and evidence by police forces and prosecutors. The messages communicated through new media have been interpreted at times as threats and associations with gangs strong enough to merit criminal convictions. In this way, mediated representations of street culture blur with real issues of crime and justice. This has furthermore created difficulties for musicians whose oeuvre spans hood and professional productions, where the police may warn off record labels or challenge their rights to perform (ibid.). This controversy may serve as either a break or a catalyst for an artiste's career depending on the scope for commodifying street cultural tropes and connections to alleged criminality.

Whilst 'Twitter beefs' may spill out into real-world violence (see Box 4.1), often these are rhetorical spats where street cultural idiom may be misunderstood by those who lack the subcultural acumen to unpick it accurately. The presence of street cultural activity within virtual space has further potential consequences for real-world outcomes. For example, messaging services such as BlackBerry Messenger were implicated in the ability of British rioters in 2011 to communicate effectively with each other and thus move through the city in such a fast and fluid manner (see Baker, 2012). In such a manner, connections can be viewed between the street cultural use of real and virtual spaces.

Box 4.1   Twitter beef, chillin' on YouTube and the creation of a 21st-century rap superstar

Nowhere has the porosity between street cultural activity and expressivity, and real and virtual environments been more apparent than in the case of Chicago rapper Chief Keef and the events surrounding his elevation to celebrity/notoriety. He came to widespread notice when his song/video clip 'I Don't Like', posted on YouTube, clocked up in excess of 18 million hits, prompting rap star Kanye West to appear on its remix and ultimately precipitating a lucrative recording deal with Interscope (Stehlik, 2012). Not only was the tune raucous and raw, but the video featured the toting of guns, smoking of weed and Keef and his friends bare-chested and tattooed, epitomizing the street cultural look. To add to the transgressive appeal of the clip, it was filmed in his grandmother's home, where he was under house arrest, an electronic tag ensuring compliance. Not only had new media served as the platform to elevate Chief Keef, but it was implicated in the lethal, allegedly gang-related violence that surrounds the young Chicago rap scene.

In the aftermath of the fatal shooting of 18-year-old rap artiste Lil JoJo, questions were asked around the extent to which his 'beefs' (or usually lyrical rivalries) with other rappers, including Keef, intertwined with conflicts between the Black Disciples and Gangster Disciples street gangs (Konkol et al., 2012). Evidence for this theory was sought online where JoJo had apparently tweeted his location (within rival gang territory) alongside taunts shortly before he was killed. He had also created his own online video insulting and taunting Keef, who for his part was said to have employed the '#300' (hashtag three hundred), which police claim is a sign of Gangster Disciple membership, on certain tweets (ibid.). Moreover, one of his song titles contained the letters BDK (allegedly Black Disciple Killer – a taunt against their rival gang) (McVeigh, 2012). Despite the contested facts within the scenario, a number of important contemporary street cultural issues become clear.

Firstly, the commodification of transgression continues at pace (certainly within the USA) where ever more explicit associations with street culture and criminal lifestyles are viewed as rap career assets (see Chapter 6). Secondly, and more relevant here, new media have blurred the boundaries between mainstream and niche/amateur media, as well as the boundaries between crime and its mediated representation. What occurs in virtual space can have powerful and tangible consequences for events 'IRL' ('in real life').

Ultimately, it is important to note that whilst the virtual is a key space to examine when studying street culture, its impacts should not be overstated. Whilst there may be a rush to speculate on whether digital media and communications will inspire some manner of street politics, they are more likely to act as a medium for voyeurism into the world of the street. Whilst this can offer researchers a crucial window onto worlds otherwise extremely hard to access, it also creates the potential for 'dark tourism' and 'chatroom gangsterism' where the included can affect elements of street cultural identity in their online personas as a quirk of identity work. As 'gang busting' toolkits of social media monitoring techniques are marketed at law enforcement agencies, it becomes increasingly clear that the boundaries between truth and fiction, empty bravado and genuine threat, evidence and lyrics are remarkably porous in virtual space and that only nuanced understanding (as opposed to 'one size fits all' approaches) are useful for the purposes of just and efficient crime control.

Reconsidering territorialism

Given what has been said here about the spatial transformations and population flows associated with late-modernity, there is a need to reconsider some of the assumptions that seem to underpin understandings of street spatial practices: firstly, the phenomenon of 'territorialism'. Both within the popular and academic imaginary, street cultural populations are often viewed as engaging in defensive practices vis-à-vis their communities of residence. In the case of strong street cultural practitioners, this can involve the development of complex, invisible spatial boundaries where violence and the threat thereof is utilized to maintain a series of competing areas or 'turfs'. Owing much to a solid conception of street cultural space, such notions of territorialism have pedigree within academia. Thrasher (1927) noted that the Chicago gangs he studied had divided their city into a 'patchwork' of territories, around which conflicts and rivalries served to reinforce the collective identity of their defenders. Indeed, the topography of the traditionally conceived 'gangland' is usually constituted by cognitive maps which divide the city into safe and dangerous spaces (Garot, 2007; Conquergood, 1994b). Gangs will sometimes take their name from their street(s) of origin. In earlier times, territorial practices were understood as a 'solution' to exclusion (in the tradition of the Birmingham School):

> 'Territoriality' is a symbolic process of magically appropriating, owning and controlling the material environment in which you live, but in real, economic terms is owned and controlled by 'outsiders' – in our society, by private landlords or the State (Robins and Cohen, 1978: 73).

More contemporary analyses have shown that such practices emerge through the habitual use of, and identification with space, which take on increased significance where there are historical connections between a community and its space, or where novel dislocations emerge as a result of urban 'renewal' (Fraser; 2013; Leach, 2005). Territorial processes have never been absolute or clear cut, however, where questions of residence and identification are complex and contingent. Research on Mexican gangs in 1980s Los Angeles revealed that: 'Almost every *klika* (gang) has some fictive residents and occasionally a majority of the members live outside the Barrio' (Moore et al., 1983: 186). Moreover, Garot's (2007) young participants report that they respond to gang-turf related challenges in a variety of different ways and for different reasons. People move, families and friendships remain durable and municipal and school catchment areas do not respect territorial boundaries. Whilst territoriality can weigh heavily, particularly on young male residents of disadvantaged areas (see e.g. Kintrea et al., 2008), restricting their movement and placing them at risk of violence, mobility can and does exist.

As late-modernity forces particular street cultural populations into more sustained migratory practices (between areas of the changing city, developing and developed countries, prison and the community) it is useful to note that territorialism can become either weaker or stronger depending on the circumstances. Thus whilst the Langview Young Team studied by Fraser (2013) eke out their territorial 'ownership' of community space that is constantly being trimmed by gentrification, the Dublin youth group I studied (Ilan, 2013), for a variety of reasons, constantly move and hone their street capital as a means of establishing safety and new networks in a changing array of street settings.

It is not helpful to make assumptions around the existence and significance of territorial practices and the violence which they might generate. As argued by Hallsworth and Young (2009) as well as myself in proceeding material, violence can also emerge within territories, between members of the same 'gang' and for a host of reasons. It is often the product of a will to violence that would otherwise emerge, discussed via 'territory', a well-understood and frequently narrated trope in street culture. Subaltern groups often relate to space in a manner that is 'vague' and specific to their own purposes, meanings and values, whereas clearly defined boundaries tend to be the product of the official or state imaginary (see Carney and Miller, 2009; Hayward, 2004). Caution must be exercised to ensure that the analogy of the nation state is not applied to street cultural formations and practices (see Hallsworth, 2011), no matter how tempting it is to view them as bordered entities with their own form of economic activity and rule enforcement. Narratives of territorialism, whilst often very real and consequential, are far from absolute. Not only are they replete with exceptions, but they do not describe the totality of street cultural experience, particularly in late-modernity.

Against 'gang discourse'

Closely linked to the idea of territorialism is that of the street or criminal 'gang'. Internationally, there is a large body of research, criminal justice policy and law enforcement activity directed at gangs and gang-related crime (see e.g. Esbensen and Maxson, 2012; Spergel, 2007; Curry and Decker, 2003; Thornberry, 2003, amongst many others). This has grown to the extent that some have labelled it an 'industry' (see Hallsworth and Young, 2009). The idea of highly organized groups of young men (and sometimes women) engaging in terrifying violence and organized entrepreneurial criminality has flourished within the public imaginary, rendering 'gangs' an ideal target for crusading politicians and police forces. As will become clear, however, the word 'gang' has been used to describe such a wide range of different street cultural group-ings and institutions that it arguably no longer retains sufficient academic utility.

Groups of young people 'hanging around' and perhaps engaging in minor vandalism, theft and petty fighting have little in common with loosely struc-tured organizations dedicated to exploiting particular drug markets, and yet the term 'gang' can be used to describe both of them. There is good cause to abandon the word within academic discourse except as the most heavily qualified of shorthand. It is a concern over accuracy, as opposed to any kind of semantic or ideological dogmatism that underpins this argument. Despite a long legacy of use within the social sciences, various problems with its use have emerged, and if we are to more usefully debate what is occurring in dis-advantaged areas globally, it becomes particularly urgent to move beyond a concept developed in US cities in the early 20th century.

Firstly, it is important to recognize the problems of this 'gang discourse' favoured in western criminal justice debates. For Katz and Jackson-Jacobs (2003) gang studies (with exceptions) have tended to overly rely on the data or at least world view of state sources, frequently neglecting a richer, more subjective view of lived realities. They show that gang studies often fail to adequately think through notions of causation (e.g. Do gangs cause violence? Ritualize and therefore reduce it? Or are gangs a product of the same social, economic, spatial and cultural factors which produce crime itself?). In the absence of an open frame of analysis, the word 'gang' thus becomes loaded with assumptions and ideological baggage (around what they are, and their nature as a problem). The authors bemoan how such an ambiguous and amor-phous concept can be deployed so casually as a research analytic, statement of social problems and target of interventions, without adequate questions being raised as to what particular manifestations mean within specific contexts.

Whilst the USA has a strong tradition both of gangs and gang research (whatever its problems), the same cannot always be said for other coun-tries, and thus the retention of gang discourse as an international convention is problematic. Notably, UK scholars were historically reluctant to import US gang study paradigms, believing that Britain had youth subcultures rather than gangs (see e.g. Downes, 1966). More recently, Hallsworth and Young (2009) have been critical of the development of 'gang talk' within the UK. They argue that despite government, media and academic claims about the existence of an increasing problem of gang membership and its related vio-lence, there is no empirical evidence to prove this causal link. Asserting the existence of a gang problem, they maintain, better serves sensationalist politico-media narratives than a genuine attempt to understand and solve issues of urban youth violence.

Interestingly when leading US-derived gang definitions are applied in a global context, they arguably begin to fray. Where Klein and Maxson's (2006: 4) gang definition was adopted by Eurogang (a network of European gang scholars), recognition of the problematic nature of the word became inbuilt:

> A street gang (or a troublesome youth group corresponding to a street gang elsewhere)* is any durable, street-oriented youth group whose own identity includes involvement in illegal activity.
>
> *For those preferring not to use the word gang (bande, etc.), the phrase 'troublesome youth group' can be substituted (Klein et al., 2006: 418).

The interesting addition of the option to use the term 'troublesome youth group' suggests the extent to which such a definition could easily apply to typical teenage friendship groups, but the adjective 'troublesome' clearly reveals an ideological position. As will become clear in the following chapter, there has been a tendency in many western jurisdictions to view typical teenage spatial and group practices as 'anti-social' in such a manner that they could fall within the above definition. This is clearly not the intention of those who deploy the definition, as the survey instrument that they were involved in developing seeks information about weapon carrying and violent behaviour (see Klein et al., 2006). It can be argued, however, that violence arises as much (if not more) due to the existence of a chaotic, violent environment, where street cultural groupings are amorphous, 'rhizomatic', internally individualistic and competitive (see Hallsworth, 2013; Ilan, 2013; Hallsworth and Young, 2009; Scott, 2004). In this way, the messy reality of street groupings and hierarchies stands in contrast to how they are conceived of as coherent and structured in state and popular imaginaries (Hallsworth, 2011).

Whilst some UK researchers claim to have found fixed, identifiable and structured youth 'gangs' in London (see Harding, 2014; Pitts, 2008), US research, on the other hand, has noted the extent to which gang identities are fluid, contingent and context specific, a resource drawn upon by young people from disadvantaged areas to assert status and navigate their way through the city: 'even hard-core gangbangers often do not claim to be affiliated with a gang when they are hit up, especially if they are deep in rival territory' (Garot, 2007: 56). Indeed, gang scholars themselves continue to engage in debates around what exactly constitutes a 'gang' (see e.g. Aldridge et al., 2012; Ball and Curry, 1995).

Australia provides another context in which researchers struggle to squeeze what they observe on the street into the existing gang paradigm, as White and Mason (2006: 55–56) have noted:

Much of what happens on the street is contingent upon specific circumstances and events. Fighting, for example, is a general feature of (male) street life, but arises due to different causes and involves different individuals and groups depending upon specific conditions...In the end, however, the issue is less one of 'gangs' per se, than one of social identity and the frictions associated with group interactions based on ethnic stereotypes...The symbolic representation of themselves as members of a gang, however, was more at the level of overt performance (i.e., presenting an image of being tough and dangerous), than in relation to particular kinds of professional criminal activity.

The extent to which these researchers found that 'gang-related behaviour' was performed by non-gang identifiers and that others merely participated in a stylistic display of 'street culture' (through music, argot, posture and dress) gives further strength to the notion that fixed gang identification and discourse is problematic. Whilst it is claimed that the Eurogang definition clearly distinguishes 'gangs' from other criminal groups such as 'prison gangs, motorcycle gangs, terrorist groups and adult criminal cartels and organizations' (Klein et al., 2006: 419), there are arguments made from a wider and more global context that suggest that this is not the case. Hagedorn (2008) notes how the 'true street gang' of American definition shares many features with groupings of armed young men across the developing world: militias and street cultural institutions which operate within disadvantaged areas, some of which are tied to political or even 'terrorist' organizations. What is more, he demonstrates how the global diffusion of street cultural styles and tropes often vest them with similar forms of stylistic expression, display and mythologies. This, he argues, is the product of late-modernity: its disruptions and exclusions, flows and hybridities.

Brotherton (2008), having studied the Almighty Latin King and Queen Nation, a well-established 'gang' with several generations' worth of history, argues that its aims of social advancement and community development render it better understood as a 'street organization'. Here too issues of political engagement and street cultural practice collide, and the traditional notions of 'the gang' again fail to accurately capture what is occurring. A danger with gang discourse is the capture of the sociological/criminological imagination where notions of a criminogenic group come to dominate explanations of and proposed solutions to urban violence (see also Hallsworth, 2013). There is a clear risk of fetishization, where 'objects' are vested with a particular significance (beyond their inherent qualities) by their observer. The very complex and multifaceted problems of urban crime and violence are reduced to a single word and focus.

Whilst Katz and Jackson-Jacobs (2004) highlight an alternative research agenda which would reanimate the utility and openness of the word as the focal point of an academic frame, there is perhaps a stronger case to be made that history and dominant paradigms are difficult to jettison, and thus the word itself should be retired. In its absence, it is important to call for an alternative language to replace it (see also Hallsworth, 2013). I suggest that the street cultural frame featured in this book provides precisely that. Sanchez-Jankowski (2003) notes that gang discourse has been used mainly to refer to groups that emerge in disadvantaged areas (groupings of included individuals which satisfy some of the dominant definitions of gangs, for example, university fraternities tend to be exempted from the categorization). Street cultural schema provide a corrective to gang discourse's assumptions around the 'oppositional' nature of gang cultures, where they arguably often conform to numerous mainstream imperatives around family, friendship, income generation and consumerism (see Young, 2007; Sanchez-Jankowski, 2003; Padilla, 1992; Chapter 8, this volume).

Expressed as a spectrum, the notion of street culture allows for a more nuanced and accurate understanding of how individuals and groups variously deploy street cultural practices and expressivity in a strong and/or weak manner. It seeks to understand not only the wider, global, macro patterns of social, economic and cultural marginalization that produce such practices, but also the significance of their local and regional manifestations. In such a way, it is attentive to the research agenda proposed by Katz and Jackson-Jacobs (2004): interested in how and why different street cultural manifestations take on different forms, and what can be learned from this. Moreover, such an approach is compatible with the questions raised by Hagedorn (2008): how is it that street cultural groupings become 'institutionalized', that is, de facto drivers of local economies, providers of social welfare, order and security in those spaces where the state is fully or partially absent? To what extent do street cultural groupings and institutions express and order local normativity and practices?

The 'gang' can refer to widely divergent phenomena: the traditional, family-orientated organized crime operations which once monopolized crime and violence within the disadvantaged areas of Britain's cities – for example, the infamous Krays (see Pearson, 2013) – and the more contemporary, chaotic violent street world in which loose instrumental groupings of young people strive for income and status (Hallsworth and Silverstone, 2009). Yet each type of group reveals something different about the operation of a range of social, economic and cultural factors at both macro and local levels. The scheme proposed in this book furthermore allows for a concurrent and meaningful consideration of stylistic and expressive practices which have been magnificently analysed by the best of gang scholarship (e.g. Brotherton and Barrios,

2004; Conquergood, 1994; Hagedorn and Macon, 1988; Katz, 1988). Moreover, it does this in a way that understands their relationship to mainstream forms of youth culture and cultural industry practice.

Labels (whilst inevitably somewhat reductive) can be assigned therefore, within this scheme, in a more accurate way. Instead of 'the gang', it would thus be possible to study the fluid youth petty-offending group; the loose friendship group which holds individuals who occasionally petty-offend; the provisionally structured territorial and entrepreneurial drug-selling group; the criminally and politically active street cultural institution, etc., indeed, even 'the true street gang' (the term used by Hagedorn, 2008). Whilst all more wordy, they are all more specific and accurate. 'Gang' will probably still find favour as shorthand, but it should, at least, be recognized as such. This alternative perspective has implications for social policy in the fields of urban and youth violence that focuses on the fetishized gang. Although an easier target to articulate, policies that avoid tackling violent street culture and its underpinnings more generally pose a risk by becoming an expensive form of tilting at windmills.

Conclusion

It can be concluded that space has a profound link to forms of street cultural practice and expressivity, but that it is important to look beyond simple, linear relationships in a late-modern era of flux, change and flow. Within such an analysis, power becomes a crucial element to consider as its absence can variously trap groups and individuals or alternatively cast them adrift (see de Certeau, 1984). Information flows may allow imaginations and forms of expression to roam, but a lack of means or control over residence can rein in movement and actual experience. What remains clear, however, is that the assumptions which underpin many understandings of territorial behaviour and gang activity are not always accommodating of the nuances considered within this chapter. It is therefore important to be mindful of the complex ways in which street culture manifests in contemporary society, and furthermore to be ready to qualify long-held paradigms. In this way, scholars of the links between urban poverty and crime can be dedicated to continuously reviewing prevailing wisdom as the nature of society, the global economy and street culture itself changes. They inevitably do and will.

CHAPTER 5

Street Life and Street Crime

Introduction

This chapter explores the ways in which street culture underpins a range of behaviours that are considered criminal. Returning to the notion of a street cultural spectrum, it demonstrates that these behaviours range from those which cause little harm and indeed may not be considered criminal when engaged in under different circumstances or contexts, to those which are inarguably harmful, detrimental and criminal. It is in fact quite difficult to define the notion of 'street crime', which should really be seen as referring to acts of criminality performed in the public sphere, but is often used solely to refer to street robberies (Hallsworth, 2005: 4). This chapter explores different kinds of street crime and begins to highlight the ways in which wider processes of exclusion manifest in the attachment of criminal meanings. The street values of accumulating and displaying wealth, carving out autonomy and seeking pleasure (which resonate with mainstream concerns) are shown to find expression through the street lifestyles and crimes explored below.

It will become clear that the more strongly individuals are embedded in street culture, the more the realization of these goals is tied to criminal and harm generating strategies. In this regard, it will be noted that youth culture in the developed world resonates with a weak variant of street culture, but whilst the middle-class young person might abandon it as he grows older and has a greater opportunity to participate in the more mainstream realms of work and adult relationships, the socio-economically excluded young person does not see these realms open up to him in the same way (see Ilan, 2013; Barry, 2006). Beginning with 'space crimes' from 'hanging around' to petty vandalism, the relevance of street culture to these less extreme social practices is explored. Theft and later drug trading are discussed in terms of their economic function within street culture, before the role of violence in street life is considered in terms of both its functionality and unpredictability. Finally, the urban riot is examined as a form of street cultural 'eruption', where an exaggeratedly strong variant of it trumps the operation of mainstream order and governance within particular spaces for limited periods of time.

This chapter and the next are centrally concerned with the foci of this book: criminal lifestyles and urban cool. A distinction, however, can at times be somewhat arbitrary where street-style and leisure activities can involve elements of criminality and criminal lifestyles are often linked to a sense of the 'cool'. As noted in Chapter 1, 'cool' involves appearing to set one's own rules and to display nonchalance to the notion of violating mainstream norms. Thus, whilst certain acts of street crime might be understood as performing instrumental functions – earning income, laying claim to sections of the surrounding environment and so on – they may also perform important emotional and existential functions. Crime has the power to conjure the pleasurable experiences of excitement, power, adrenaline and control (see Fenwick and Hayward, 2000; Katz, 1988). This adds an emotive seduction to the practical appeal of street lifestyles. The sense of power and images of 'cool' that accompany the street lifestyle contribute to the ability to hold a persona and sense of worth that are otherwise very difficult for the excluded to realize. Such associations go some way to explaining the appeal of weak street cultural lifestyles to included youth populations, who experience some amount of socio-economic exclusion within their current life stage.

Space crimes

Given that street life often takes place in the spaces that give the phenomenon its name, it is not surprising that congregating in public is an important facet of it. What is more surprising, however, is the extent to which the social use of the streets can become the basis on which labels of criminality are assigned. Whilst the criminalization of 'hanging around' in public spaces is not automatic, its deployment has had a long relationship with exclusion and marginalization. Historically, laws against loitering and vagrancy were a means for agents of law enforcement to censure those who appeared to be in public without what was seen as a valid and productive reason (see e.g. Carney and Miller, 2009; Pearson, 1984). In the contemporary global north, the social use of public street spaces can expose individuals to the risk of being classified as engaging in 'disorder', 'nuisance' or 'anti-social behaviour'. This deployment of criminal (or at least pseudo-criminal) meanings owes much to prevailing socio-economic thinking.

Groups of working-class, young men congregating on street corners in industrial revolution Britain were perceived of as threatening by the respectable classes. They were clearly not engaging in what were perceived of as approved behaviours for individuals of their class: work and structured leisure. The casualness of street life posed a threat to the order and rationality of modernist, industrial society. By contrast, in contemporary consumer society where public space has been increasingly colonized by privatization and business, congregating outside of commercial leisure areas does not just deprive such ventures of business, but it potentially deters the movement of other (better heeled) customers who might otherwise visit and spend (Bannister et al., 2006). Street cultural uses of space, which involve seemingly economically non-productive and aesthetically damaging activities become an anathema. In the material that follows, I set out the cultural logic of 'hanging around' and petty vandalism (excluding the case of subcultural graffiti which will be considered in detail in the next chapter) in a manner which explains their wider resonance with general youth culture, whilst considering how and why these activities are increasingly criminalized.

Studies of youth and street subcultures abound with descriptions of street life: groups of people gathered on street corners, sitting on walls, standing around green spaces, parks and playgrounds. Sometimes alcohol and drugs are consumed in these spaces, other times they are simply the site where conversation cultures are enacted and enjoyed. Whether organic or instrumentally designed, these congregations can also be the 'spring board' for mischievous and transgressive play, petty theft and vandalism, street violence and/or drug dealing. Popular culture bulges with images and incarnations of these sorts of groupings and scenes.

The meanings of various public congregations and the activities they participate in are varied and context specific. As will become clear, 'hanging around' could be classified as the lack of activity rather than an activity in its own right. 'Space crimes', however, are easily misunderstood, whilst theft, drug dealing and other crimes which yield an income are fairly easy for the general public to understand as a means of earning a living (however disagreeable). Why, many wonder, would anyone 'wantonly' destroy property or 'hang about' doing very little, if not motivated by some kind of inherent flaw such as destructiveness, idleness or laziness? The early subcultural theory of delinquency articulated by Albert Cohen (1955) described such behaviour as 'negativistic', whilst later petty disorder became understood as the precursor to greater crimes as part of the regressive notion of 'broken windows' (Wilson and Kelling, 1982).

What those who are perceived of as using public space in a transgressive manner tend to share is a lack of power, resources, ownership and control. Those who possess these qualities can usually define the space's appropriate use. A clear tension thus emerges between those who congregate in particular areas (and for further emotional and existential purposes mark these spaces) and those who are legally favoured and desire to see the space used and maintained in its 'proper' manner (see Malone, 2002). 'Hanging around', however, performs numerous important functions within street lifestyles which are considered below:

Spatial: At a basic level, congregating in public space is a result of its availability and/or suitability for informal street and youth cultures and the casual, unstructured activities that are viewed by their members as desirable. As noted earlier, living quarters may be cramped or formalized and dominated by 'civilizing' influences such as parents and 'respectable' family members. Where they exist, leisure facilities provided by the state or voluntary sector may be viewed as overly controlled and surveyed; whereas commercial spaces may be prohibitively expensive or may indeed exclude those who do not possess a particular status, be it of age, appearance or membership. The relative freedom and potential of street spaces offers a free-to-access space which can be temporarily used to practice and celebrate street values. This includes evading the 'respectablizing' forces (e.g. education, formal employment and supervised leisure) to which street culture is antithetic (see e.g. Gillespie et al., 1992; Jenkins, 1983; Corrigan, 1979; Gill, 1977; Chambliss, 1973). The literature cited tends to draw distinctions between working-class youth cultures which particularly emphasize street cultural values of autonomy and collective congregation and middle-class youth cultures which tend to be more regulated by structured leisure (sports teams, youth clubs etc.) and extra-curricular education. Nevertheless, the universal imperatives of youthful identity-work and boundary-testing will create a desire for young people to use space independently and for their own purposes (see Holloway and Valentine, 2000: 10–11). To this end, the streets are essential (see Matthews, Limb, and Taylor, 2000: 64). As will become clear, regional variations weigh heavily on this process.

Temporal: De Certeau (1984) famously theorized that the powerful can enact 'strategies', that is plans and decisions based on an ability to define and determine the use of space, whereas the powerless can only deploy 'tactics', to define and determine their use of time. The unstructured leisure of 'hanging around' provides just this opportunity for the autonomous expenditure of time: time for the individual and his/her friends, not for employers, teachers, family or other more establishment demands. This, in turn, ironically leads to a need for activities to fill this time. As vividly described by Paul Corrigan (1979) in relation to the *lads* he studied in northern England, warding away the boredom of 'doing nothing' becomes a central concern. For these young men, the discussion and performance of 'weird ideas' such as petty vandalism and play-fights came to animate the otherwise empty time and furthermore provided fuel for hours of humorous conversation in their aftermath. The imperative to seek excitement thus butts up against the inevitable boredom accompanying the hard won empty hours spent on relatively entertainment-free streets. For these reasons passer-bys might be interrupted or loudly commented upon, bottles may be smashed, endless cigarettes smoked and various forms of criminality take on a particular appeal.

Performative: The milieu of the social, friendship or street cultural group provides the ideal arena in which individuals can perform and lay claim to their identities. Its relative freedom allows individuals to distance themselves from the expectations of family members, teachers, employers etc. and provides them with the space to perform in front of peers. This may involve enacting particular variants of the street gender identities considered in Chapter 3 and/or the street stylistic practices that will be discussed in the following chapter. Indeed, engaging in either petty or more serious acts of criminality may become part of the performance.

Utilitarian: Complex analyses should not necessarily preclude simple explanations. 'Hanging around' is not just free, it is very often local and convenient. Personal, local and group geographies will tend to yield a variety of favoured spaces to gather, often governed by a variety of factors such as convenience, familiarity, distance from sources of surveillance, and facilities such as street furniture. Kate O'Brien (forthcoming) describes the 'bucket stations' where her participants congregate to consume alcohol and cannabis situated within green spaces proximate to their homes, whereas the drug dealers studied by Bourgois (1995/2003), their friends and associates gather in or outside the front businesses for their drug sales, or indeed local parks and stairwells. Importantly, without the widespread availability of mobile phones, predictability provides an important logic for the choice of gathering areas. This was a concern for the Whyte's *Corner Boys* (1943). Finally, an issue which is frequently under-considered is the importance of 'hanging around' in groups to individual safety. As Hallsworth (2005) notes, those involved in street crime are often also its victims, whilst Crawford (2009) describes how young, female participants in his study cited the presence of their peers as mitigating the risk of assault.

Whilst 'hanging around' public spaces is thus central to street lifestyles, its contribution to 'visibility' ensures that it is inextricably linked to debates around appropriate behaviour and crime problems. As noted by Gill Valentine (1996), in the global north a simultaneous but contradictory view of young people as vulnerable and threatening contributes to a desire to restrict their presence in public places. This has dovetailed with the rise of criminal and pseudo-criminal sanctions against perceived instances of 'disorder', 'nuisance' or 'anti-social behaviour' (see Mooney and Young, 2006). Inherently difficult to define, these concepts are arguably a means of enforcing the dominant section of the populations' aesthetic judgements and behavioural expectations on the excluded (Millie, 2008, 2011): both the poor and the young. The famed 'zero tolerance' policing practices of New York City in the 1990s have been framed as a shift from policing criminality proper in an era of declining rates of serious crime, to censuring vexatious quality-of-life conflicts which were not previously viewed as meriting intervention (Curtis, 1998). In the UK, the New Labour government introduced 'Anti-social Behaviour Orders' as a means of deploying law enforcement against the neighbourhood ills of everything from public drug dealing to perceived 'excess' noise. The inherently subjective nature of this new legal measure saw them deployed disproportionately against the young and where once young people playing football on the streets of Britain was greeted as emblematic of post-war regeneration it could now lead to formal interventions (see Squires and Stephen, 2005).

Ultimately, the subjectivity of these kinds of policing tactics and legal provisions can serve to conflate 'innocent' youthful sociability with the kinds of 'hanging around' that are a springboard for violent or intimidating behaviour. According to Presdee (2000) the transgressive, hedonism-centred 'second life' of the public is the 'first life' of youth: where middle-class adults might try and 'let their hair down' at the weekend, young people in the developed world are often involved in these behaviours on a daily basis. The autonomy and potential excitements of weak street cultures thus hold considerable appeal to young people from the more included sections of society. The publicly present are more open to criminalization, significantly more so when they are from demographics associated with strong street cultures and disproportionate captured by the criminal justice system.

Whilst negative encounters with law enforcement may be a particularly serious concern for young people in the global south, there are significantly different youth cultural concerns that apply in many of its regions. There, young people can enjoy far higher degrees of independence compromised by a lack of leisure that stems from participation in the labour market as well as higher rates of youth homelessness that casts many into a struggle for survival (see Holloway and Valentine, 2000). In these regions, furthermore, as will be discussed in Chapter 8, debates and initiatives around urban aesthetics revolve around expelling poor communities totally, rather than focusing on issues of 'space crime'.

Vandalism is similarly underpinned by street cultural concerns and is indeed frequently tied to 'hanging around'. Vandalism takes various forms from the political to the vindictive or playful (see Cohen, 1973) and it is these two latter aspects that are most relevant for consideration here. Cohen rightly states that some kinds of what we might call street cultural vandalism attack the symbols of authority (schools, youth clubs, CCTV cameras). His assertion that certain other vandalism targets 'middle-class' property is,

Figure 5.1 Various acts of vandalism photographed in Dublin, Ireland. A public phone box is smashed; a police van has been attacked with battery acid; a bicycle wheel is kicked in—thieves also made off with its saddle

however, arguably somewhat more dated in an era where the excluded often desire the same material goods as the included. Thus, it is unlikely that 'maliciousness' is always in operation here, but instead either frustration or 'play'. Indeed, vandalism can be both instrumental and expressive: it can generate a sense of transgressive excitement whilst at the same time communicating a message of sorts. In Figure 5.1, from my own research, we can see how police vehicles have been attacked out of vindictiveness, telephone boxes smashed for the thrill (there was nothing to be gained materially and the young men I researched are unlikely to have 'resented' the presence of a facility they used when they had no mobile phone credit) and indeed bicycle wheels stamped out of shape when my participants were frustrated that they could not snap their locks to steal them. Thus whilst acts of vandalism can mean different things, they are arguably all part of a process by which the excluded negotiate their relationship with the spaces that they inhabit and pass through but within which they feel little power or control.

This assertion of presence is often no more apparent than in non-stylized graffiti which proclaims to the world the names of the young people who have been within a space. This creation of a link to space can conjure a certain amount of illusory mastery of surroundings, conveying street cultural status, demonstrating that sufficient autonomy has been attained to both escape and defy the supervision which would prevent or punish the acts of graffiti. Thus, seemingly 'negativistic' crimes such as vandalism, but extending to joyriding (driving/racing stolen vehicles at speed) in fact also correspond to a logic of 'edgework' and 'transgressive thrills'. Playing at the edges/boundaries of risk (around capture and injury) provides in itself strong emotional attractions (see Lyng, 1990, 2005; Presdee, 2000).

Economically motivated street crime

Given street culture's relationship to conspicuous consumption, the rapid earning and spending of money, the informal economy as well as the valorization of leisure, it is unsurprising to see a range of economically motivated street crimes featuring as part of the street cultural lifestyle. Again, these activities range on a spectrum from those which closely trace legitimate entrepreneurialism (undocumented labour from shoe-shining to street vending; see e.g. Duneier, 1999), the more 'amateur' and playful (stealing items of low value for own use; see Katz, 1988), the frequent, criminal and quasi-professional (routinized theft; see e.g. Ilan, 2013; Parker, 1974) to the high end and high value (e.g. integrated drug trading networks; see e.g. Gunst, 2003). The extent to which the different varieties of economic street crime become established within different areas arguably owes much to context, both local (see Chapters 3 and 4) and global (see Chapter 7). Ultimately, it is useful to remember the important findings of Cloward and Ohlin (1960) that demonstrate how community characteristics shape illegitimate offending opportunities. In the absence of the appropriate street cultural competencies and networks it is extremely difficult to engage in economic street crime to any great level of dedication and success. The material below focuses on two key examples of 'stronger' street criminal practices: theft and drug selling.

Much like the pettier forms of criminality discussed above, these crimes are tied to street spatial practices, often utilizing the areas that groups habitually use. A number of logics underpin this, where familiarity, local knowledge and geographies permit the optimum sourcing of appropriate targets, their surreptitious surveillance, and potential 'getaway' routes (see e.g. Box 5.1; Parker, 1974). The technical acumen, embodied competencies and steely nerves that are required to successfully conduct thefts with any kind of consistent efficacy resonate strongly with street cultural notions of masculinity. Locks, wiring, electronics, dogs, victims who might defend themselves as well as a range of detection and apprehension risks might need to be overcome in one way or another. Moreover, the awareness and attitudes that facilitate success in doing this can lend a sense of canniness to its practitioners, further affirming them as street culturally competent, as well as 'mature' and independent (see Parker, 1974: 91).

Box 5.1   The bicycle thieves

As part of my PhD research, I conducted participant observation with a group of young men who frequently engaged in theft. This extract from the dissertation illustrates the methods and unwritten rules which tended to order their engagement in it:

By the end of fieldwork The Crew have settled into a more or less regular practice of stealing mobile phones and bicycles, for which they have developed a well-established customer base. The act of 'cruising' (walking around) doubles as an opportunity to review the locality and establish opportunities for theft. Ideally, one member of The Crew would have an item, car or shed 'sussed' (cased) before any attempt at theft is made. This process involves first identifying the item as something that is worth stealing. Secondly, ensuring that there is a viable manner in which it can be stolen. Thirdly, where possible, to maintain vigilance over a certain amount of time and establish the kinds of security measures or surveillance that is evident in the immediate vicinity. In the case of a locked bike, initial strain might be placed on the lock to break it more easily at a later time. At this stage the Crew member will refer to the item as his own: 'I have this bike, you want to take a look?' There are rules that operate delineating objects that may be stolen from those that should not. As a rule of thumb, the property of someone they know, and know to be on a similar economic level, is not targeted unless as part of a particular vendetta or disagreement. Where the owner cannot be identified, the property is fair game, but the enquiry is always made: 'Anyone know who owns this bike?' Although the influence of immediate opportunity is strong, cultural rules, planning and forethought form the basis for a large proportion of their thefts.

The act of theft is generally undertaken collectively. There are multiple tasks to be assigned. 'Keeping sketch' is the method by which a lookout is kept for Gardaí (police), owners or concerned citizens and one member will take this lesser role. Another 'clips' the ignition wire or 'snaps' the bicycle lock (depending on the vehicle in question), or alternatively smashes the car window with a projectile or an arm wrapped in a tracksuit top. Another person then 'takes' the item they are stealing, someone else may then be called upon to 'hold' it. If they then decide to continue 'cruising' the object will be offered for sale on the street to those who seem like potential customers. Otherwise the goods will be sold to shops whose owners display a lack of curiosity in relation to their origin, to local criminals, or door-to-door in housing complexes considered appropriate. The prices generally sought by The Crew are very low: usually €20–50 for a bicycle or mobile phone, depending on its quality. Where goods are of exceptional quality they can be sold at a higher price. The proceeds of the sale can be in cash or cannabis depending on the customer and are divided between those who participated in the theft. Towards the end of fieldwork, the researcher is told that each member centrally involved in 'robbing' is earning approximately €150 per week (Ilan, 2007: 65–66).

As is frequently discussed in criminology (and indeed the industries that exist around crime control) the opportunity to steal is a vital component of any theft. There are problems, however, with the rational choice theories which often underpin the situational crime prevention techniques that are now orthodoxies of crime control thinking and practice (see Hayward, 2007, 2012). Notable amongst these problems is the failure to consider the cultural factors that prompt and permit criminal opportunities to be exploited. Indeed, Simon Hallsworth in his comprehensive account of British street robbery stresses the need to address this imbalance:

Learning requires an apprenticeship, a process by which a nonpractitioner is equipped with skills that will enable them to become an active and motivated offender. This in turn requires the existence of a culture where these deviant skills may be transmitted and internalized (2005: 6).

On the one hand, thus, street cultural networks can provide the necessary technical 'education' to exploit opportunities. On the other, street cultural factors may make one person more likely to be motivated to exploit such opportunities than another. Shover and Honaker (1992), for example, consider the extent to which those who commit robberies are deeply embedded in a heady 'easy come, easy go' culture of earning through crime and 'splashing out' on expensive consumer goods and partying. Through valuing a mode of expressive consumerism that would only be supported by high wages or illicit income, street culture provides practical motivations in itself. This is complemented by the existential appeal of theft. On the one hand there are pleasing emotions which accompany the triumph over the threat of detection (Katz, 1988) and on the other it provides some opportunity for the cultivation of 'cool' (no doubt assisted by the voluminous gentleman/expert thief tropes that abound within history and popular culture).

'Stick-ups', robberies and 'muggings' where victims are directly confronted (often with the threat and/or actuality of violence) allow for a further sense of power, control and mastery to be experienced (see Katz, 1988) – again emotions in short supply amongst the excluded. Such acts furthermore allow for the inversion of the social structure, where a victim higher on the socio-economic spectrum can be made to feel weak in their lack of street cultural acumen: lower on the scale of traits that matter in the moment of robbery/potential violence. This situated moment allows for a host of emotional satisfactions to be produced where victims are forced to walk a thin tightrope between safety and danger. The robber for his/her part is free to exploit the power imbalance this creates to exhibit whatever demeanour they wish: humorous and jocular to contrast their lightness to the victim's fear; or pseudo-kindliness as if to imply that the act of robbery is not what it is (there can be a thin line between robbery and the confidence trick when the victim only realizes late in the process that an unspoken threat of violence is present); or indeed plain menace, whether aggressive or understated.

Similarly, street-level drug trading offers a combination of instrumental and expressive resources that those with the requisite street cultural acumen and connections (i.e. capitals) can exploit. As noted in Chapter 1, intoxication and the general celebration of visceral, embodied pleasures tend to be a feature of street life and culture (indeed, this is also the case with particular youth cultures). Preferred intoxicants are frequently legal or quasi-legal (e.g. alcohol whose consumption may not be legal in public spaces or for certain age groups) although illicit substances can occupy places of varying importance. Moreover, the heavy consumption of intoxicants is again a form of 'edgework', involving the assertion of competence and mastery to maintain control at the edge of what one's consciousness and psyche can tolerate (see Lyng, 1990, 2005). Within street culture, not only is intoxication understood as inherently pleasurable (which it is not necessarily), but one's ability to display competence in its appreciation and management becomes a measure of street capital.

Indeed, distinguishing between preferred intoxicants is part and parcel of establishing street capital as well as 'cool' more generally (a fact not lost on alcohol marketeers – see e.g. Measham and Brain, 2005). This may entail displaying a preference for marijuana and powder cocaine over crack cocaine and heroin which can be associated with 'weakening', debilitating addictions (see Ilan, 2011; Curtis, 1998). Forms of street cultural expression such as rap and Jamaican dancehall music provide clues as to the role of historical cultures in establishing the use of marijuana (often referred to in ethnic folk vernacular as 'cheeba', 'collie' and extolled as both intoxicant and medicine) as well as contemporary youth cultures in popularizing 'dance' drugs such as ecstasy (see the recent references to 'molly' (MDMA) in pop culture). Street cultural expression has similarly paid tribute to the figure of the drug dealer as both villain and/or paragon (Bogazianos, 2012) whilst drug dealers themselves around the world look to US street cultural expression as a means of understanding their lifestyles (see e.g. Sandberg and Petersen, 2009).

Socio-economic exclusion as the driver of street culture thus to some extent provides part of the demand for drugs, whilst simultaneously creating strong instrumental motivations to become involved in the drug trade as a means of generating income. The drug dealer, in some senses, becomes the embodiment of the (strong) street cultural ideal. He/she is the entrepreneur operating within local street spaces (e.g. Bourgois, 1995/2003); displaying the trappings of wealth and consumerism (e.g. Gunter, 2008); present to bask in the 'respect' of peers and 'taking care of business' through displaying the optimum degrees of canniness and physical menace (see e.g. Jacobs, 1999). Padilla's (1992) description of drug dealing as an 'American enterprise' should be taken seriously, recognizing that in drug dealing like many other aspects of the neoliberal society/economy, there is very much a culture of winners and losers: large profits as well as underpaid drudgery; consumers in a perpetual state of desire and demand as well as consumers harmed, discarded and replaced; all underpinned by the pursuit of pleasure and the dream of becoming vastly wealthy (see further, Chapter 7). Of course, the ideal rarely transfers to reality in a straightforward manner.

It becomes useful to consider the diversity that exists both in terms of drug markets and the roles that individuals play within them. Firstly and obviously, there are numerous levels of drug dealer, from smugglers and 'wholesale' distributors (see Adler and Adler, 1993), to those who supervise and participate in sales to customers. At this latter level, strict 'consignment' systems frequently operate where individual dealers and collective 'crews' essentially buy the product from their superiors and sell it on at a relatively small profit. In this situation there is both less scope to earn meaningful amounts of money and considerable risks where money must be repaid irrespective of seizures, arrests, robberies, fraud and fluctuations in the market (see Jacobs, 1999). Those lower down the dealing pecking-order can be exploited to the extent that they view their trade and/or the group that orders it as a 'suckers outfit' (Scott, 2004). Famously, those working in lower and supporting roles may well merely earn a minimum wage and remain dependant on parents, partners or others for their subsistence (see e.g. Bourgois, 1995/2003; Venkatesh, 1997). Indeed, the income from drug sales may simply fund the purchase of luxuries and the fulfilment of inflated material desires to supplement a life otherwise devoid of this kind of material autonomy.

Markets themselves vary between the open and closed. The former operates much like its name suggests: in public space, where a general drug-buying public can access the dealers. This creates opportunities to sell to a wider customer base, but opens up the operations to a greater degree of risk. Street capital becomes a crucial asset in this context (see Sandberg and Pedersen, 2009), deployed to ward off predatory robbers, menace those tempted into forgoing payment and spot undercover police officers who might catch a dealer in the act. Closed markets are both considerably less risky and increasingly viable with recent developments in telecommunications. What closed drug markets require in abundance is street social capital – personal networks in the street and drug-using worlds which funnel customers to the dealers' doors (indeed home spaces are often utilized as staging points, although this creates its own risks in terms of an individual's residence and respectability being threatened; see Fleetwood, 2014).

Within O'Brien's (forthcoming) study of drug using young people in the north of England, community, kinship and friendship networks are important resources for accessing drugs as few of the local dealers would be willing to sell to someone they do not know. This is a luxury that is likely to exist in closed markets much more so than in their open equivalent. The informal relationships of acquaintance that order street culture map onto the patterns of interaction that order drug sales. Assessments tend to be conducted quickly based on existing knowledge of another and judgements around how they hold and present themselves. Individuals should expect to be tested and if found wanting in terms of violent potential or mental agility, may well suffer some form of exploitation or mistreatment. With that said, drug markets (their open variants particularly) can be competitive and dealers may well find themselves forced to cultivate good customer relations by ensuring a quality product at a fair price and dispensing small favours and credit in order to maintain a flow of business (see Jacob, 1999). The business analogy can extend to the 'branding' of drugs with names (e.g. 'Terminator', 'Rambo', etc. presumably as testament to their strength; see e.g. Bourgois, 1995/2003: 125) as well as colours and symbols in an effort to secure the preference and confidence of customers.

Clearly, although business analogies apply, the unique position of economic street crimes should not be understated. They can involve exploitation, loss and harm (then again so too do certain legal business). Their illegality, obviously, vests them with particular risks, which can in some instances feed the desire for excitement that is frequently a part of street culture, but also can compound the exclusion of their practitioners who are moved away from the potential to attain socio-economic inclusion as they gain criminal records and ingrained street cultural dispositions. In contrast to much of the work that (if available) might be open to those on the socio-economic margins, which is often characterized by tightly proscribed rules, strict surveillance and a lack of trust in the ideas and acumen of the employee (see e.g. Newman, 1999), drug dealing calls for the individual to display ingenuity in organizing their activities (secreting away their 'stash' of product, ensuring payment etc.) in such a way as to minimize risk and maximize profitability. Those who participate in it are more able to adhere to the street cultural imperatives of autonomy and entrepreneurialism.

Although often entered into for instrumental economic reasons, such crimes do not replicate the role of legitimate employment in mainstream culture. For example, the proceeds of crime are often spent on maintaining an extravagant street lifestyle as opposed to making the kinds of investments in education and property that are so tied to standard middle-class advancement strategies. The world of the 'Cocaine Kids' as described by Terry Williams (1990) is one where drug sales and violence sit within a wider lifestyle of socializing with similarly orientated friends in nightclubs and 'jump-offs' (after-parties) also frequented by other free-spending members of disadvantaged groups. What the experience of his participants furthermore suggests is that economic street crimes such as drug dealing can be difficult to retire from, where earning is relatively 'easy' and the risk of punishment sufficiently avoidable. The emotional pleasures and existential lure of street culture can be too strong in such instances, where wider 'desistance' factors such as decently paid employment or a family one is committed to (see Maruna, 2001) do not adequately compete.

Violence, hierarchy and the regulation of the street world

Violence is a key criminal behaviour within street worlds. The level of violence that prevails within particular localities, regions and contexts exercises considerable influence over the strength of street cultural variants in those environments. In the case of less-excluded youth friendship/leisure groups (as considered earlier), violence may be primarily ludic (play-like): an activity to pass the time, generate some excitement and populate conversations (see e.g. Corrigan, 1979). In the case of open drug markets or in communities 'controlled' by militia-like 'gangs' violence can be lethal, ever-present and necessary to negotiate in some way merely to subsist (e.g. Goldstein, 2003; Anderson, 1999). Much like the other aspects of criminal lifestyles considered in this chapter, violence has both instrumental and expressive functions, which although examined in turn, again are often difficult to separate. As will become clear, violence is seldom a desired end in itself, instead, it is used to achieve various different goals within street life and culture. Indeed, as Paul Willis (1977) noted with the tough English school boys he studied in the 1970s and Elijah Anderson (1999) observed in the ghettos of Philadelphia in the 1990s, this violence need not necessarily be actualized: it can exist merely as the potential for violence read on the body of the street competent individual.

As Anderson noted, and indeed as has been discussed since (see e.g. Wright and Decker, 2006), the antipathy to the forces of state authority that is often a part of street culture creates the need for an alternative, independent form of settling disputes. This underpins the 'might is right' ethos of street dispute resolution, where contested matters are often settled by those with street capital enough to speak and act authoritatively in a context where academic learning tends not to attract a particularly large amount of respect and recourse can hardly be had to the courts. Moreover, the will and potential to use violence effectively is a key component of this form of capital. Indeed, where the state and formal laws have relatively little penetration, governance and discipline continue to operate, albeit generated 'from below' (within the excluded community itself; see Lea and Stenson, 2007). This, in turn, creates an overall cultural context in which interpersonal violence, actualized, implied or threatened is normalized as a means of establishing authority (as opposed to the legal and ideological forms of authority wielded by the state).

Applying Elias' (1969/1994) notion of the 'civilizing process' here (the argument that as the sovereign/state increasingly took up the sole right to deploy violence, it began to decrease within everyday life), it could be understood that strong street culture operates outside of this monopoly on violence. Indeed, this is a further application of the idea set out in Chapter 1 that street worlds are to varying extents excluded from socio-economic modernity. This is in part due to the lack of disadvantaged populations' meaningful inclusion in the state institutions which reduce the normative use of interpersonal violence. With that said, street cultural institutions and personalities can attempt, with varying degrees of success, to claim this monopoly power, reserving onto themselves the power to deploy violence. Hallsworth and Silverstone (2009) indeed make a comparison between UK criminal organizations, where 'old firms' in years past were said to keep street violence to a minimum in order to both gain community support and avoid unwanted police attention, to contemporary street groups who cannot and do not institutionalize themselves to an extent that creates strict rules and rituals around when violence might be deployed.

Scholars of street culture sometimes describe its violence as operating according to particular rules. In this reading, levels of street capital (linked to the deployment or ability to deploy violence) are seen as establishing ever-shifting hierarchies that are carefully read by others who craft their response accordingly (e.g. Silverman, 2004). In such a manner, men in particular are keen to avoid being labelled in the US context as 'punks', i.e. lacking in violent potential and thus an easy mark for various kinds of exploitation: being robbed, forced to perform menial or not so menial tasks, or forever being the butt of jokes (see Mullins, 2006). Street slang in the Anglophone world offers a variety of insults to be levelled at such individuals. In this sense, 'respect' gained through a proven or perceived capacity for violence is viewed as a sort of currency. Moreover, the rules that operate in these situations are often viewed as 'clear cut': sleights and insults must be responded to, lest they deprive an individual of respect in the eyes of street peers; female relatives are to be 'protected' (both their person and reputation); retaliation should similarly follow when a friend, relative or fellow group member has been harmed; an issuer's version of events is to be accepted. Indeed, Kubrin (2005: 366) sees this 'code of the street' (see Anderson, 1999) articulated within American rap music, whereby: 'rap lyrics are discursive actions or artifacts that help construct an interpretive environment where violence is appropriate and acceptable'.

The 'street code' model of understanding the motivations to violence can be very useful in both academic and everyday life contexts. For example, the question: 'what are you looking at?' is a well-known precursor to potentially violent interactions. This occurs because a 'strange look' can be perceived of as a slight or insult. This insult can then be answered by either psychically or physically besting the issuant. The former might be understood to have occurred where the looker lowers their gaze and acts submissively, whereas the latter might involve the instigation of a fight. As mentioned earlier in the book, however, it is important not to overemphasize the rule-bounded or ritualized character of street cultural violence, which by its nature is open to ample amounts of chaos and unpredictability. This stems from its expressive and existential qualities.

In this regard, reading Simon Winlow's *Badfellas* (2001) and Winlow and Hall's *Violent Nights* (2006) in tandem can be particularly instructive. By doing so, it is possible to compare the instrumental use of violence by street cultural entrepreneurs in the course of their economically acquisitive criminality, with the weekend violence of aspirant men of working-class extraction for whom the potential for violence is part of their nightlife and alcohol-related leisure. In the former context, violence underpins an entrepreneurial logic where decently paid, stable working-class employment has all but vanished. In the latter, those elevated to the margins of the newly expanded middle-class punctuate the monotony of their tightly controlled call-centre employment with the unpredictability and excitement of a night on the town where anything can happen, and violence is an exciting and emotionally grabbing experience, whether observed or participated in. As noted in Chapter 3, notions of masculinity and adulthood (i.e. identity) are, for many of those participating in street cultures, deeply intertwined with attitudes to and/or practices of violence. Leaving aside the pleasurable experiences of control and power that can be gained from besting another (see the discussion of robbery above), the ability to convincingly wield violence, or its potential, offers resources for the demonstration of a particular kind of selfhood: a person to be 'taken seriously'. Indeed, Jack Katz (1988) posits that the violence of street gang members detracts from the potential absurdity and childishness of their other activities: the donning of costumes, creation of mythology etc.

With personhood and power at stake, it is problematic to assume that individuals will restrict themselves to acting according to strict rules. Again, as briefly mentioned in earlier discussions of gender, unpredictability remains a key resource on the street. The trope of 'insanity' (see Anderson, 1999) thus finds expression across various street cultures where an individual perceived of as 'mad', 'loco' etc. earns a certain amount of respect and deference simply because it is difficult to read how they will react to a particular situation. Returning thus to questions around the extent to which violence and the rules around its deployment might be institutionalized within a given community, it is important to recognize a number of factors. First, the emotional dynamics of an individual person or situation may well trump the overarching street cultural norms in play. Katz's (1988) consideration of 'righteous slaughter' traces the ways in which individuals when they feel deeply humiliated by a perceived injustice can lash out in rage and kill for reasons that do not hold up to rational scrutiny.

Secondly and more prosaically, the deployment of violence is not an act that is easy to control and manage. As pithily put by Felson (2002: 2) murder is often the result of a 'lethal weapon too near and a hospital too far' as opposed to planning and premeditation: people get hurt more than the perpetrator of violence might have intended. Given also the extent to which retaliation for violence against one's friends is expected (see e.g. Gunter, 2008), interpersonal conflicts can rapidly spill over to involve greater numbers of people. Such incidents are open to being inaccurately interpreted as 'inter-gang' violence. Third, as noted earlier in this book, the institutionalization of street cultural groupings requires a number of factors to be in place. Frequently, there may be less order within street worlds than some might imagine.

Simon Hallsworth (2013) has recently critiqued a tendency to overemphasize the understanding of urban violence as relatively rule bounded. Commenting specifically on assumptions that have been applied to the operation of 'gang' rules within street worlds, he notes that it is often their absence or their expedient evocation that contribute to violence and not, in fact, their presence. Simply put, his argument is that strong rules and institutions within the violent world of the street would tend to ritualize violence and limit the circumstances in which it can occur. Applying analogies he argues that whilst the world of the state is 'arboreal' (tree-like: ordered by clearly demarked levels, hierarchies and structures), the street world is 'rhizomatic' (more akin to the growth of fungi: tangled, horizontal, amorphous and messy). Thus rather than ordering the use of violence, notions of hierarchy and territory become issues of dispute that are invoked to lend normative/ethical weight to explain violence that would have occurred in any event. In other words, fights occur within the violent street world for many reasons when matters of respect are at stake: traded insults, suspicions of impropriety towards a persons' significant other, jokes gone wrong, misunderstandings, a perceived need to heighten one's image in the eyes of one's peers, or indeed for little discernible reason other than a desire to make 'something happen'.

Post facto and in the disputes that may arise between peers on either side of the conflict, matters of territoriality and hierarchy might be raised to justify or interpret the violence: assertions that a person should have known better than defying A or going to place B or indeed wearing clothing C. Hallsworth and Young (2008) had previously argued that street violence is often defined by default as 'gang' violence because of the demographic of those involved and the assumptions that are held about the rules they operate under. A more nuanced understanding recognizes the extent to which well-established tropes within street culture, such as notions of 'territoriality' and 'gang-banging' become a 'grammar' to articulate and make sense of what is essentially violence that stems from the harsh ethos and chaotic unpredictability of street life, not necessarily causes of that violence in themselves.

Whilst interpersonal violence plays functional, emotional and existential roles within street cultures (and in particular its stronger variants) it is especially potent in stoking the 'respectable fears' (Pearson, 1984) of included groups. Violence deployed by the state tends to be shrouded in technocratic language, held at a distance from 'ordinary citizens' or obscured through slow and symbolic application (see Young, 2007) which is in stark contrast to the immediacy, viscerality and unpredictable nature of street violence. Where this violence is moreover associated with excluded groups that tend to be the target of disparagement and fear, it becomes a ready 'lightning rod' for a wide range of social anxieties and contributes to the calls for social control that are explored in more detail in Chapter 8.

Riots as street cultural eruptions

On the topic of respectable fears, it is useful to finally consider 'rioting' as an example *par excellence*. Whilst riots have featured throughout the world and across many different historical periods (see e.g. Horowitz, 2001; Gale, 1996; Thompson, 1963), there have been more recent manifestations of the phenomenon that might be usefully understood through a street cultural analysis. This applies both to the logics and appeals of rioting as well as the fear of them, which arguably stems in part from the seeming triumph of street culture over official and mainstream forms of control and order. Riots powerfully illustrate the divisions between included and excluded populations divided by class, ethnicity or both. These should be distinguished from the riots that are associated with explicitly political protest.

Western examples such as Los Angeles in 1992, Paris in 2005 and England in 2011 represent occasions in which resentments around over-policing and the other privations associated with racism and ghetto living erupted into aggressive destruction. In Los Angeles, for example, the growing disparities in income and mass unemployment generated by neoliberal economics of deindustrialization, together with black and Latino populations experiencing excessive police attention, simmered for some time before the acquittal of the police officers who were videotaped beating Rodney King (see Davis, 1992). This event was merely the 'tinder-box' spark which ignited the combustible 'powder keg' of excluded peoples' frustration (for more on this analogy, see Abrams and Hogg, 2002). The looting, arson, assaults and murder that took place during the six days of rioting highlighted the extent to which the ordinary police force was powerless in the face of such a potent street cultural outpouring.

Indeed, as mainstream forms of order maintenance (such as police forces) fail, the logic of street culture takes on a greater significance as personal acquaintances and violent potential become increasingly important to exist safely. The emotional and existential seductions of street culture in the context of rioting attach to an expanded and untrammelled range of extreme spatial, economic and violent crimes. Thus, for example, arson may become a possible means of responding to these feelings within a riot situation, where petty vandalism would be the limit of what would seem possible within everyday life. In contrasts to riots which follow on from political demonstrations, or are part and parcel of transitions between different models of governance, street cultural riots tend to be viewed as destructive affairs, devoid of transformative political potential. For Treadwell et al. (2013), the English riots of 2011, which were marked in particular by looting, were a form of aggravated acquisitive consumerism. The authors view the events as lacking a politics, instead expressing the ubiquitous insatiable desire that underpins the psychology of living within the neoliberal state.

For others, however, the same events could additionally be understood as a response to similar 'powder keg' factors as those considered above, sparked this time by the failure of the police to adequately respond to their shooting of Mark Duggan, a young black man suspected of links to 'gang' crime (see e.g. Youth Justice Board, 2012). Indeed, and as might resonate with the analysis offered in Chapter 8, there is cause to understand even the most seemingly nihilistic of riots as informed by some politics, no matter how under-articulated or inchoate. Mere expressions of vast discontent can arguably be considered political, even if they are not accompanied by a sense of transformative politics. Thus, for example, the Paris riots, marked in particular by the burning of cars and conflict with heavily armoured French riot police were understood to represent a consequence of the move away from concerted efforts to integrate immigrants, to containing them within multiply-stigmatized ghettos (Haddad and Balz, 2006).

Conclusion

This chapter has demonstrated the extent to which street culture manifests across a range of criminal behaviours. Importantly, thus, the exclusion experienced by those participating in what is viewed as street crime provides important clues as to why they engage in it, and also why such behaviours seem to become law enforcement priorities. As discussed earlier in the book, it is issues of exclusion that can explain the forces pushing an individual to particular points along the street cultural spectrum. Stronger levels of material deprivation and social marginalization can precipitate involvement in more harmful forms of crime, whereas weaker variants of street culture may be linked instead to behaviours that are defined as criminal due more to the identity of those involved or the contexts in which they are performed. Where street cultural practices are more leisure orientated, then they are more likely to have resonances with, or even some place in, more general youth lifestyles. The stronger and more economically/survival orientated street cultural practices can be more exclusively located within the criminal realm.

Ultimately, it is the sense of danger and threat associated with street culture that to some extent informs the prioritization of efforts to censure its adherents, but also that which animates its decontextualized image's connections to 'cool'. This will be explored in more detail within the next chapter, dedicated to issues of street cultural expressivity.

CHAPTER 6

From Street Expressivity to Commodifiable Cool

Introduction

This chapter examines the street cultural concerns underlying a wealth of expressive activities from graffiti writing and 'streetwear' fashion to urban music and street sports. Furthermore, their relationships to the realm of 'cool' and the mechanisms of the cultural industries are analysed to better understand the use of (particularly weaker variants of) street culture in contemporary commercial practice. It is ultimately argued that the authentic and transgressive nature of street cultural practices (or decontextualized images and tropes derived from them) is an invaluable resource to those who produce a range of products, particularly targeted at youth markets.

As previously discussed, street expressive activities can have an extremely ambiguous relationship with criminality: they may have origins in or continue to contain elements of criminality (e.g. graffiti writing can be a form of criminal damage if no permission has been obtained); they may have associations with criminal individuals but come to be practised and/or consumed by a far wider audience (e.g. the prison styles that have had a considerable influence on mainstream fashions); they may depict criminal themes which may be fact, fiction or a combination (e.g. particular variants of urban music); or they might be actively 'criminalized' (e.g. street sports within particular urban areas). Indeed, as was noted in the previous chapter, there are particular acts of criminality proper that may in part occur due to their own inherent expressive qualities. The focus of this chapter, however, lies on those forms of street expressivity which can be executed without criminality (e.g. if all necessary permissions are in place) and thus have commercializable potential well beyond 'the street' itself.

Whilst the Birmingham subcultural scholars of the 1970s (see e.g. Hall and Jefferson, 1976) considered issues of fashion and lifestyle side-by-side with criminal deviance, the evolution of disciplinary boundaries, in particular between youth studies and criminology, has meant that this occurs less in contemporary scholarship. Of course, detailed ethnographies of young peo-ple who offend (e.g. Sanders, 2005) and of subcultural scenes (e.g. Snyder, 2009) continue to do so, whilst cultural criminology has reinvigorated under-standings of the relationship between transgression, marketing and the leisure industries (Ferrell et al., 2008). What remains missing is a broader account of the styles and activities which emerge from the disadvantaged inner-city and spread, not just to be appropriated by mainstream entertainment industries, but to actively shape them.

Whilst particular strands of scholarship note the extent to which the urban poor are in effect victims of a consumer culture within which they lack the finance and taste to adequately participate, less attention is paid to the ways in which sections of the disadvantaged are in fact an inspiration not just for particular products, but for business techniques and production architec-tures. It is important to remember, however, that such opportunities for the socio-economically excluded to play decisive roles in the entertainment and leisure industries are infinitely rare compared to the obstacles faced by the vast majority of the excluded in terms of securing decently paid employment. The material below does not contradict the notion that poverty and exclu-sion are extremely difficult to transcend. Rather, it demonstrates the extent to which the street values born of these conditions are not so ultimately different from the principles underpinning the successful participation in contempo-rary forms of business practice. It furthermore speaks to the ethical flexibility of establishment actors where profits are at stake.

A brief history of street cool

Though long a feature of African-American culture and further immortalised in classic film depictions of gangsters, cowboys and such like, it would not be until the youth marketing revolution ushered in by the 1950s that notions of 'cool' would be so explicitly identified and injected into characters and products (Pountain and Robins, 2000). During this period, the notion of 'cool' and the 'hipster' who sought it became topics of public debate.

> You can't interview a hipster because his main goal is to keep out of a soci-ety which, he thinks, is trying to make everyone over in its own image. He takes marijuana because it supplies him with experiences that can't be shared with "squares." He may affect a broad-brimmed hat or a zoot suit, but usually he prefers to skulk unmarked. The hipster may be a jazz musi-cian; he is rarely an artist, almost never a writer. He may earn his living as a petty criminal, a hobo, a carnival roustabout or a free-lance moving man in Greenwich Village, but some hipsters have found a safe refuge in

the upper income brackets as television comics or movie actors. (The late James Dean, for one, was a hipster hero.) ... ('Born, 1930: The Unlost Generation' by Caroline Bird, Harper's Bazaar, February 1957, cited in Mailer, 1957).

The above quote is from a magazine article that was in turn quoted by Norman Mailer in writing 'The White Negro', a noted early text on cool. It posed questions as to where a culture he identifies as primarily hedonistic, anarchic and psychotic might have come from. The racialized language of its title and content, whilst a product of its time, nevertheless reveals a key relationship between exclusion and cool that has persisted over the decades. Furthermore, issues of 'authenticity' were central to early understandings of cool. Polsky (1967/2007: 150–152), for example, distinguished between 'hip beats' and 'hipsters'. The former, he argued were part of the latest developments in transgressive music and drug subcultures, whilst the latter tried hard to create the impression that they were similarly connected.

Mailer viewed the hipster of his time as emulating the tastes of black jazz culture: its 'out-there' music, appetite for drugs and distinct image. For him, a sense of cool is generated through sporting the trappings of groups that are excluded from the socio-economic mainstream. The jazz musicians that Becker would later term 'Outsiders' (1963) were a group whose deviance he argued was not inherent, but ascribed to them by the more powerful culture from which they were excluded. The fear-fascination duality that accompanies this ascription then had further cultural resonance. Essentially, cool has historically been the domain of racially marginalized and/or criminalized groups, which 'hip' individuals (those seeking the 'next big thing') from more dominant racial/class groups would emulate. One need not go to the lengths that Mailer did to try and explain this phenomenon. It is simply that those who seem to be concerned mainly with pleasurable experiences and looking good despite the judgements of others naturally attract the admiration of those from included populations who are adventurously inclined and in-tune with the subterranean (present, but less acknowledged) aspects of mainstream culture (see Matza and Sykes, 1961).

Black American culture continued its hold over the popular imaginary of 'cool' throughout the 1960s and 1970s. The nonchalant flair of Jimi Hendrix, the righteous funk of James Brown and the 'stone cold cats (men)' of Blaxploitation cinema each contributed something to an ideal type that seemed to change outfit and soundtrack but not ultimate essence. The geographic centre of the cool aesthetic similarly shifted; as Harlem jazz lost dominance to Southern rock 'n' roll and later Midwest funk and soul, New York would once again become the epicentre of a movement which would more closely than ever before fuse the aesthetics of the street into the cultural products of everyday life. Hip-hop's emergence in late 1970s New York seemed to usher in a totalized expressive movement encompassing music, dance, art, fashion as well as a variant of street cultural philosophy (see Chang, 2005). As hip-hop graffiti entered galleries, rappers and break-dancers reached the uptown clubs, hit records sold to mainstream audiences and television cameras (and later cash-in movies) recorded the sights and sounds of this vibrant Black and Latino youth cultural movement, the world watched, first in curiosity and eventually with desire.

Hip-hop's reverence of skill and mastery (street cultural concerns *par excellence*) to a certain extent ritualized some of the brutal gang violence that characterized the 1970s 'Rotten Apple', with DJ/MC luminaries such as Afrika Bambata preaching a doctrine of unity and nationhood to street-orientated youth. On the other hand, there is a tendency to over-state and romanticize the notion of a coherent hip-hop movement, which to some extent has always been a piecemeal combination of a variety of expressive subcultures and individuals (see Snyder, 2009). By this stage, variants of cool had arguably diverged along different (largely racial) lines with white pop-cultural producers continuing to draw on older black tropes as their inspiration, whilst excluded populations of colour remained intensely innovative in response to the street's voracious demand for new ways to conjure a sense of dignity against the backdrop of their exclusion.

Between the mid-1980s and mid-1990s, the focus of street cultural cool shifted towards the US west coast, where an aesthetic more attuned to a fine climate and Central American influences began to develop: smooth rap songs dedicated to stories of crime and tussles with justice, low-rider car culture, patterned bandanas and elaborate gang signification (see further Quinn, 2005). Similarly, the daring outdoor pursuits of Californian 'outlaw' surfers had made the transition to mainstream youth cultural fare: skateboarding (see *Dogtown* and *Z-Boys*, the 2001 documentary film by Stacy Peralta) and a range of extreme sports captured the imagination of the youth market. This, once massified, offered the optimum balance of wholesome exercise, regulatable leisure and seemingly anti-establishment thrill-seeking.

The US cultural hegemony that has held sway for the last seven or so decades continued to see its street expressivity act as a decisive influence on pop-culture. As rap music charted and sold amongst a mainstream audience, the more business-savvy artistes were able to profit. The music would, from the late 1990s on, reference designer goods and luxurious, exclusive lifestyles out of reach to all but the wealthiest. Household names in urban music sought to become synonymous with jewellery, champagne and private jet lifestyles: the style of the ghetto raider and that of the City trader, together at last.

As time passes, however, the global influences that have always patterned street culture in the USA and elsewhere arguably have become more visible beneath American cultural hegemony. As will be explored in this chapter and the next, there is a truly global current of street expressivity flowing in and out of the creative-industrial complex. There is, however, a relative singularity in the ways in which it is harnessed for commercial purposes. The cover story of marketing trade-sheet 'American Demographics' in November 1996 indeed was titled 'marketing street culture', within which author Marc Spiegler wrote:

> Scoring a hit with inner-city youths can make a product hot with the much larger and affluent white suburban market. But to take advantage of this phenomenon, you have to dig into how hip-hop spreads from housing projects to rural environs, understand why hip-hop is so attractive to suburban whites, and discern the process by which hip-hoppers embrace products (1996: 2).

The embodiment of 'Cool'

Following the material considered in Chapters 1 and 3, at its most essential level, street culture's 'cool' stems from the bodies and beings of its practitioners. Pountain and Robin (2000) observe that cool is an attitude of casual indifference, seemingly effortless control, inherently authentic with astute taste, cold-burning defiance and even a hint of disdain for those who fail to exhibit these traits. These are qualities that tend to be embodied to varying extents by street cultural practitioners at various points in the spectrum. Leaving aside the issue of taste, which itself is highly open to being shaped by street cultural practice, it is useful to reconsider how various street cultural concerns are manifested in both passive states of being and particular expressive activities.

Remembering that street culture operates as a value system parallel to the mainstream, where different resources (capitals) and opportunities are available for individuals, the street cultural practitioner automatically performs something of a 'devil may care' or daring identity. This is fuelled by those attitudes which are valued in the street but are viewed ambiguously or as problematic within wider society: the preference for 'street smarts' over formal education, the embodiment of violent potential; the search for excitement which might readily involve acts of law-breaking. More than existing as an ephemeral attitude, however, such traits tend to be written onto the bodies and mannerisms (the physical and verbal habitus) of the street cultural individual: in the way he holds himself, walks and stands, his accent, intonation and vocabulary. These actions are performed unconsciously; they are difficult to imitate; they are authentic and 'cool'.

In terms of bodily posture: the stony, indifferent 'yard face' of the ex-convict (Caputo-Levine, 2012); the wide, flamboyant 'b-boy' stance of the break-dancer (Verán, 1999), the swaggering walk of northern English men marked as 'trouble' by security workers (Hobbs et al., 2003), the challenging crouch of the Chicano gang member (Katz, 1988) and the 'gangster lean' of the proverbial pimp (Quinn, 2000) are all part of a repertoire of physical street cultural performance. The 'cool pose' (Majors and Billson, 1992) innately captures and communicates the street cultural acumen of its holder: nonplussed, contained, physically imposing, relaxed but ready.

More than this, street culture is connected to a rich body of verbal communication which is linked to exclusion from mainstream or dominant forms of culture. These can consist of accents (Charlesworth, 2000), dialects: e.g. Jamaican Patois (Stolzoff, 2000), linguistic variants and slang (see e.g. Baugh, 1983 on black American street speech and Doran, 2004 on French 'Verlan'). Socio-economic exclusion and participation in street culture thus pattern the ways in which people speak, again often compounding their exclusion through signifying this position. On the other hand, these verbal repertoires become the grist to the mill of the entertainment industry featuring heavily in movies, music and video-games. Overall, these patterned modes of being become the most basic level of expressivity, connecting a person's body to their position within society (see further Shilling, 2012). Once again, those styles associated with the street tend to disadvantage street cultural practitioners, marking them with their exclusion. They are, however, also transposable (with varying degrees of accuracy), creating emulatable modes of posture, movement and speech that can be imitated in an attempt (however successful) to vest either individuals or products with a greater sense of 'authenticity', 'grit' and/or cool.

Style and (bodily) pattern

The body can act as another locus of street cultural expressivity through the ways in which it is modified and adorned. In the case of the former, altering body shape through the regular repetition of exercise and various forms of bodily marking stand out as examples. American street culture, its most ubiquitously visible variant, is often manifested thus, through the development of prominent muscularity in men and in the acquisition of stylized street tattoos. Considering first the informal body building that visibly marks some of those who participate in street culture, its logic is relatively easy to grasp. Bulging muscles communicate physical strength and psychic discipline whilst also appealing to ideal rugged masculine aesthetics. More than this, however, the development of extensive musculature can imply time spent in prison where there is little else to do but exercise and thus constitute part of a stylistic practice that seeks to link prison and street life. Indeed, a recent phenomenon is the celebration of the 'prison workout' amongst fitness enthusiasts who view it as a simple and cheap means of improving form (see e.g. www.menshealth40plus.com/prison.html). This involves exercises that are performed without weight-lifting equipment (which is easily weaponizable and thus generally not allowed within individual prison cells). This has further spawned the availability of commercial instructional videos where those who claim to be ex-convicts lead customers through the steps.

American street feminities are also associated with particular forms of body shape which have spawned their own mythologies and industries. In particular, and problematically related to one of the ways in which black femininities are almost dismissively physicalized in the public imaginary, curvaceous figures which include a large posterior become something of an ideal type. Such matters are discussed (often by men) in various rap songs, not least Sir Mix-a-lot's 1992 single *Baby Got Back* (Def American Records). Indeed, an industry has emerged around the provision of buttock enhancement treatments, whether injection or implant, that is said to draw heavily on the aesthetic of key women in US urban music (Vaidyanathan, 2011). Even the embodied physicality associated with the American prison/street is readily commercializable.

Tattoos are another street/prison tradition in many parts of the world. They are, for example, a colourful aspect of East Asian institutionalized criminality both Triad (Chinese; see Lim et al., 2013) and Yakuza (Japanese; see Raz, 1992). It is again, however, US street tattooing which has become more publicly recognizable. The gothic style lettering which spells out 'thug life' on the stomach of the late rap icon Tupac Shakur is, for many, an apparent example of this phenomenon. The sheer variety and scale of this tattooing tradition, however, runs to greater depths and extremities than this popular image (see DeMello, 1995). The Mara Salvatura, a US–Central American street gang (see Arana, 2005), are known for their extensive all-over tattoos which include the letters, numbers and iconography that constitute their visual repertoire: the gang name and/or its initials, the number '13' and devil horns (their hand signal).

In a classic subcultural sense, street and prison tattoos can thus represent a complex system of codes, a form of 'street literacy' (Conquergood, 1994a) that can be read by those similarly embedded within particular street cultures. This much is evident from the Russian Prison Tattoo Archive constructed by London graphic design studio and publishing house Fuel (based on drawings by Danzig Baldaev and photographs by Sergei Vasiliev, http://fuel-design.com/russian-criminal-tattoo-archive/). Here the iconography of political critique, spirituality and violence communicates the stories of inmates. The collection, furthermore, has been displayed in exhibition, book and postcard format. This is one example of the extent to which the aesthetic of street tattooing has increasingly infiltrated the interests and visual palette of more mainstream aspects of cultural production. There is also the story of the iconic Los Angeles tattooist Mister Cartoon, known not just for his work on the body of various celebrities but his design collaborations with a range of global brands from Nike to Casio (see http://www.mistercartoon.com). These striking examples are mere aspects of a wider aesthetic that has left a mark not just on the skin of street cultural adherents and their emulators, but on wider practices of graphic design, fashion styles and the content of art galleries.

More than this, body adornments such as clothing and accessories are very much connected to the performance of street identities on the one hand, and influence wider youth fashion trends on the other. Whilst the speed at which urban fashion moves (which will be later discussed) renders much of the material outlined below somewhat dated, the principles discussed remain relevant. Ultimately, the street cultural concern of attaining 'distinction' can be achieved in a number of different ways. Most obviously, through spending money to consume brand name clothing and gold jewellery street cultural individuals can assert their earning and violent acumen through procuring and keeping hold of such goods (see Hall et al., 2008; Anderson, 1999). An issue here previously noted, however, is that such a style is easily stigmatized as gauche and of poverty.

The imperative to be distinct, however, can equally be met through the deployment of 'originality' and improvisation, deploying a heightened sense of aesthetic taste combined with an intuitive sense of what will appear stylish on the street: to select and customize clothing and seek out diverse influences in a manner that forges new modes of street cultural style. A clear example of this phenomenon can be seen in the origins of hip-hop fashion stalwarts April Walker and Angela Hunte-Wisner's enduring careers (Williams, 2013). The designer and stylist cite black designer pioneers as well as 'fashion forward' individuals in their neighbourhoods as key influences in establishing looks that would prove highly influential. Similarly, Bobbito Garcia (2006) in his painstaking catalogue of classic 'sneaker' culture in New York City notes the ways in which local young people hunted for rare shoes in desirable colours and furthermore customized their footwear with paint, markers and innovative lacing. Not only would this font of improvisational innovation become highly influential on sneaker design, but Nike even released a line of plain white-on-white shoes, together with markers as DIY customization kits.

This DIY aesthetic has been inherently worked into streetwear brands (e.g. FUBU – For Us, By Us), which have grown to challenge those brands from outside of street culture which seek to sell into it. Indeed, there has been a rather complex pattern of interactions between traditional luxury brands and the members of the urban poor who favour them. On the one hand, the Tommy Hilfiger brand which inadvertently became a streetwear favourite in the 1990s sought to actively capitalize on this position with the effect of 'alienating' both its street and traditional middle-class customer base (Sherman, 2010). Evidently, the authenticity of appropriating clothing designed for more opulent nautical/outdoor pursuits chaffed against blatant attempts to court street consumers. On the other hand, the Burberry brand was reported as disappointed with the extent to which their distinctive check pattern became associated with the UK lower working-class 'chavs' and adjusted their designs accordingly (Jones, 2008). Ultimately, however, it is clear that global brands, particularly those with an eye to the youth market, actively seek out street fashion developments to influence their products.

'Cool merchants' or 'cool-hunters' working on behalf of such brands have been shown to observe the stylistic practices of inner-city youth (see Rushkoff, 2001; Anderson, 1999; Gladwell, 1997). Street tastes are thus not only attuned to the consumption of noted brands, but they actively shape the design decisions of brands who want to sell to wider youth markets. Individuals who have developed particular skills and influence in terms of street expressive aesthetics may find themselves sought out as creative partners or employees. In this way exceptional members of the urban poor (or as likely keen observers or emulators of this group) can be producers more than consumers of the cool aesthetic.

Broader criminal/justice phenomena, often linked to street culture, themselves feature as influences on streetwear. Juliet Ash (2009), for example, has noted the way in which elements of prison uniforms are lifted out of context and woven into fashionable garments. More than this, however:

> The manner in which prisoners wear clothing, rather than the garment itself, has also traversed the prison walls. In the early twenty-first century for example, low-slung jeans that revealed the bum became fashionable for young men and women in Europe and America. The style took as its inspiration the way prisoners were not allowed belts. Similarly, shoe laces, forbidden in prisons, disappeared from the street. These youth styles signified their wearers' distinction from elitist fashionable circles. They also revealed an ironic disreputable allegiance to the hierarchical fashion system through the exposure of designer underwear labels such as Calvin Klein (Ash, 2009: 171).

In this latter example, the author is referring to the uniformed prisoners' sole opportunity for sartorial innovation in their choice of socks and underwear, which is then used to maximum effect through visibly exposing these garments to earn distinction. This style of wearing designer underwear (with branded elasticated band proudly exposed) is a familiar 1990s streetwear trope whose significance was no doubt lost on many who adopted it. In the former example, suicide prevention protocols are converted into styles of wearing attire. These stylistic practices, much like certain forms of tattooing, illustrate the manner in which street expressivity can traverse prison and street spaces.

Scholars have examined the extent to which street criminal imagery from guns and grenades to drugs and drug taking paraphernalia features within fashion designs, music publicity and marketing strategies (see Ferrell et al., 2008; Blackman, 2004). There remains more to say, however, about the role of street fashion practices in acts of criminality themselves. Cultural criminologists such as Hayward (2004) have correctly reflected on the consumerist pressures that exist for those who do not have the legitimate means to realize them resulting in a kind of animated strain which acts as a strong motivation towards criminal behaviour. This is particularly the case where individuals adhere to a variant of street culture which places high value on 'fresh' clothing and shoes: always on trend and preferably brand new. Observe, for example, the trend of retaining authentification holograms on branded baseball caps which signal the garments' newness. Indeed, this preference for 'boxfresh' (fresh out of the box) attire is no doubt known to the streetwear brand which has taken this word as its name. More than simply creating a need to consistently spend a lot of money on clothing, this generates a cause of potentially violent disputes when one individual (accidently or otherwise) damages another's clothing or shoes (see e.g. Kramer et al., 2014) and indeed makes such items the targets of crime themselves.

Garment choice has also been long associated with membership of particular street cultural groupings such as gangs. Beyond the colours which can indicate affiliation with one set or another, within the USA, for example, a complex code has been said to exist around sportswear where team names and logos are plumbed for deeper meanings which reveal something about a gang's particular mythologies, identities and rivalries. The ways in which such practices continue to feature in the same way in a contemporary 'remixed' US street culture are open to question (Moore, 2013). Indeed, streetwear can be read by agents of law enforcement as a sign of criminality even where its signifying power of such is highly tenuous (see Ferrell, 2004). Style can become criminalized based on outdated or misunderstood impressions of what it is supposed to represent. This is no more clear than in particular reactions to the 'hoodie', a garment which arguably becomes a channel for anxieties around the people who might wear them. Whilst this includes students, athletes and indeed university lecturers, these items of clothing have been banned in particular UK shopping malls (see Marsh and Melville, 2011) and have been discussed in the wake of the infamous killing of Trayvon Martin in Florida (Giroux, 2012).

The movement(s)

Beyond the body itself and how it is adorned, street culture extends into a range of movements and activities (at times through proxy objects) that are performed variously in dance and competition. These have evolved into identifiable tropes and genres that have extensively infiltrated the mainstream cultural industries. Although it is open to be viewed as an excessively 'decorative' topic, 'some of the most richly coded class practices in contemporary society can be observed in leisure and in dance' (McRobbie, 1997: 211). Much the same might be said in relation to issues of ethnicity. Beginning by considering dance, it is clear that the practices (and perceived intimate indiscretions) of the urban poor and ethnically different have long been a site of contest between popular taste and mainstream, 'respectable' normativity (see e.g. McBee, 2000). Once again, a degree of US cultural dominance applies to this area of street cultural practice, where hip-hop dance emerged from areas of disadvantage in New York City to a place within mainstream media products.

Breakdancing, the acrobatic, combative form of competitive dance, succeeded to some extent in ritualizing the rivalries between different groups of young people in 1970s New York (Chang, 2005). In such a manner, those who previously participated in the identity work inherent in street gang culture found an alternative means to express distinction and earn street capital. Contemporaneous with the spread of hip-hop music, the spectacle of young people aggressively taunting each other into evermore elaborate feats of limb-twisting exhibition demonstrated how street cultural environments incubate niche forms of expressivity. Here practices were honed and exaggerated intended primarily for an audience of peers, not wider tastes. The less ritualized (and it must be said spectacular) genre of hip-hop dance emerged in part from breakdancing and its 'popping and locking' variant on the US west coast. Indeed, the form has gained global ubiquity and respectability. Its practitioners may or may not be aware of the extent to which it shares roots in street cultural expressivity with the extravagant motions of 1920s jazz dancing (see Osumare, 2002).

The performance of up-to-date urban dance moves requires intense physical competence and aesthetic nous. It embodies thus key street cultural concerns and vests the performer with a cool persona. Moreover, as exemplified by Henry's work on Jamaican dancehall culture in the UK (2006), dancing, music and the sociability that goes with it is part of a process of community building and space making, where those who experience intense exclusion in their everyday lives can be together and where themes relevant to their experience are aired. Again, the 'hothousing' of styles that emerge from such a crucible ensures constant innovation. Remaining 'on trend' will often require a deep knowledge of niche urban music scenes and thus a high degree of street stylistic acumen (although now the internet has had a significant role in facilitating such knowledge acquisition more broadly). Dances such as the 'crip walk' have become part of the non-textual communication practices of particular US street 'gangs' (Phillips, 2009). On the other hand, street dance such as hip-hop has undergone a process of appropriation whereby it has become adopted within the mainstream cultural industries, albeit in diluted form (Back, 1997). As pointed out by Boyd (2004: 71) this changes the meaning of the dance, stripping it of its particular significance and rendering it simply a means of lending an edge to otherwise relatively staid musical acts or films.

The path tread by breakdancing/hip-hop dance in this journey is fairly well chronicled (see e.g. Verán, 1999). B-boys (breakdancers) featured in early hip-hop tours and in the early 1980s movies which either reverently or cynically attempted to harness its energy for visual appeal. Indeed there emerged a notable genre of street dance movies such as 'Honey' (Universal, 2003) which narrate the tale of dancers from middle-class backgrounds who secure the redemption of their art form by invigorating both it and their wider lives through their immersion within tough street dancing scenes (Boyd, 2004). Controversies over popular, mainstream white entertainers attempting to import sexuality and 'edge' into their act through appropriating black street dance abound and were very much present in Miley Cyrus' provocative 'twerking' during a performance at the 2013 MTV Video Music Awards (see e.g. Mazelle, 2013). Much as this performance seemed to lay claim to the images of black femininity that are used to denigrate black women, it also revealed the cultural currency of niche forms of street dance. In this case, 'twerking' a style associated with New Orleans' more obscure 'bounce' music scenes, could serve. Disadvantaged communities in the USA (e.g. within Chicago with juke music and footwork dancing) and worldwide (e.g. within Rio de Janeiro with baile funk music and its distinctive dancing style) house styles of movement which are ripe for vesting more conventional pop cultural products with seeming distinctiveness and cool.

Sport equally plays a prominent role in street life and, depending on local tastes, a wide variety of 'official sports' casually played feature in the everyday life of disadvantaged urban youth. Whether this is the casual football (soccer) 'kick-about' favoured by the Liverpool boys studied by Parker (1974) or the highly charged 'pick up' variant of basketball lovingly documented in New York by Bobbito Garcia in his 2012 documentary *Doin it in the Park* (Goldcrest Films), street sports draw on the premium placed by street culture on physical prowess, generating excitement and spending time in organic activities. Of course, such activities dovetail with the worlds of professional sporting and sports merchandizing. The place of the street in honing the talents of future mainstream stars is noted in the Garcia film, and there exists a widespread belief that many of the world's urban disadvantaged see only sports and music as their routes out of poverty. Indeed, the preference within streetwear for sporting goods provides further evidence of this link, where perhaps the professional athletes' ability to earn a massive income from participation in a 'leisure' activity arguably resonates with certain street cultural concerns (and indeed wider neoliberal values).

Sports merchandizers can take solace in the vast market provided by street cultural practitioners. The casual nature of sportswear contrasts to the formal garments of those in many forms of corporate employment. Beyond the sphere of mainstream sports, however, is where street cultural expressivity has had a key influence in the proliferation of practices and markets that have deeply impacted on the contemporary youth cultural industries. Whilst admittedly less significantly linked to urban poverty, the urban extreme sports tradition both exhibits a number of street cultural concerns and is often featured alongside true street cultural practices in range of youth-orientated events and products. Here, I refer to practices such as skateboarding, BMXing, etc. With a premium placed on an ability to perform complex, acrobatic tricks, the display of attitude and an institutionalized 'disrespect' to the rules which tend to govern ordinary transport and urban civility, these youth cultural practices have been marketed alongside baggy streetwear, adorned with street-style graffiti and thus without a close examination seem part of a similar repertoire. Much like graffiti writers (on which more later) skateboarders have turned an obscure, underground subcultural practice into a lucrative mass market and suite of subcultural industries (see Snyder, 2012).

With phenomena such as the XGames boasting huge global audiences and skate brands such as Vans as high street institutions (Rinehart, 2008), the attempt by urban extreme sports to lay claim to a level of authenticity, whilst simultaneously constituting a form of 'wholesome' (structurable) outdoor pursuit would seem to ideally position them as a commodifiable form of street culture 'lite'. Here a fascination with the aesthetics of the street is revealed as a vesting products and activities with the requisite 'cool' to become the drivers of consumerist trends. A further example of the ways in which street aesthetics float to rest on activities viewed by some as 'street' (even if they are not necessarily so) is observable around the French sport of Parkour (or 'free running'). Whilst developed as a form of physical and mental discipline and as a means of reimagining the urban environment, it has arguably taken on the 'edge' of a transgressive street sport. This may be to some extent due to its presence within the ghetto-dystopian film *District 13* (2004) or indeed the streetwear, daring and disregard for urban etiquette demonstrated by some of its practitioners (see e.g. Atkinson, 2009).

Another key plank to the transgressive image (and possibly even the 'outlaw' appeal) of urban extreme sports is the reaction to them by certain private property owners and indeed particular law enforcement agencies. Where skateboarding is made illegal in public spaces, or indeed property owners cry trespass over free runners vaulting around their roofs, this will add an extra degree of risk and excitement to such activities (see Hayward, 2007) and will arguably cause certain individuals to admire them more. The impressive aesthetic of free running, combined with its (at times) death-defying riskiness and attributed urban edge all arguably thus contribute to its cinematic appeal, where it featured as part of the renaissance of one of film's most enduring characters: James Bond (see *Casino Royale*, Columbia Pictures, 2006). Of course, these variants of urban extreme sports are essentially linked to more minor, often self-generated forms of law breaking. There are people both within and outside of areas of urban disadvantage who showcase their physical and acrobatic abilities using their bodies and varieties of pedal, foot and motor powered vehicles. Those truly trapped in conditions of socio-economic exclusion, however, tend to seek their thrill seeking in more extreme activities (see Fenwick and Hayward, 2000).

The street cultural practice of 'joyriding', for example, is deeply steeped in illegality and yet it possesses certain similarities to forms of extreme sports (see O'Connell, 2006). Cars or other kinds of motorized vehicles are stolen and driven at speed or raced for purely expressive purposes. The goal here is not to sell on the vehicle for a profit but to generate the maximum amount of excitement in the moment through risking both injury/death and apprehension/punishment. The act represents a carnivalesque disregard for typical consumerist pressures (i.e. to have a car), instead celebrating their wilful destruction, particularly where it is completed by the burning of the vehicle (see Presdee, 2000). Skilful vehicle handling can be yet another signifier of potent and sure masculinity, whilst overt displays of daring signal a disregard for safety and conformity that can become a means of boosting street capital. These activities dovetail with the more consumerist forms of car culture linked to the street, where speed, power and handling retain particular salience, tempered by a regard for the condition of legally owned vehicles which become signifiers of status themselves.

In Chicano 'lowrider' culture, for example, cars have their suspensions modified and are often painstakingly customized to act as a symbol of the street acumen of its owner. The culture is replete with exhibitionist and spatial logics: vesting the owner of the car (and its passengers) with a mobile space from which pride can be derived (Chappell, 2010). In a similar manner, the 'boy racers' of the UK preen their modified vehicles, meeting in real and virtual spaces to exhibit their pleasing form and powers of speed and acceleration (Lumsden, 2013). The 'delinquent driving' and street racing that can sometimes link to these practices render these cars into targets for the traffic police. Undoubtedly, the socio-economic and/or ethnic status of their owners is intertwined with this process. Marketers, moreover, are very well aware of the symbolic appeal of outlaw vehicle culture and regularly incorporate it into advertising campaigns (Muzzatti, 2010). For those street cultural practitioners, however, who invest in these practices (and vehicles) their cars become important proxies for themselves. Here there is a particular resonance with mainstream 'middle-class' culture so taken with investment in home properties. For the more financially precarious, vehicles are a far more viable (though far less fiscally productive) investment than property, serving as a repository for surplus wealth during times of plenty, but readily saleable/pawnable during times of scarcity (see similarly Skeggs, 2011, on gold jewellery).

The art of survival

Beyond the body and its extensions, street cultural expressivity has manifested in a number of artistic practices that now too are globally ubiquitous. Chiefly recognizable within this lexicon is the subculture of hip-hop graffiti (which bleeds into wider forms of street art) and various forms of urban music (a term which can denote diverse genres with different levels of renown). Central to the development and spread of both these disciplines is the veritable cultural powerhouse that is hip-hop. Despite the mythologization of its emergence from the 1970s New York slums, there is no doubt of its potency in terms of badging together a range of street stylistic expressivity and demonstrating the extent to which these could eventually shape mainstream industry practices and aesthetics.

There is a rich tradition of studying graffiti and its practitioners. For most urban dwellers the swirls, bubbles, patterns and lines of hip-hip graffiti fade into the background of their consciousness: a ubiquitous presence, perhaps perceived as chaotic and ugly, perhaps as vibrant and beautiful. What has emerged from the literature is a sense that this form of 'vandalism' is not

Figure 6.1 The mighty FOES crew are represented here by an elaborate 'piece', the ultimate expression of the graffiti writer's vision and skill. Photo by Killan 'Kube' Walsh

simply about the defacement of private property, but instead is concerned with aesthetic principles and behavioural norms, themselves deeply intertwined with the logics and illogics of street culture. For MacDonald (2001), hip-hop graffiti operates on the basis of 'an economy of prestige', whereby 'writers' (as they call themselves) vie against each other to become the most renowned and respected. Their murals (usually prominently depicting their 'tag' or pseudonym) compete with corporate billboards for brand visibility in the late-modern city. A key component of a writer's arsenal is thus his/her technical skill and aesthetic vision which allows them to attain prominence within a subculture that is essentially rather tightly bound by convention.

Ferrell's (1996) study of Denver graffiti writers sets out in detail the tripartite division of graffiti craft into 'tags' (a writer's signature rapidly painted, often in a great variety of places); 'throw ups' (a rendering of a tag or initials in larger and more elaborate lettering); and 'pieces' (elaborate murals often including complex graphic work and/or illustrations, often in colour – the true exhibition of a writer's skill – Figure 6.1). Depending on visibility, competitions over writing spaces and the risks of getting caught, writers tend to make judgements as to the most appropriate form of graffiti writing to perform in particular spaces. This should not, however, be necessarily interpreted as implying that a form of 'rational choice' is operating here. Both the location and content of graffiti may be selected precisely because they entail a greater likelihood of apprehension or offence. In this way the street cultural imperative to seek a visceral sense of excitement animates the activity (see Hayward, 2007). This can especially inform the painting of graffiti that involves trespassing on the upper levels of particularly tall buildings. A sense of daring, producing street capital, can be generated in this manner.

Ferrell furthermore mentions the extent to which graffiti subcultures have grown considerably past the limits of the disadvantaged inner-city and tend to involve a great many middle-class individuals (a number of which will tend to have formal art school qualifications or indeed operate thriving small businesses). The relative privilege of some of its practitioners, however, does not detract from the fact that it emerged as part of the efforts of the under-privileged to make a greater visual impact on the city around them (see MacDonald, 2001). Snyder (2009) furthermore importantly points out that violence can surround the conflicts that erupt between practitioners and rivals demonstrating the extent to which street cultural logics continue to operate within this milieu. It is, however, flair, originality and skill with their visual output that remains the ultimate arbiter of status within the graffiti world. Hierarchies and etiquette tend to dictate how one subcultural member will treat the work of another, variously leaving it unmarked, painted over or commented upon.

Whilst this system explains how a criminal art scene is capable of producing an impressive and evolving body of work, Millie (2008) demonstrates the extent to which wider aesthetic judgements, as well as the spatial logic of consumerism (with its demands for precisely rendered environments) operates to define graffiti as vandalism in a great majority of cases. This is despite its porous boundaries with 'street art', a genre finding particular favour amongst mainstream art critics and buyers. The antics of Banksy, the mid-20th century styles of OBEY and the lesser-known but vitally influential interventions of Blek le Rat all animate the commerce and conversation within the mainstream art world. Nevertheless, street-style graffiti tends to remain a law enforcement and crime prevention priority, despite questionable results in this regard.

Indeed, it has been argued that the aggressive cleaning or 'buffing' on the Metro carriages that acted as the original canvasses for NY graffiti saw it migrate to a much greater extent to buildings (see Snyder, 2006). This demonstrates the weaknesses of crime control policies that are built on abstract notions of 'broken windows' (that failing to counter lesser incivilities leads to serious criminality thriving; see Wilson and Kelling, 1982). Instead, the crime is obviously merely displaced to different targets. Indeed, where writers have fewer opportunities to flourish through creating impressive murals (which would be an aesthetic asset to any urban or transit space), other fields of competition open up. More prevalent tagging and attempts to throw-up onto riskier and more dangerous walls can become part of this, perhaps even exacerbating the originally identified 'problem'. Of course, as Snyder (2009) and Alvelos (2004) note, graffiti aesthetics and tactics have been harnessed by the mainstream marketing world to render products more 'edgy' or indeed to add transgression to their medium if not their message.

As ubiquitous as this street-stylized graffiti adorning cities is the urban music which has drawn heavily on street cultural logics, themes and aesthetics to become a fundamental force in the contemporary cultural industries. I use 'urban music' here in reference to the more contemporary musical expression of marginalized groups (although it can be used in more historical contexts too). It is usually used as a form of music industry shorthand to refer to rap, R'n'B, dancehall, afropop, etc., all forms of black music, which has caused Henry (2006) to object to its failure to properly acknowledge this cultural context. The racism of western society and its imposition of exclusion and control on black populations has served at various points in time to construct their cultural expression as 'low' at worst and 'exotic' at best (Ramsey, 2003). This has been compounded by the marginalizing effects of poverty. Originally thus, such genres of music were more or less exclusively available to a tightly knit network of performers and audience members who shared similar aesthetic tastes and themes of interest. This allowed for the relatively rapid development of niche genres, sheltered from the tumultuous tides of the pop charts.

The tight bond between audiences, entrepreneurs and performers within geographically and socio-economically limited spaces allows for a responsiveness that cannot be achieved by a music industry architecture several times removed from its customers. The street cultural imperative towards 'sporting the latest' applies similarly to music where it is a mark of acumen to know and appreciate the most current trend. Performers and promoters will thus become rapidly aware of the consequences for failing to immediately cater to audience preferences. Important here is also the improvisation that has long been a feature of music forged in conditions of poverty. The documentary film tribute to the art of 'MCing' (or rapping) is indeed entitled *Something from Nothing* (2012) – a reference to the extent to which this massively successful genre was creatively spun out of playful interjections over already produced records. Jamaican music, moreover, produced in a developing country over decades elevated the requirement of extracting maximum impact from limited technical resources to an art form, producing thus the notions of the producer as *auteur*, the version (or remix) and indeed 'toasting' the precursor to rapping (see e.g. Bradley, 2001).

Contemporary genres of urban music tend to be at the forefront of exploiting technological advances, where hip-hop embraced sampling and electronic production (see Quinn, 2005) whilst British grime music has made good use of virtual networks and platforms (Ilan, 2012). The notions of niche audiences and self-referentiality have arguably underpinned the ways in which such developments unfolded, where it is the urban music of previous generations that is often re-versioned to suit the tastes of the next. Thus, for example, disco, funk and soul loops formed the basis of hip-hop (Rose, 1994), classic Jamaican tunes (and wider hits) became the 'riddims' on which a raft of newer music was built (Bradley, 2001) and electronic dance music owes a great debt to various analogue predecessors (see e.g. Thornton, 1995). Ultimately, whilst this kind of imaginative reinterpretation speaks to the improvisational qualities of urban music, it also created tensions and conflicts with the mainstream industry who take a somewhat more proprietorial attitude to matters of copyright (see e.g. Manuel and Marshall, 2006). This represents a further instance where forms of street cultural expressivity run into the constraints of the law.

Urban music's lyricality tends to embody the dissonance of life in the disadvantaged inner-city, its joys and pains, raucous parties and bitter desperation, uplifting determination and grinding pressures. Indeed, as scholars such as Jeffries (2011) and Quinn (2005) demonstrate in relation to US rap music, the seemingly incongruous themes of intense spirituality, political consciousness, brutal violence, the sexual objectification of women, and crass consumerism jostle for space within the oeuvre of single artistes. In the niche urban music genres of the developing world, for example, Jamaica or Brazil, it is not uncommon to hear coded or direct references to large-scale, well-institutionalized, street cultural groups (see e.g. Charles, 2009). Whilst references to the cocaine trade are frequent within the American rap genre to the extent that a book has been written on this precise phenomenon (see Bogazianos, 2012), there are countless references to Rastafarian spirituality in the similarly violent Jamaican dancehall (see Stolzoff, 2000). In this manner, music which forms part of street cultural expressivity contains extremities in its lyricism that mirrors the intensity of the experiences within the street lifeworlds that spawned it.

The search for respect at the heart of street culture extends to its music, where a competitive attitude permeates the ways in which MCs (rappers) and DJs 'battle' or 'clash' in an attempt to gain superiority over their rivals. The mock threats and violent metaphor that can be part and parcel of its performance can be taken as literal by outsiders. Indeed, Charis Kubrin (2005) identifies the extent to which street codes permeate rap music, which itself becomes a rhetorical device to articulate the normative circumstances within which violence occurs in street culture. This, she maintains, must be clearly delineated from any 'cause' of violence and crime, which of course exists within a complex web of factors. Nevertheless, the lyrical content of urban music has tended to be the subject of respectable opprobrium, targeting especially references to sexuality and violence. The Jamaican government, for example, banned all lyrical references to the sexually suggestive (in the extreme) dance style of 'daggering', despite its existence as a distinctive, organic component of the island's internationally popular, own urban music genre (see Watson, 2011).

Looking to rap music, furthermore, there are numerous moral crusades observable where records have been ruled obscene, concerts cancelled and various voices calling for further action (see Keyes, 2002). Rather than stymieing its commercial appeal, however, references to crime and violence, if anything have made American rap music all the more appealing to middle-class suburban consumers (see Ilan, 2012; Quinn, 2005). As cultural criminologists such as Ferrell et al. (2008) and De Jong and Schulenburg (2006) rightly suggest, this exemplifies the commodification of crime that is rife throughout the cultural industries, where rappers with supposed links to urban disadvantage now boast of attaining the trappings of the hyper rich. This raises questions as to the extent to which these sorts of articulated values can be identified as oppositional or conformist (to be explored in more detail in Chapter 8). It also indicates the commercial nous of those artistes who realize that controversy serves to sell more products to a youth market hungry for what become perceived as symbols of rebellion (McRobbie and Thornton, 1995). Indeed, as Bakari Kitwana (2005) has argued, rap music (and this applicable to wider urban genres) now occupies a stable position as part of the pop pantheon, appealing to alienated young people wary of commercial artifice and relatively eclectic in their tastes. With its mantra of 'keeping it real' hip-hop can consistently lay claim to authenticity and thus 'cool' and this applies further to even more obscure or extreme forms of urban music.

The subcultural career and the commodification of authenticity

Greg Snyder (2009), in following the careers of his graffiti writer participants, noted the extent to which they had moved into employment as magazine editors, marketers, designers, etc. Coining the term 'subculture career' and following this up with similar findings in relation to professional skateboarders, Snyder (2012) captured the extent to which the contemporary cultural industries are indebted to the subcultural experience of its new breed of employees and agents. With the speed at which street trends develop amongst closely knit communities of taste, those industries seeking to stay abreast of what is 'fresh', 'hip' or cool must rely on the inside knowledge that such individuals provide. Thus more middle-class entrepreneurs with street cultural acumen (e.g. rap mogul P Diddy) or indeed those who have experienced urban poverty (e.g. his colleague Jay Z) can reap the rewards of standing at the apex between perceived authenticity and commercial mass production/consumption. TV phenomena such as *American Idol* and *Pop Idol* ooze material ultimately derived from street cultural expressivity: urban music and street dance (however watered down). Urban music has not simply featured frequently in the pop charts, but its production techniques of sampling and sequencing, synthesizing and remixing are now contemporary pop music staples. Street cultural expressivity has become (in street parlance) a 'game changer'.

Where Frank (1997) explains how the 1960s explosion of 'youth culture' involved changes in business culture beyond the mere appropriation of youth stylistic expression, similar points can be made regarding street culture and significant sections of the cultural industries in contemporary times. He identified a 'cult of youth' that undercut previous orthodoxies around the authority of seniority, demanding that creative professionals 'think young'. In the contemporary cultural industries, the requirement to be aggressively authentic, relevant and on trend can arguably be achieved through attentiveness to developments within particular fields of street cultural expressivity. The proliferation of relatively cheap digital media production and distribution technologies has elevated the potential of street cultural artistes to make increasingly ambitious and polished products and market these directly to an audience, a far cry from selling hand-recorded cassette tapes from the trunk of a car. Successful careers are arguably now available to those who can effectively curate and navigate these information flows.

Google, the information age commercial force par excellence, has been keen to link itself to those who have successfully marketized street stylistic expression. A 2011 advertisement for its 'Chrome' web-browser charts the rise and rise of Jamal Edwards and SB.TV, a young black British entrepreneur and his urban music YouTube channel. Combining the DIY ethos and entrepreneurial hustle of the street cultural artistes it originally showcased with a savvy understanding of the new-media industries, Edwards has secured private equity capital for what has become a successfully growing youth media company (Sweney, 2013). Whilst large multinationals continue to dominate the new mediascape (note Google is represented here as the facilitator of business), authentic voices and curators carry currency as the conduits through which young people might be reached. Indeed, UK urban music is notable for the fact that some of its artistes have been able to capitalize on their superior use of virtual commerce and community building to pioneer successful careers and have seen major labels offering their patronage as a consequence (see Ilan, 2012, 2014).

From around the globe, the Internet hosts an abundance of street stylistic expressivity: recorded music, videos, photographs of art, fashion and bodies. The key art for the cultural industries becomes tapping into the genres, platforms and products that will resonate. Advice on such matters can be provided by those in a range of subcultural careers: niche communication companies and brand consultants. Arguably, this does not quite compete in terms of energy (and often charisma) with the street cultural entrepreneurs who bring their or others' creative work to commercial realization. In rap music, for example, there was a marked rise in independent labels, heavily affiliated with the majors, who handle a stable of artistes and retain a portion of profits. Particular rappers such as P Diddy and Jay Z are noted for their business acumen in heading such operations as much as lyrical ability.

Where what is cool is that which is authentic (organically created) and current (relevant to key audiences at the key time) street stylistic capital can be a very useful resource to possesses. Attaining the necessary balance between street capital, creative talent and/or contacts and the skills necessary to operate within the legitimate business world (in a sector as specialized as the cultural industries) is, however, difficult to the extent that those who achieve it are exceptional. Urban poverty, as previously noted, tends not to promote a successful media career in the vast majority of cases and is more likely to yield outcomes covered elsewhere in this book.

What is far more common is for those who are in media/communication careers to take an active interest in global developments in street culture, to indicate a level of 'subcultural capital' (Thornton, 1995) and a cutting-edge awareness of trends. The quintessential embodiment of early 21st-century cool, 'the hipster' can be understood as revelling in being 'the first to know' (Hujić, 2010) about new cultural developments or the particular obscure retro fashions that are currently *de rigueur*. In this arena, street cultural expressivity provides a rich bank of obscure variants on which to draw, whether contemporary and exotic or historical and iconic. In this sense, the blogosphere that acts as the scrapbook for the formation of future mainstream trends abounds with accounts of richly expressive street cultures. Meanwhile, particular forms of street cultural expressivity have comfortably intertwined themselves with hipster culture. The A$AP Mob, for example, deftly meld high fashion and hip-hop creating a musical and visual aesthetic that appeals beyond the traditional hip-hop market to those with more eclectic, but on-trend tastes.

Finally and importantly, marketing strategies, a cornerstone of the mainstream cultural industries, have also been altered by street culture. Once again where the street is viewed as an alternative to commercial artifice, marketeers have become aware that messages may be delivered in a more 'subversive' manner by embracing the tactics of street expressivity, be it graffiti or urban music videos. Thus, for example, mainstream industries can use temporary graffiti or even reverse stencilling by cleaning away patches of dirt to communicate a brand message through means that may stick in the mind of the audience (see Alvelos, 2004). Cutting-edge film collectives can work one day shooting videos for urban music artistes and advertisements for leading brands on others (see e.g. www.studiomurmur.com). Indeed, the power of well-received videos to 'go viral' can be harnessed, where, for example, a 2010 spoof music video featuring the then favourite British urban comedians Shadrack and the Man Dem was produced by streetwear brand Boxfresh, very subtly showcasing its products through a skit that generated wide viewership and discussion. The branding campaign analysed in Box 6.1 is an example of how street culture, film and the online world can be brought together to bolster the image of particular commodities.

Box 6.1   Advertising hits the streets

An analysis of this interactive advertisement, photographed in London, demonstrates the ways in which street cultural expressivity is harnessed as a marketing strategy. It asks for (presumably younger) members of the public to actively contribute to a street sports brand's corporate identity through performing one of the many styles of street cultural expressivity listed. It furthermore draws on the imagery of urban crime ('graffiti' – the legal stencil on the ground, featuring the brand's logo, which becomes the stage on which the participant performs, and also a CCTV camera – similar to those which survey the disadvantaged inner-city in particular western regions). The participant is asked to take part in something that seems street cultural and transgressive, but in reality is quite likely to be both effective advertising on the one hand and a means of gathering 'authentic' material for use in promotions on the other.

The activation of the camera by text message, the multimedia nature of the competition and its association with a particular website all exemplify the additional opportunities for the commercial exploitation of street expressivity in virtual space. This innovative but careful branding serves to indicate how street culture stripped of any real link to urban poverty is a boon to those cultural producers who seek to sell to youth markets. The name of the website on which these performances were featured was 'prostreets.com' (site no longer active).

Conclusion

Stemming from the bodies, beings and expressive practices of those who live within areas of urban poverty is a rich bank of culture and creativity that has moved beyond merely informing and on to influencing the activities of the cultural industries. Alongside accounts of poverty's privations and the criminality linked to these, this other story should be born in mind (although it should not be used to either romanticize or gloss over the problems that exist). Crucially, because this body of expressivity is often linked to notions of transgression and authenticity it takes on a quality of 'cool' that can be appealing to those who produce and consume particular products. Ultimately, it can be seen that much as illegal entrepreneurialism underpins particular street criminal activities, its legal counterpart continues to animate cultural industries that are keen to exploit urban cool and expressivity to sell its products, in particular to youth markets.

CHAPTER 7

Street Flows in the Global Ghetto

Introduction

This chapter examines the ways in which street culture is intertwined with globalization. In doing so it highlights the processes which give rise to the socio-economic conditions underpinning street culture across the globe. It furthermore analyses the ways in which particular local street cultural manifestations are shaped by flows of people, goods, money, images and ideas. Overall, these analyses achieve a number of goals: developing the arguments around the links between socio-economic exclusion and street culture introduced in Chapters 1 and 2; locating these in broad socio-economic structures as opposed to individual or community pathologies; advancing an understanding of how street cultures are both similar and different on a global scale; deepening the book's analysis of inclusion/exclusion offered through considering the role of exoticism, othering and desirability in a globalized context; and finally sharpening the understanding of how particular kinds of criminal lifestyle and urban cool come to be, again in the context of globalization.

The chapter begins with a theoretical account of the contemporary neoliberal, globalized, socio-economic order with particular references to its effects (and affects) on urban poverty in both the developed and developing worlds. This includes a spatial analysis which examines both immigration and migration. It also examines consumer culture's ubiquity: how it manifests in the desires of the excluded in the developing world and the preferences of those in the developed. The roles played by the movement of people, goods and money are analysed as drivers of street culture in both regions of development. Indeed, population flow produces its own illicit opportunities, culture clashes and imaginaries that impact on manifestations of street culture. Finally, the manner in which street-expressive tropes, images and ideas globally circulate is considered to understand the ways in which they style (rather than create) various forms of criminal lifestyle and urban cool in various different global regions. This issue simultaneously signals the hegemony of western (particularly US) culture and its openness to (if not desire for) 'exotic' influences from elsewhere in the world. Ultimately, it is again argued that street culture resonates with the logic of globalized neoliberalism and that a firm understanding of its macro-structural underpinnings necessitates an analysis of global developments.

By means of introduction, it is useful to consider the designer running shoe, trainer or sneaker (see Ferrell and Ilan, 2013). As mentioned in Chapter 6, these are both highly desirable items of street fashion and indeed, even at times, the subject of violent conflict. Much like one aspect of Henri Lefebvre's (1991) analysis of sugar, although everyday and banal in some ways, these objects are in fact telling products of global capitalism. Naomi Klein (2000) in her famous critique of globalization, *No Logo*, views trainers as the product of dual processes of exploitation. On the one hand, cheap labour in the developing world produces a relatively low-cost product, whilst on the other, sophisticated marketing techniques (attentive to the ways of cool) stoke up consumer desires that can see them sold at a high price. Crucially, this process is global and underscored by legacies of colonialism, where the developing world acts as both workshop and ancillary (although increasingly significant) market for goods and services which profit companies based in the developed world. Meanwhile, those urban centres across the global north, which once housed mass manufacturing industries offering decently paid employment to its working-class residents, are now repositories of surplus labour: the kinds of places in which street culture flourishes. Here, for example, a second-generation immigrant, whose parents moved to the country in the hope of securing a life they viewed through films but could not attain at home, may be robbed for their shoes. Whilst a group of young men 'hanging around' a particular street wearing such shoes might be seen as an obviously local phenomenon, their worlds are profoundly shaped by the processes of globalization.

Globalization and neoliberalism

It is not the aim of this book to give a comprehensive account or definition of globalization, but as indicated above, it is impossible to understand contemporary street culture without considering its relationship to these overarching macro processes. The term 'globalization' is not without its contentions and controversies, but in common with a range of social theorists I use it to refer to the increasingly unbounded and networked nature of contemporary economic and social existence, where people, goods and information flow between spaces with greater speed and frequency. On the one hand, these developments are seen as a product of modernity (Giddens, 1991) and technology (Castells, 1996), where transportation and digital connectivity are such that 'time-space compression' (Harvey, 1990) occurs and people can interact, know and have over greater distances and more immediately. On the other hand, this occurs within specific political and economic conditions and within a particular point in history, where capitalism had defeated its rival communist ideology and was freed thus to spread-eagle the globe in a particularly pronounced manner. Debates about globalization thus generally refer as much to its overarching ideology of neoliberalism: the belief that economic markets, unencumbered by states, are the best drivers of progress, development and efficiency and thus next to everything should be open to being commodified and traded with minimal interference (see Harvey, 2005).

Neoliberalism, of course, did not begin with contemporary globalization, but was incubated by particular thinkers and politicians to begin its practical application in and around the 1980s (Harvey, 2005). With the USA under Reagan and the UK under Thatcher as its champions, this mode of governance was gradually expanded and exported (some might say imposed). Over time the weight of Anglo-American power within the international sphere, in negotiating trade treaties and through their influence over development institutions such as the World Bank and International Monetary Fund, ensured that a near global ubiquity of this 'Washington consensus' was achieved (ibid.).

For Harvey, thus, this project is an explicit effort to redistribute wealth upwards to financial elites, and whether or not one accepts this proposition, such a result to some extent been undeniable. The deindustrialization that has occurred throughout the developed world is a key example of these processes. Outsourcing manufacturing jobs abroad to developing countries with lower levels of wage expectation, labour organization, employment protection and statutory regulation allows for companies to profit more. With freedom for capital to move, multinationals can pit states against each other to compete for jobs and investment. Ultimately, corporation taxes (which can finance public spending) and decently paid employment are the casualties of this process. In sectors and services as diverse as agriculture and software programming, global multinationals (some with turnovers greater than the GDPs of small developing countries) have been freed to disrupt previously established patterns of economic activity and stability in order to compete more effectively on a global scale.

Concepts such as globalization and neoliberalism, of course, can be somewhat abstract and it is useful thus to say something more about their tangible consequences. For Bauman (1998) these principles create specific inequalities where flows and freedoms attach to the privileged, whereas immobilities are imposed on many of the disadvantaged. Here the material considered in Chapter 4 becomes particularly pertinent as whilst the underprivileged do move through space, it is often not as a consequence of their power over it, but a reaction to its changing nature around them. Equally, imprisonment and tough immigration procedures do much to limit the range of mobility for many of them, whilst simultaneously protecting the ability of those with disposable income to travel the globe: a world of 'tourists and vagabonds' (ibid.: 77).

These spatial consequences of globalization, considered again later in the chapter, are accelerated in part through its governmental consequences and also due to wider, intertwined aspects of late-modernity. For Bauman (1998) and others (see e.g. Lea and Stenson, 2007) nation states have had their ultimate power to govern dissected by transnational rules and treaties as well as neoliberal pressures to divest their assets and functions to the market. As a consequence, some have sought to bolster their flagging power through building their criminal justice capacities and extending them furthermore to deal with issues of immigration (see Aas, 2007). With a reduced financial capacity and political willingness to engage in inclusive policies of welfare, such exclusive policies of control become more pervasive (Garland, 2001; Young, 1999). This chimes with many peoples' and states' experiences of globalized modernity as a series of 'risks' that to some extent must be managed rather than overcome (see Beck, 1992). The poor and immigrants become such risks to exclude rather than populations to embrace and include.

Where this occurs simultaneously with wealth being redistributed away from key population groups, for example, the urban poor in the developed world, and information flows which bombard the developing world with images of bounteous wealth, a 'perfect storm' is created (see Young, 2007). The privations and desires of the poor are inflamed, contributing to crime on the one hand (see Hayward, 2004), and immigration on the other (see Aas, 2007). This is met by harsher controlling and excluding policies: more imprisonment, less emphasis on 'rehabilitation', stringent and criminalizing immigration measures and ultimately thus generates a greater degree of socio-economic exclusion. This, in turn, fertilizes the ground for the growth of street culture. The economic efficiencies and profit growth facilitated by globalization, the opportunities it produces and the living standards it raises are but one part of the story, where, as Borja and Castells (1997) argue, great swathes of the global population do not see such gains and are in fact surplus to the requirements of the new order. In such a manner, globalization simultaneously includes and excludes, distributing its benefits to those who facilitate the neoliberal project and discarding those who do not to the sorts of warehousing described in Chapter 4.

Indeed, the consequences of neoliberalism are such that they have become echoes of historical processes of colonialism and empire, effectively reconstituting them in contemporary terms (Escobar, 2004). The entire notion of 'economic development' becomes a discourse through which developing countries are expected to promote conditions conducive to the enrichment of western enterprise at the expense of their own marginalized populations (see e.g. Coleman, 2007). Globalization's generation of social exclusion is not merely the unhappy product of structural circumstances, but is driven also by the cultural logic of neoliberalism, an ideology at home with the concept of 'winners and losers' and seemingly willing to allow the latter to suffer its consequences, even if it is produced by circumstances beyond their control (see Sassen, 2010). As Elliott Currie (1997) eloquently demonstrates in his work on market societies and crime, this contributes to the incubation of a harsher culture and world view whereby the cut-throat competitiveness evident in global markets manifests on the streets.

Undoubtedly, another consequence of globalization has been the spread of a more ubiquitous form of consumer culture, where particular goods and brands are seen as important to have by a wide section of the global population despite the vast disparities in wealth that exist. Thus, Jock Young (2007) describes late-modern society as 'bulimic': both partially inclusive and harshly exclusive. He refers in one case to the urban poor who share in the universalized desire for consumerist distinction, but who are precluded from attaining it through legitimate routes which are rarely available to them in the hyper-competitive global economy. The lure of the wealth of the developed world is strong, creating a 'pull' factor that tempts certain people into immigration (Aas, 2007: 40).

Street culture indeed is underpinned by operation of such dual principles. On the one hand, it stresses the wealth acquisition and consumerism that are prime values across a range of mainstream social institutions (inclusion). On the other, it speaks to lives marred by the operation of multiple disadvantages (exclusion). Similarly, decontextualized activities, images, tropes and genres are harvested from street culture by the global cultural industries to sell products (a form of cultural inclusion), whilst those populations who invented them continue to face the privations of poverty, and are subject to the forms of social control examined further in the next chapter.

One world, different spaces

Globalization has particular consequences for movements of people through space, as well as for the nature of space itself. To better understand the constitution of contemporary street culture, it is useful to consider how this unfolds in both the developed and the developing worlds.

The spatial consequences of globalization are such that borders do not disappear, but are made porous, allowing capital and information to flow with relative ease, but placing restrictions, either formal or informal on individuals, and indeed particularly on the disadvantaged. The experiences of those seeking asylum or engaging in immigration into the developed world could hardly be described as free of restriction (see Aas, 2007). Illegal immigrants face particular pressures in this regard. If fear of detection and deportation prevents them from accessing state services then this creates the conditions for their abuse on the one hand, and on the other, potential motivation either to practice stronger variants of street culture or to seek the patronage of those who do. Legal or otherwise, immigrants face particular excluding discourses, via the media, politics and, within certain circles and/or contexts, public opinion. Arguably, facing these particularly excluding tendencies, coping with living far away from a country and community of origin and attempting to project a persona that is relevant within a new milieu are all pressures that for some can be met to some extent through the adoption of street cultural practices. This applies especially in the case of young men (the more likely demographic to practise street culture) who can be particularly economically disadvantaged when emigrating from the developing world to the developed (see Aas, 2007: 43).

Large urban centres in the developed world are particularly significant spaces in which the consequences of globalization manifest in human terms: where the disadvantaged who have been resident for generations meet the newly arrived disadvantaged, who much like money flow to those spaces that signal the greatest potential for material gain. Sassen (1999) identifies the convergence of globalization's winners and losers within such spaces as creating the potential for particular tension. Such concentrations of difference, disadvantage and visible wealth not only provides impetus for the practice of street cultures, but introduces a range of diverse cultures from around the world to supply influences for how street cultures might specifically manifest:

> Global flows traverse national boundaries, creating a constant flux between the inside and the outside, resulting in hybridity of what before appeared to be relatively stable entities. Increasingly, the boundaries between the inside and the outside are being blurred and we are faced with the question of how to deal with the constant influx of sometimes unfamiliar and undesirable people, ideas, images, objects and activities in our midst. The meanings of home, community, nation and citizenship become transformed beyond the recognition by the global, creating hybrid identities and 'glocal' belongings. Minority youth across the world have to juggle multiple belongings, not only to the nation states they live in but also to the places of their and their parents' origin as well as other cultural and political influences (Aas, 2007: 8).

The claiming of/identification with ghetto spaces, discussed in Chapter 4, becomes more logical when considered as a means of bridging these complex issues of identity. More than this, however, street culture provides a repertoire of expressive practices and tough behaviours that can act as an overarching means of identification, allowing individuals to better cope with their travels through space (Ilan, 2013) and different 'glocalities'. This notion of glocality is useful, describing as it does the way in which particular spaces support specific, niche practices despite the existence of connectivities to broader flows of people and information. Les Back's (1996) research on multi-ethnic young people in south London, for example, highlighted the manner in which hybrid forms of slang, style and music were part of the process by which individuals from disparate backgrounds formed cohesive friendship groups within a particular locality and region. Where street cultural practices gain traction by their inclusion in media products, there is ample scope for them to become part of processes of 'translocalization' (see Sassen, 2007) by which they become part of local variants of global culture in other parts of the world.

In some ways, this process is akin to aspects of Appadurai's (1996) notion of de-territorialized culture. Much like the idea of the ghetto as discursive space discussed in Chapter 4, 'the streets' as an abstract notion becomes a globally mobile category of identification. As will become clear later in the chapter, however, both the USA's cultural domination and local tastes play into this, and although themes, genres and practices can be readily identified as broadly similar and comparable across different localities, they take on other distinct characteristics. In this way, street culture does not always produce practices that are quite globally ubiquitous, they often retain their own accent, correspond to specific flows and are produced by the specific cultural and ethnic influences at play within particular areas (Figure 7.1). In Chapter 3, for example, it was noted that hip-hop was a fusion of coexisting Hispanic, Black American and Black Caribbean youth cultural forms in disadvantaged New York. It has now become more globally ubiquitous through media flows, but is, however, performed somewhat differently in various countries and localities (see Neate, 2003).

Whilst flows of immigrants into major urban centres in the developed world style one way in which street cultures come to be constituted (although, again, it is important to note that it is exclusion and not immigration which is the significant factor in their formation), population flows into what Mike Davis (2006) calls the 'megaslums' of the developing world can contribute to its even stronger manifestations. Undoubtedly, and as will be further explored, it is the heightened struggles for material subsistence, weaker/less-funded/less present state institutions and often a rule of violence in place of the rule of law regulating the lives of the urban poor, which raise the stakes in these contexts. With neoliberal development packages (loans, etc.) linked to agricultural deregulation and the reduction of state subsidies

Figure 7.1   A youth in Blois, France demonstrates the extent to which street aesthetics can fuse the fashion popularized by American rappers with the traditional garb of communities of origin. Photo by Simon Wheatley

and support, agrarian livelihoods in the developing world were increasingly open to the shocks of extreme climate events and competition from western agribusiness, driving more and more people into urban centres, despite the lack of opportunities for economic advancement that existed within these spaces (ibid.: 15–16). Moreover, in certain regions, geopolitical conflicts and internal wars created a great impetus for people to seek the relative shelter of the city (ibid.; see also Sommers, 2003).

Davis catalogues how this mass warehousing of economically surplus individuals often takes place within the most sparsely serviced shanty-towns, where the competition for subsistence and work is such that the most exploitative of practices can flourish. Again, he points squarely to neoliberal development regimes which prescribe 'flexible labour' as facilitating a race to the bottom in terms of pay and conditions, where desperate individuals will engage in a wide range of informal labour practices and diverse strategies to obtain the material means for survival. This, he concludes, has manifested in a breakdown of traditional solidarities and the flourishing of a tough and violent world view:

> Those engaged in informal-sector competition under conditions of infinite labor supply usually stop short of a total war of all against all; conflict

instead is usually transmuted into ethnoreligious or racial violence (Davis, 2006: 185).

On the one hand, thus, much like the demise of the western industrial classes described in Chapter 3, changing macro-economic conditions have a profound effect on traditional ways of life, opening up space for the more chaotic practices of street culture to grow. For certain scholars of development spaces, this is a process that is linked to the politics of developing countries which simultaneously neglects and violently oppresses those in areas that challenge the image of nations progressing forward (Coleman, 2007; de Sousa Santos, 2002). In the barrios, favelas, townships and shanty-towns, inhabited by the most marginalized of the developing world's urban poor, this potent combination of subsistence disruption, community decimation/re-aggregation and violence from above (whether by state police forces, armies or politically connected militias) account for the particularly extreme variants of street cultural institutionalization and violence that will be discussed in the following section. Whether channelled through ethnic, religious or political conflict, strong street cultural norms around the deployment of violence and the presentation of self would seem to be observable phenomena.

This is not just symptomatic of developing nations who seem in thrall to the narratives of neoliberalism, but also those which at least utter words of defiance towards them, such as Venezuela. Caracas, its capital city, has its own iconic squats and slums that house various street cultural practices (see e.g. López, 2014).

Deviant globalization and illicit flows

Globalization's contribution to the state of contemporary street culture is further realized through its 'deviant' elements:

> The unpleasant underside of transnational integration, deviant globalization describes the cross-border economic networks that produce, move, and consume things as various as narcotics and rare wildlife, looted antiquities and counterfeit goods, dirty money and toxic waste, as well as human beings in search of undocumented work and unorthodox sexual activities (Gilman et al., 2011: 1).

For these authors, deviant globalization is an inextricable part of the neoliberal move towards more open borders and voluminous trade. The demand for various illicit goods and services (particularly in the developed world), according to these authors, can create the opportunities for the generation of wealth and raising of living standards in the developing world that at times dwarf the possibilities offered by licit commerce or donated aid. It is not simply a matter of states failing to adequately regulate and patrol borders and flows, but a reality that legal flows also facilitate the existence of their illegal counterparts. Whilst the chapter thus far has primarily considered the consequences of licit, legal flows (which themselves have profound impacts), illicit flows of people, products and money as part of criminal enterprises should also be considered.

Traditionally discussed in reference to more established networks of institutionalized organized crime (i.e. 'the mafia', 'firms', 'cartels'), there is evidence to suggest that at least in some parts of the world, these relatively stable institutions have minimal presence at street level (Hobbs, 1998), and if present, they operate 'behind the scenes' to a greater extent as arms-length importer/exporters or wholesalers (see e.g. Hallsworth and Silverstone, 2009). Deviant globalization instead tends to take place at a 'glocal' level (Hobbs, 1998) where existing street cultural institutions or discrete but loose, semi-organized criminal networks use the resources and advantages of their structures, contacts and/or street capital to generate income (see Silverstone, 2011; Morselli et al., 2010). Rather than the spectre of sophisticated and organized, international organized crime networks responding to the demands for illegal goods and services they detect, it is far more common for groups to coalesce into various forms of organization and institution in order to capitalize on the economic opportunities that emerge as a result of deviant demand.

This has important consequences for understanding street culture: as a more organic, socio-economic response to conditions of exclusion, it takes shape around the deviant opportunities available for the generation of income, rather than existing as the diffusion of shadowy 'organizations' importing immorality. Recalling the links between urban space, illicit opportunity and street culture, the nature of inherently international markets in narcotics, weaponry and people vests many local variants of street culture with this globalized dimension. They remain, however, locally specific, 'glocalized', as it were. As one character in the famous cinematographic reflection on American street culture, that is, Mario Van Peeble's (1991) 'New Jack City' reflects: 'Ain't no Uzi's made in Harlem. Not one of us in here owns a poppy field.' Local, street cultural institutions deal in drugs and weaponry that are often imported from abroad, involving complex international illicit flows.

Specific examples can be seen in John Pitts' (2008) examination of 'gang' life in London, whereby groups of young people distribute the drugs that are imported by more established and organized criminals who remove themselves from the cut and thrust of the street. Here, street cultural logics order the everyday sale of imported commodities such as cocaine, or indeed marijuana, which may well be grown by farmers of Vietnamese origin domestically (see Silverstone and Savage, 2010). The Jamaican 'yardie posses' in America and England exist at the apex of various global flows, facilitated by Jamaica's geographical, post-colonial and cultural position between South America, the USA and the UK (see Gunst, 2003). Glocal structures, in New York, for example, trace the contours of their parent organizations in Jamaica receiving and distributing product and remitting cash and consumer goods.

There is thus evidence of street cultural institutions (traditionally discussed in reference to 'gangs') growing complex transnational webs and linkages. A classic example is the 'Maras' spanning between the USA and various Central American countries (see Miguel Cruz, 2010; Arana, 2005). These sprawling street cultural institutions, such as the Mara Salvatrucha and M-18, apparently emerged as a by-product of disastrous US juvenile crime and immigration policy, which saw young people born in Central America but raised in the USA jailed for long periods of time in tough conditions, then immediately deported to their countries of origin (Arana, 2005). Here without language skills or economic or educational prospects, it was easy for them to remain within the street cultural institutions which had supported them in prison. Spanning a key route for the trafficking of people, weapons and narcotics and operating within spaces of deep disadvantage, groups claiming affiliation with the two rival Mara structures were able to profit from the significant illicit global flows moving through their 'territory' (ibid.).

Whilst the Maras may seem on one level to be sophisticated, transnational criminal entities, questions remain around the extent to which they are more like rather loosely connected networks of glocal street cultural institutions that share iconography, mythology and, where advantageous, resources and contacts. What cannot be disputed is the extent to which the Maras clearly represent the product of both licit and deviant forms of globalization that have hollowed out the governing capacities of Central American states, seen the imposition of tough criminal and immigration policies and facilitated the illegal flow of drugs, people and money which represent opportunities for profit.

A world of street cultural difference

With the neo-colonial interference by western governments in the governance and economic advancement of particular developing countries, combined with a *pax Americana* (the lack of wars between nation states in an era of one global superpower), the types of threats and targets identified by most state governments have changed. In place of enemy armies or the spies of rival factions, relatively informally constituted and loosely organized groups of 'armed young men', running from street gangs to militias and terrorist organizations, are occupying the efforts of many national defence and security services (see Hagedorn, 2008). Suggesting the futility of retaining outdated notions of gang crime (see Chapter 4), this development demonstrates furthermore the extent to which it is useful to understand a range of violent phenomena through the street cultural spectrum.

For particular African militias, South American barrio/favela gangs, Middle Eastern resistance groups and western street criminals, there are similar structural and cultural underpinnings to their behaviour (Hagedorn, 2008; see also Cottee and Hayward, 2011). These stem from the degrees to which they encounter material deprivation and socio-cultural marginalization, the product of various degrees of state neglect and oppression. Here, the extent to which such street cultural groups form stable and durable institutions can be related to the extent to which they can provide ranges of services and infrastructure to local communities, provide meaning and purpose to those otherwise lacking it and create economic opportunities where none others existed.

Importantly, this perhaps challenges a particular orthodoxy around the chain of causation used to explain the erosion of developing countries' capacities to govern. For Sullivan (2011), and as one assumes the military and security sources he cites, these problems stem from the growing power of criminal 'gangs' to generate profits on a global scale and to disrupt and/or corrupt local and national institutions of state authority. The position of Hagedorn (2008) and indeed Davis (2006), along with my own, however, would instead point out that these 'gangs' emerge in the vacuum left by a lack of state services, legitimate economic opportunities and routes to inclusion in the trappings of modernity. For the political scientist James Buccellato (2014) indeed, the American street gang is an 'obscene remainder' of the exclusions that neoliberal markets and politics inflict. They emerge as neoliberal entities par excellence.

The power that street cultural institutions acquire perpetuates itself in the developing world through subverting and challenging states that were already weak (see also Sanchez, 2006). Elizabeth Leeds (1996), for example, sets out the extent to which drug-trading gangs in the favelas of Brazil emerged as a form of 'parallel power' in the face of state neglect of, and violence towards, the urban poor (see also Dowdney, 2003):

[I]n exchange for the 'protection' and anonymity a community may offer a drug group, it can often expect in return an array of services ranging from internal security, to money for an ambulance or taxi to hospital, to money for medicines, soup kitchens, day-care centres, parties for children on special occasions, and other emergency funds in cases of extreme hardship (1996: 61).

State violence, viewed as oppressive, arbitrary, widespread and deadly, was thus perceived differently from the violence of the drug gangs, which whilst brutal could at least at times be construed as consistent with community interests (see also Winton, 2004). Thus, as these gangs grew sophisticated and organized crimino-entrepreneurial and violent apparatuses, they operated a parallel system of care and governance where the state did not. Informal and unofficial, sometimes at least nominally associated with leftist political symbolism and rhetoric, such organizations both embody and apply street cultural logic, whilst at the same time making it difficult to classify them as purely criminal. Returning again to the example previously discussed in Chapters 1 and 4 around the links between political parties and gangs in both Jamaica and Haiti, the propensity of street cultural institutions to fill gaps in civil society and state provision are furthermore highlighted.

It is this presence/absence of the state as a protective force that would seem to be so important in the extent to which extreme street cultural logics can take root. At times, indeed, the ability to appropriately apply and negotiate violence can become the central facet of a de facto system of governance. Danny Hoffman (2007), for example, in studying cities in war-torn West Africa—Freetown, Sierra Leone and Monrovia, Liberia—charts the extent to which 'the barracks' becomes a key site of production: 'security service offers one of the few stable sources of income and as a wage earner's dependents crowd these structures. They are becoming important locations for political life' (Hoffman, 2007: 408). Redolent of the colonial goals of economic exploitation and coercive rule, improvised barracks housing armed young men created spaces of power essentially removed from the state where the individual capacity for violence is a key determinant of a capacity to earn. As armed conflicts wound down, ex-combatants could flow readily into the requirements of the diamond industry through leaving the city for rural locations. Where profitable industries are largely unregulated and city streets teemed with violent danger, street cultural acumen can be harnessed to take up risky but economically promising ventures.

Even 'terrorist groups,' often conceptualized as advanced forms of organized political criminality, cannot so easily be categorized as entirely different from the institutions produced by prevalent strong variants of street culture. For Hagedorn (2008), for example, particular dissident/terrorist groups operating within the Middle East function to additionally provide security and services to disadvantaged communities where operating within governing regimes viewed as hostile. For Cottee and Hayward (2011), the same kinds of existential gains and pleasurable excitements that inform particular kinds of street criminality can be seen again within certain acts of terrorism. Indeed, radical subcultures have at times drawn on the tropes and imagery of street culture, whether to form hybrid Islamist and 'rudeboy' subcultures (Qurashi, 2013; Vidino, 2010) or indeed politically laden rap lyrics (see e.g. Lombard, 2007 by contrast see Box 7.1). Understanding this seemingly disparate range of phenomena through the lens of street culture is not a case of conflating them to the extent that the phrase becomes meaningless. Their differences always remain significant. The effects (and affects – the more existential and emotional facets) of globalized neoliberalism, however, can be identified as key drivers of street culture's prominence and various manifestations both within the deprived inner-cities of the global north as well as the burgeoning slums of the global south. Moreover, and as will be further explored, the imagery and tropes of street culture flow between these different spaces, giving style and accents to what occurs there.

This book is not attempting to unreflexively impose a dominant western form of knowledge to explain what is occurring within the developing world. Instead, I would argue that street culture in the developing world has flourished precisely in part due to the imposition of orthodox forms of western knowledge. Firstly, neoliberal discourses of economic development gauge the worth of developing nations in a neo-colonial manner and promote policies that further disadvantage their most marginalized populations. Secondly, exported logics of crime control impose the priorities of particular western governments over the material and existential well-being of those who, for example, engage in the narco-economy to subsist in conditions where traditional agriculture is no longer viable. The book is seeking to draw connections rather than to set down universal rules in stone. Indeed, research on Lagos' 'area boys' (street cultural groupings which span legal and illegal enterprise) by Daniel (2012) made use of concepts developed by Anthony Gunter (2008) in relation to London 'road culture' (street culture with a British accent). Moreover, Goldstein (2003) saw similarities between the principles ordering the lives of young men within a Brazilian favela and those articulated by Bourgois (1995/2003) in relation to East Harlem drug dealers of Puerto Rican descent.

It is necessary to flag up the extent to which this book and its arguments have been written from a western perspective, albeit critically, but with the intention of trying to understand what is occurring in both developed and developing spaces. There remains a need for the articulation of critiques of this street cultural paradigm from a developing world perspective, in such a way as to achieve the 'double critique' which may challenge the subordination of southern forms of knowledge to its northern counterparts (see Mignolo, 2012).

Box 7.1 Rap music goes to war

It seems incongruous that rap music would have a part to play in the most significant military actions of the early 21st century. This is precisely what musicologist Jonathan Pieslak (2009) found in his research on US soldiers, music and the war in Iraq.

For US soldiers, alongside hard metal music, rap (especially that of a particularly street cultural nature) was used in the preparation for battle. The bellicose, belligerent backing tracks created the right mood and complemented by aggressive lyrics about violence and triumph rendered the genre a staple across servicemen's iPods. In this way, it could be part of individual rituals, but favourite songs also became part of certain collective rituals. Here close comrades in arms would shout/sing the lyrics of particular rap tunes in unison before heading out. Pieslak found that whilst rap music often referred to small arms use in confrontations over personal matters, the aggressive sentiment could find resonance with events in war.

Indeed, using portable laptops equipped with relatively sophisticated music recording and producing software, soldiers were able to produce their music whilst in active service. Whilst Pieslak does not specifically mention rap music being produced in that way, he noted the extent to which 'freestyle cyphers' were a feature of army life. One of the earliest forms of the rap genre, this is a social interaction where people stand in a circle, taking turns to chant rap lyrics improvised on the spot. The author noted that this became a means of soldiers expressing some of their feelings about the threats they faced and their task at hand.

A subcultural capital rush? Raw cool in the global ghetto

Whilst the structural underpinnings to various forms of street criminal/violent behaviours can thus be clearly understood as tied to processes of (neoliberal) globalization, the extent to which global flows manifest in street expressivity and ultimately urban cool merits further exploration. As earlier indicated, many well-known forms of street expressivity are products of various urban 'melting-pots'. This is particularly clear in the case of urban music whose historical and contemporary manifestations are replete with cross-fertilizations and hybridities. The black music of the USA from blues to jazz to hip-hop carries African, European and at times Creole notes (Ramsey, 2003), not to mention the Jamaican music which went on to establish so many of the techniques which would inform the production of contemporary urban music

(Stolsoff, 2000). More contemporary forms of urban and dance music voraciously consume influences and exhibit the global flows of ideas and sounds in an exemplary manner. They do so, moreover, in ways that highlight particular patterns within glocal scenes and, ultimately, the global cultural industries.

Within street cultural spaces, in both the developing and developed world, hybrid forms of urban music reflect both global population movements and the ways in which urban cool is dependent on modes of expressivity associated with ever more extreme forms of socio-economic exclusion. Devereaux (2007) explained how the popularity, at the time he wrote his article, of both the critically acclaimed HBO drama *The Wire* set in Baltimore, Maryland, and the niche urban dance music genre 'Baltimore Club' are both related to their embodiment of a raw ghetto authenticity. In his article, he correctly identified the ways in which tastemakers and subsequently audiences are increasingly drawn to forms of extreme 'ghettoness' as a means of increasing 'subcultural capital' (see Thornton, 1995). The logic follows that as established urban music genres such as hip-hop become ubiquitous, those seeking 'the next big thing' or at least something more substantial seeming must seek out more extreme forms. He made reference thus to a growing interest at the time in niche urban music forms from various disadvantaged areas across the world. Thus 'kudro' from Angola (Brown, 2010), 'baile funk' from Brazil (Sneed, 2008) and 'grime' from London (Ilan, 2012) became part of the repertoire of particular American DJs who commanded ever more prominence internationally.

The coming to prominence of 'exotic' urban music genres from spaces of ever greater deprivation is perhaps best exemplified by 'reggaeton', a fusion of Jamaican dancehall and various Latin American musical traditions, which became immensely popular within US urban music scenes and markets in the mid-2000s (see Rivera et al., 2009). Though pan-South American and already a decade old, this genre – which had endured a tense history with the governments of a number of its host states – seemed to arrive as an exotic novelty, with Spanish lyrics and Latin timbres conjuring an air of transgressive sexuality. Leaving aside the various politics of gender, development and respectability that this occurrence raised, it signalled the extent to which the global south represented a veritable gold mine of commodifiable cool for the cultural industries of the global north. Beyond the opportunities that such developments signalled for a minority of artistes and various creative workers, it signalled the extent to which the exploitation of street expressivity had gone global.

Street cultural expressivity from the most marginalized communities in the developing world would thus seem to have particular 'authentic' and obscure qualities, which greatly increases the capacity to wring cool out from them. This trend continues in some ways. *Vice* magazine, a world-spanning, sometimes ironic, hive of urban cool (arguably commodified and further commodifiable) has made a virtue of attending to extreme manifestations of street culture and indeed crime and violence across various regions of development (see www.vice.com). A scan through its YouTube videos (and those of its sister brand Noisey) reveals, on the one hand, talented film makers cataloguing the atrocities of Liberian warlords and, on the other, extraordinarily on-trend music videos.

This notion of commodifying the 'exotic' in popular culture is nothing new and indeed its scale and speed in contemporary times has been noted by Hutnyk (2000). An interesting facet of the phenomenon is the extent to which expressive hybridities form at the point at which young people from different ethnic backgrounds converge on facilitating technologies. The initial intention of communities of production might be to carve out something unique to their experience, reflecting both their inherited stylistic forms and the techniques and aesthetics they encounter in a new setting. Thus, for example, in Britain young people of South Asian descent fused traditional music from the subcontinent with the house, garage, hip-hop and dancehall they encountered to create 'bhangra', 'desi beats' and other hybrid genres (see e.g. Bakrania, 2013). The subsequent tendency of large American artists/production teams to incorporate elements of this music in their own material (at least for a time) suggests a somewhat complex relationship between the core and periphery, at least where cultural production is concerned.

Whilst the USA still occupies a central position in forging and marketing street cultural expressivity, it is also a vast repository into which various different strands of street expressivity flow from around the world. It is consumed in its raw forms by its loyal co-ethnic followers or by tastemakers expanding their subcultural capital and nous. Alternatively, it might be spliced into a pastiche of various 'world beats' by particular DJs and producers keen themselves to present something 'fresh' or indeed appropriated as an influence by the vast cultural production companies.

This phenomenon, however, remains both qualitatively and quantitatively more benign than some of the scenarios into which street cultural tropes from the west have become intertwined internationally. The street cultural rhetoric of US rappers has found considerable resonance with members of street cultural institutions, gangs and militias in different parts of the developing world. Hagedorn (2008) has noted the extent to which American hip-hop resonates with the violent realities of those in both Brazillian drug gangs and African militias. Sommers (2003) cites journalistic accounts of how American gangsta tropes were adopted by elements of militias fighting in Sierra Leone, forming the bizarre, incongruent backdrop to indiscriminate slaughter:

'The rebels [RUF] wrote Tupac's [renowned American rapper] lyrics on the sides of their vehicles' during the Freetown invasion, one Sierra Leonean refugee later recalled during a field interview. According to the refugee, 'they wrote "Death Row," "Missing in Action," "Hit em Up," "Only God can Judge," and "All Eyez on Me" on them.' Junger (the journalist in question) also notes that the rebels 'favoured Tupac T-shirts and fancy haircuts' (2003: 9).

The scale and ferocity of the 'mayhem' wrought by this army faction, described by Junger (2000, cited in ibid.), to some extent make western concerns around the ill-effects of violent media seem misplaced. There is no evidence to suggest that the consumption of violent media contributed to a conflict on a continent riven by the legacy of colonial mistreatment, but the power of US street cultural tropes to resonate in this context suggest the extent to which spaces separated by vast amounts of space and countless degrees of deprivation and violence respond powerfully to similar rhetoric. The appearance of Tupac song titles in this scenario, much like Hagedorn's (2008) accounts of militia-men writing their own rap lyrics, signals the connections between street cultures, however different. Indeed, the associations that exist between notions of conspicuous consumption and American street cultures ensure that its trappings are much in evidence even in countries and contexts where wealth is a far less widespread state of being.

Nyamnjoh (2000) articulates a sense that Africans, living in poverty but nevertheless facing strong consumerist desires emanating from the west, are essentially subject to forms of neo-colonialism. The solution is to resurrect second- or third-hand, older objects, so that symbolic participation in the consumer culture can be maintained despite the general privations suffered by the 'masses'. Indeed, there is little that seems to preclude impoverished 'area boys' in Lagos (for example) from sporting the trappings of street style in the form of designer clothing, however past 'fresh' these might seem to a western street stylistic devotee (see Daniel, 2012). These groups of young men graft considerably across the grey and illegal economies in order to finance this aspect of their lifestyles as well as maintaining their subsistence in one of the world's fastest growing cities. Once again, street cultural principles can be viewed as underpinning this lifestyle of multifaceted subsistence strategies and dedication to particular stylistic practices. Indeed, even the notorious pirates of Sudan have been seen to display a particular penchant for western streetwear as well as the kind of brand new all-terrain vehicles that would not look out of place in rap videos (see Bahadur, 2011).

Conclusion

'Globalization' and the 'global' can thus be understood as playing key roles in street cultural styles and practices. From a macro perspective, the wide socio-economic realignments that are the result of neoliberal globalization have contributed to vast inequalities as much as flows of people, images, goods and services. The erosion of traditional working-class and agrarian livelihoods have variously given rise to the warehousing of the urban poor within economically moribund inner-cities or desperation-filled megaslums. Linking the misery of the poor in the developing world with the relative deprivation of those within the developed, the neoliberal consumerist economy creates in both types of space the confluence of low economic opportunity and strong consumer desire that gives shape to contemporary street culture. More than this, the flow of street cultural tropes, styles and ideas ensures that there is constant circulation, appropriation and hybridization occurring. This in turn ensures that there is the constant generation of new, 'fresh' forms of street stylistic expression that can be harvested by global cultural industries to produce 'cool' and ultimately add greater edge, transgression and subcultural capital to various brands. Ultimately, the global flows between areas of disadvantage across the world are an important facet of how contemporary street culture functions and, indeed, came to be in the first place.

CHAPTER 8

Resistance, Ghetto Politics and the Social Control of the Slum

Introduction

This chapter is concerned with building an understanding of the political significance of street culture, whilst analysing its relationship to more mainstream, dominant, governing values and institutions. As such, it examines two main themes: firstly, whether or not street culture might be viewed as a means of 'resisting' dominant regimes, and secondly, the extent to which the urban poor are subjected to social control mechanisms. To do so, the chapter considers existing arguments around subculture, resistance, power and governance to locate street culture in its relationship to the establishment's norms and values. The chapter furthermore examines not just modes of criminalization and policing, but the extent to which dominant and subordinate cultures relate to each other, in essence, reproducing and exacerbating inequalities and exclusions.

I develop the argument that it is problematic to assume the existence of fundamental value differences within late-modern human cultures that exist, within the boundaries of history and social-economic structure, to facilitate meaningful existence. What will be argued instead is that material conditions and existing capacities to become included heavily shape the adoption of, and attitudes towards, particular norms and/or behavioural expectations. As elements of culture, these become part and parcel of world views, aspirations and interpretations of various events, coalescing as part of a habitus (or patterned way of being) that prompts various responses to stimuli, which may be 'street' or 'decent' to varying degrees and extents.

Does responding to police questions in a surly manner, or indeed street crime itself, constitute a form of 'resistance' against oppressive socio-economic factors or governmental attitudes? If these behaviours are 'oppositional' but not quite 'resistance' (with its overtones of politics), then how might they best be conceptualized? If the disadvantaged often feel marginalized by the state institutions that are a product of mainstream politics, do other forms of politics exist in their neighbourhoods? Does the fact that criminalization tends to echo existing patterns of inclusion/exclusion say something about the way in which the forces of law and order treat the excluded? What consequences does this have for the ways in which everyday life on the street plays out? Finally, are there less adversarial ways of dealing with street culture? The chapter deals with these questions and is furthermore attentive to the fact that the stakes, both in terms of the politics of the disadvantaged and their social control, are greatly raised in the developing world where they are more frequently and dramatically directly related to issues of life and death.

The disadvantaged, conformity and resistance

Where street culture exists as a set of norms, styles, values and dispositions that are held and practiced by some of the most excluded, questions around the extent to which these might run counter to their more widely held and dominant equivalents tend to arise. To some extent, this might stem from ways in which street cultures are often wrapped up in overt displays of aggression, which stand in contrast to the more indirect, proxy or legitimated forms of violence that are associated with elite groups or the state. In this way, such direct violence might be seen as challenging the authority of the state, which holds to itself a monopoly on the use of legitimate violence (with certain rare exceptions such as notions of 'self-defence', narrowly construed to exclude acts of criminal violence that might be conceptualized as defensive acts from a street cultural perspective). It is important to note, however, that much as street cultural violence might be viewed as problematic by the state, it generally operates and is deployed for street cultural rather than overtly political purposes. As will be further explored later, what is considered a problem does not necessarily equate to a form of resistance. This will depend, however, on how resistance is defined.

There is a legacy of Marxism, both as a sociological theory and as a political force, which bears on this question (see also Carver, 1991). In Marxism the urban poor represents, on the one hand, a mass of revolutionary potential and, on the other, a self-destructive force which holds themselves and their wider communities back from the egalitarian utopia that awaits them. This latter understanding was particularly associated with what was called the *lumpen proletariat* or 'lower working-class'. Such Marxist overtones arguably, whether explicit or implicit, continue to resonate within debates around the resistant nature of street culture. It is useful thus to trace how such debates emerged, before seeking to bridge some of the tensions that exist through the suggestion of a more operationalizable middle ground.

The 'conflict criminologists' that explicitly drew on Marxist thinking tended to view criminality as emerging from the schisms in cultural norms and power interests that existed between elite and marginalized groups in society (see e.g. Turk, 1969; Sellin, 1938). According to this perspective, the modes of being, world views and patterns of behaviour associated with the wealthier and more powerful would become enshrined in law, whilst those associated with the poor and marginalized became criminalized. From this position, criminality might be viewed as an assertion of the interests of the excluded against those groups and agencies which exercise control over them: a clear case of resistance. A more moderate stance seemed to emerge from the work of Robert Merton (1938) who tended to view the street criminal as an 'innovator', exercising fiscal entrepreneurialism to attain wealth which was difficult to acquire through legitimate means. For Merton, 'resistance' occurred where there was an explicit attempt to challenge both the behavioural norms dominant in society, and its overall cultural values, in his case 'the American dream' of a pleasant life full of consumer goods. Whilst street culture cannot be understood as a challenge to capitalism-consumerism as a fundamental value, this does not mean that it should be merely understood as a coldly rational economic innovation. Indeed, its emotive and existential qualities suggest a deeper significance.

The subcultural theory offered by Albert Cohen (1955) began to capture something of the more visceral qualities associated with street culture. He argued that the 'delinquency' of tough, young, disadvantaged men was a form of 'status frustration': a means of lashing out against the dominant society that excludes and marginalizes them through its institutions of education and employment that ultimately reproduce the class structure (see also Willis, 1977). Similar to notions of street culture, as articulated by this book, he saw this subculture as emerging specifically as a 'reaction' to exclusion. In this sense, though not referring to an explicit form of politics, it would constitute a form of resistance as it does target for attack (even if by proxy) the institutions that are viewed as wielding power over them. By contrast, Miller's (1958) assertion that the 'lower classes' adhere to their own cultural code (whilst resonant in some ways with conflict criminology) suggests instead the operation of independent imperatives and thus an absence of an explicit resistance.

Marxism similarly underpinned the perspective of the Birmingham School, whose work tended to view the stylistic expressions of working-class youth as brimming with resistance to a socio-economic structure that limited their inclusion in the benefits generated by capitalism. This approach was avowedly Gramscian where they viewed political potential within this mass population, emerging as a series of codes and signs which expressed their ultimate discontent (see Hall and Jefferson, 1976). With frustration, however, they noted the power of capitalism to ultimately co-opt these symbols of 'resistance' into cultural products marketed to middle-class young people (see Hebdige, 1979). Indeed, their notion of resistance was somewhat problematic in that it was conceptualized as unconscious and 'magical', ultimately hollow where young people simply tended to occupy the same socio-economic position as their parents.

In more recent times, contemporary cultural criminology (see Ferrell et al., 2008) has been criticized for apparently romanticizing the activities of particular street-stylistic actors (skateboarders, graffiti writers, etc.) as a form of 'resistance' (see Hall and Winlow, 2007). For critics such as Hall et al. (2008), the world of acquisitive street crime is brutal, competitive, entirely apolitical and obsessed with matters of narcissistic consumerism – entirely removed from any notions of resistance. Rather, the street world, these authors would argue, demonstrates the extent to which individuals in the socio-economic margins have absorbed the prevalent mores of neoliberal capitalism and consumerism. Their argument points to the colonization of the self by the individualistic competition such philosophies encourage. Meanwhile, there have been numerous critiques of Birmingham School conceptualizations of subcultural resistance. Post-subculturalists tend to view youth groups as conformist, non-political, hedonistic, consumerist and primarily social (see e.g. Hayward and Ilan, 2011; Muggleton and Weinzierl, 2003; Muggleton, 2000). Clearly, there is a lot of contention around the notion of 'resistance' residing within both street criminal and youth cultural lifestyles.

A complementary point was made by Hollander and Einwohner (2004), who reviewed a wide range of sociological literature. They noted the inconsistencies in the ways in which the word has been used, as well as the extent to which it has received inadequate conceptual development. 'Resistance' tends to be variously attributed based on the intention of those who are said to exhibit it, its recognition by its targets and its recognition by others (ibid.). Additional complications with the word's past use include the extent to which it has been deployed to describe both passive and active behaviours: those which challenge the status quo and others that merely reinforce it. In such a manner, the foot-dragging, sullen attitude or impertinent mockery that might be exhibited variously by 'peasant' farmworkers and industrial shop floor workers, whilst nevertheless performing the duties demanded of them by their lords or paymasters, has been categorized as 'resistance'. This is despite the fact that such behaviours do little to challenge the power inequalities that exist within such relationships (see Scott, 2008; Willis, 1977). What those who react to power in such a manner ultimately gain, however, is a sense of agency:

a subjective sense of control and mastery within circumstances that make such feelings difficult to achieve.

Clearly, thus, there are significant schisms between a notion of resistance that involves an overtly political desire and effort to redress power imbalances, and that associated with subjective, seemingly less political and ultimately minimally challenging variants. These latter instances might be viewed as scenarios in which there is not an overt Marxist (in style or substance) politics, but instead an effort to protect a feeling of autonomy in adverse circumstances, to carve out a space for one's own dignity and to cling to a self-defined identity. This process can occur at the group level as much as the individual and may account for some of the more cultural and existential motivations to participate in street culture.

There are some (see Hall et al., 2008), however, who label as 'liberal' attempts to read resistance into what they see as destructive, exploitative and brutal street criminal behaviours. Arguably, this label is meant to denote a naïve tendency to lionize sections of the urban poor as revolutionaries-in-waiting, when in fact there is little more to their criminality than an internalized and impoverished variant of the neoliberal, competitive free-for-all that defines mainstream economic life (see previous chapter). Perhaps a more charitable reading is that there is some tendency on the part of particular sections of the political left to conflate various forms of 'resistance' identified earlier. This too was a tendency of particular Marxists where, for example, Eric Hobsbawm (1959/2010) viewed the Robin Hood-style bandits of old as proto-revolutionaries. There can be an aspirational element of particular leftist thought that perhaps views the anger and aggression of street culture as the seeds of a politically transformative force (see Ilan, 2014). The challenge for cultural criminology remains to distinguish between movements which are creative/transformative and those which engage in mere communication and thus change little (see Schuilenburg and Hayward, 2014).

Particular works in cultural criminology have focused on instances where political resistance and expressive practice coexist. For Jeff Ferrell (2001), a diverse range of disruptive/expressive activities can be understood as a form of direct action: attempts to deny the interdictions of governing forces and to demonstrate the possibilities that exist beyond those sanctioned or condoned. His analysis considers politico-cultural activists that espouse the anarchist sensibilities of 'fighting and singing' (2001: 23) and a DIY culture that facilitates creativity and commerce outside of capitalism. Here he correctly identifies the possibilities for those who are more politically aware to resist the values and norms of mainstream culture, either by directly challenging them or by carving out spaces free from them. In relation to street cultural activities, however, it is difficult to assume that such intentionality exists, consciously or unconsciously. For sure, as Ferrell suggests, graffiti writers may well be resisting the aesthetic dictates of the commercial-government mainstream. They operate, however, according to well-developed aesthetic principles which are alternative to those more widely held and enforced. It is more difficult to identify a similar intentionality and distinctly coherent philosophy amongst those who, for example, steal phones or deal drugs.

Arguably, however, there is a strand of cultural criminology, which much like Hall et al. (2008) notes the extent to which the concerns of contemporary street culture seem to echo those of neoliberal capitalism: the elevation of the accumulation of wealth to prime value, where achieving such and exhibiting as much through the display of consumer goods represents a lifestyle to be envied and aspired to by all (see Young, 2007; Hayward, 2004). The parallels between street culture and elite 'mainstream' cultures abound. Sanchez-Jankowski (2003), for example, demonstrates the extent to which frequently employed definitions of 'the gang' could apply equally to American college fraternities. Dick Hobbs (2013) articulates the extent to which crimino-entrepreneurialism is simply a form of unlicensed capitalism, demanding many of the same qualities that underpin much of its legitimate counterpart. For him, the major differences have tended to centre on the fact that unlicensed capitalism tended to be undertaken by certain excluded groups to profit from servicing the appetites of others.

It is also interesting, as earlier noted, that the accounts offered by those operating within elite levels of the financial system articulate a kind of ruthless dedication to profit that resonates with attitudes expressed by hardened street criminals:

> What I had seen was the most horrific side of City life – suited men using cash to make women debase themselves for their own animal desires. In many ways, I think, that experience sums up what the City does so expertly across the world: using its cash or the promise of cash to rape natural resources – be it coffee plantations in Brazil, oil reserves in Iraq or any other sellable commodity (Anderson, 2008: 83).

Here, a former member of an elite banking/trading culture honestly reflects around the destructive and harmful nature of both his business and leisure practices (see also Lewis, 1989). Such unflinching dedication to profit, divorced from its consequences resonates strongly with the dictum of 'Get Rich or Die Trying' (Aftermath/Interscope/Shady Records, 2003), uttered by famed gangsta rapper and victim of gun crime 50 Cent. Indeed, certain American criminologists have been attentive to the extent to which a society which places economic markets and success above all else are likely to contribute to the strengthening of criminal cultures (see Currie, 1997; Messner and Rosenfeld, 1994).

Where Hagedorn (2008) applies Castells' (2010) notion of 'resistance identity' to refer to the existence of street cultures in the impoverished inner-city, he is not referring to the existence of transformational politics but indeed its absence. For these scholars, essentialized identities emerge as a response to a lack of political agency, a lack of a sense that individuals and communities can have any bearing on the decisions that impact on their lives, which are ultimately determined by more transnational, neoliberal concerns. In reaction to this, such communities, it is argued, coalesced around a sense of what is distinct and different about them (in relation to what is seen as the colonializing, homogenizing force of the globalized consumer culture). For those in impoverished urban communities, this can be the street culture, which despite its ultimate sameness at the level of values, nevertheless contains relatively distinctive normative and expressive components.

Ultimately, however, there seems to be a tension at the heart of what might be described as mainstream culture. Whilst the 'Protestant Work Ethic' which was said to underpin modernist, industrial capitalism (see Weber, 1962/2002), continues to hold rhetorical value—championing notions of sacrifice, the deferment of gratification, hard work, prudence and meritocracy—in reality consumerist notions of instant gratification, untrammelled desire, indulgence and leisure are in fact dominant (see Hayward, 2004). Social and material worth are not distributed according to merit and contribution, but arbitrarily on the basis of an ability to exploit existing privilege (Young, 2007). In this way, the subterranean values of leisure and pleasure seeking, which have long constituted the under-articulated section of hegemonic culture (see Matza and Sykes, 1961) are in fact central to both ghetto streets and executive suites (see Densley and Stevens, 2014).

Where it is clear that there are not any great value distinctions between street and mainstream cultures, this provides some better impetus through which to consider the level of resistance within it. Hall et al.'s (2008) rejection of any kind of oppositional meaning within street culture beyond individualistic narcissism is perhaps arguably a step further than is necessary. Indeed, I have previously argued for a middle-ground between the subcultural resistance and colonized-self positions (see Ilan, 2014). As argued in that paper, and indeed demonstrated by a range of research cited at various stages within this book (not least Bourgois, 1995/2003), street culture is replete with meaning: the search for respect, a sense of autonomy (however subjective), the deployment of creativity, humour in the face of adverse circumstances, in short, 'defiance'.

Research by Eleni Dimou (2013) further problematizes the post-subcultural tendency to overlook the significant meanings inherent in particular leisure and deviant practices. Examining two different music scenes in the socialist state of Cuba, she demonstrates the extent to which intoxication, dance and friendship provide momentary liberation from the travails of life. The subcultural, radical rap music, which urges the state to remain true to its stated ideology and alleviate the suffering of the poor, is appreciated thus in similar ways to the raunchy raggaeton which celebrates the consumerism that has become the de facto ideology of the rich. Ultimately, whilst they challenge the reality of the state (in the former case) and its supposed socialist ideology (in the latter), their most pronounced affects are amongst fans enjoying the music in the moment. Indeed, by forensically examining the theories and principles around which conceptualizations and denials of resistance have been built, she concludes that these share much in common, and in all cases, the significance of leisure and/or deviant practices must be considered in light of structural inequalities. Blackman (2005) notes that post-modern critiques of subcultural theory still see energy and creativity in the activities they simultaneously see as relatively empty of resistant momentum.

I thus argue for an understanding of street culture as 'defiant' rather than a form of resistance. In this way its embodiment of frustration and discontent, fleeting emotional satisfactions and refusal to obey normative imperatives can be understood, whilst at the same time decoupling it from aspirations that it might represent some kind of transformative force in the absence of political organization (see Ilan, 2014). The affective/emotional satisfactions of contradicting the imperatives of the powerful (i.e. that one should work hard and avoid trouble, excessive sensuality, etc.) are arguably most potent in moments of defiance. In an earlier study, I noted the extent to which young offenders who defy the rules of their youth justice service conjured a sense of power and control for themselves, although outside of this momentary flush of emotion, these young men were effectively moving themselves closer to prison (Ilan, 2010). In short, contemporary understandings of the 'defiance' inherent in street cultural actions should be attentive to the counter-dominant qualities of their performance, as opposed to seeking a counter-narrative to dominant socio-economic principles. Where individuals or groups act in a manner that incites condemnation and/or fear from powerful institutions, they are in effect expressing their discontent with the role that social, economic and cultural forces seem to be resigning them to. There is no real attempt, however, to change these forces.

Returning then to Merton's classic typology, it is arguably the case that street cultural actions do not sit comfortably in either 'innovator' or 'rebel' categories. They are often motivated by a desire to have the trappings of inclusion by any means necessary as per the innovator, but these are not solely material goods and include the desire to express agency (achieve a sense of autonomy) even if this might disadvantage them ultimately (see also Hayward, 2004; Young, 2003). To some extent thus, Agnew's (1992) restatement of this traditional strain theory as creating the capacity for negativistic emotions – that is, frustration, rage, etc. – seems somewhat restrictive, where a wider spectrum of emotions can similarly operate. Equally, a lack of participation in forms of transformative politics seems to preclude the application of the 'rebel' definition. Street cultures are, however, multifaceted, potentially volatile and subject to various forms of institutionalization and organization given the right circumstances, as previously noted. Thus, for example, Brotherton (2008) notes the extent to which certain long-standing American street gangs have transformed themselves into politically active, community development groups.

Power and politics in the ghetto

Linked to the demise of the traditional working and agrarian classes earlier discussed, the spread of ubiquitous values are a consequence of the neoliberal global order described in Chapter 7. As alluded to by Hall et al. (2008) this order significantly weakened the material base for class politics and the kind of broad leftist movements which achieved so much in the 20th century to foster greater egalitarianism. Arguably it was previous levels of collectivism and communitarianism that opened up more democratic opportunities for income and dignity in the developed world. These underpinning modes of being were ultimately replaced by more middle-class notions of individual advancement. As such, the achievement of political change that disrupted and reversed previous configurations of power is considerably more elusive in late-modernity. This goes some distance to explain contemporary street culture's lack of potential to underpin meaningful transformative resistance. The triumph of the neoliberal-capitalist ideology over its socialist-democratic rival, moreover, significantly reduced the scope for a coherent and powerful politics of opposition.

In effect, thus, a certain bifurcation of the traditional leftist constituency occurred, whereby its upper reaches were increasingly identified with middle-class values and politics, whereas the residualized rump of this group became viewed as a dysfunctional and apolitical 'underclass' (this meta-narrative should be treated with a certain amount of caution, the reality is somewhat more nuanced – see Savage, 2000). Even such a broad brush strokes explanation, however, offers some historical purchase when one considers the significance of changing working-class communities and the cultural dynamics that are intertwined with them.

As noted previously, there has been a tendency amongst scholars of urban poverty and slum life to draw distinctions between what might be conceptualized as the 'respectable', 'decent' and 'conformist' sections of the lower-classes and those labelled as 'rough', 'street' and 'non-conformist' (see also Ilan, 2011). These somewhat normative classifications reveal the extent to which the more socio-economically included/successful individuals, groups and families within the working-class area were inherently praised for their ultimate adherence to 'governance from above' (see Lea and Stenson, 2007). Dutifully adhering to the dictates of the formal law and less formal norms of respectability (e.g. around behaving well in and completing school) was viewed as vesting them with greater moral and personal worth (see e.g. Willis, 1977 – this did not necessarily translate into social mobility).

Not only could this moral authority underpin a politics which sought better material conditions for the working-classes, but structured through the trade union movement in an era of mass industrial employment (in the global north), organizational and rhetorical capacities similarly existed. The kinds of working-class structures and institutions described in Chapter 3 thus not only served to order life in the inner-city, but to make some manner of contribution (however limited and challenged) to national modes of governance. The contemporary urban poor, however, largely exists without these community institutions and political structures, without a constituency more widely viewed as respectable and deserving and without socio-economic mobility. The extent to which these traditional working-class modes of order and politics offered an alternative to middle-class notions of individualist careerism and/or consumerist notions of competitive display is open to question, but they arguably did provide a certain symmetry between the forces that governed such communities from above, and those institutions which did so from below. Arguably, there is little such symmetry within contemporary society. Indeed, drawing on Manuel Castells (2010) and Cornel West (1993), Hagedorn (2008) views contemporary 'gang culture' (what this book classifies as street culture) as stemming from the failed promises of modernity: greater equality for all; leaving the excluded with little choice but to retreat into a culture concerned with the most immediate of needs.

It is within this context of the less formally governed and governable area of disadvantage that street culture flourishes. Where trade union chapters or social clubs might take minutes and constitute by-laws in a manner comparable to state, corporate or legal institutions, street cultural institutions function on the basis of primary personal interactions, unwritten rules readily mutable and contestable, ephemeral and shifting hierarchies, rumours and gossip, force of will and/or violence, and indeed, often very indistinct notions of membership. Returning to Anderson's (1999: 10) notion of street culture as continuing an ancient notion of 'people's culture', it becomes reasonable to understand the phenomenon as a form of normative order, albeit usually incapable of providing stability and security in an open, democratic and non-exploitative manner. Where the formal economy fails to provide the material resources necessary for stable, decent lives and communities and where official forms of governance variously neglect, ignore, violently and/or symbolically repress large swathes of the poor, it is simply the case that meaningful engagement with and inclusion in political processes becomes extremely difficult.

Street cultural concerns and normative practices can thus be understood as a form of 'governance from below' (see Lea and Stenson, 2007; de Sousa Santos, 2002). Often seemingly antithetical to formal modes of governance, they create taboos around cooperating with state authority (the police) as well as particular respectabilizing institutions (e.g. the formal education system). They are nevertheless concerned with attaining a similar set of values/goals around the accumulation and display of wealth as well as the attainment of dignity and respect. The cultural and economic division of the world into a minority of winners and a larger class of struggling losers deposits its most deleterious consequences amongst the urban poor who are thus more strongly drawn towards an orientation disinterested in incremental collective transformative politics where there are opportunities to speak a narrative of individualistic success, bolstered by momentary opportunities to feel powerful and defiant.

In such a manner, it is clear that the contemporary economic order impacts significantly on the cultural conditions and political aspirations of the urban poor. Importantly, however, the specific conditions in various regions of the world give shape and character to the ways in which this occurs. Thus, for example, the consumer-thieves in the north of England studied by Hall et al. (2008) reject the leftist militancy of their parent culture for the pleasures and status that can be garnered from spending money. Meanwhile, the criminal gangs in the favelas of Brazil examined by Leeds (1996) represent additionally a source of (brutal and perhaps arbitrary) security and welfare in spaces that the state will not govern by means other than oppression. Their aspirations, however, are crimino-entrepreneurial rather than political (no matter the rhetoric and historical links to radical groups that some of these groups might exhibit). Both phenomena, despite their wide differences in impact on their wider communities are arguably a consequence of the 'crisis' in national governance described in Chapter 7, whereby states govern often in a manner that places the interests of transnational capital above those of citizens.

The criminalizing gaze

Another consequence of this transnational-capital-focused mode of governance, as noted, has been the state's recourse to muscular criminal justice policies as a means to assert power, which in absolute terms is decreasing. Once again, this manifests differently according to global region and takes shape around political realities, such as electoral demands amongst liberal democracies in the global north and neo-colonialism in the south. Jock Young, in regards to the former case, wrote eloquently about the ways in which insecurity amongst the 'precariously included', mainstream majorities across the English-speaking west contributed to the flourishing of a more exclusive society (1999, 2007). Here the expanded middle-classes, fearful for their own material future, view the poor through the emotive lens of sensed lost privilege and fears of falling further. Bev Skeggs' argument that 'respectability' defines itself against what it is not (1997) seems particularly apt here, where there is a mobilization of a politics that rejects the so-called 'unearned indulgence' (Young, 2007: 62) of the poor (welfare, perceived high rates of substance use, perceived refusal to engage in sexual propriety), rather than a variant that challenges that of global elites which is held out as an (albeit impossible to reach) aspiration for all.

There is historical pedigree in operation here, where numerous studies have demonstrated the extent to which fears of 'the street' amongst majority populations have underpinned first media outcry and then legal/law enforcement action against the urban poor (see e.g. Gilfoyle, 2004; Pearson, 1984; Cohen, 1972). For centuries, thus, the privileged have spoken out against what they see as the moral and behavioural failings of the poor, with this narrative supporting an understanding of the world as justifiably unequal (see also Elias and Scotson, 1994). This renders as logical the proposition that the criminality linked to street culture should be firmly punished whilst the socio-economic structures underpinning its existence need not be altered too quickly or radically. There has been a long tradition of examining social control (more recent works include Innes, 2003; Cohen, 1985) and the intention of this book is not to rehearse it, but instead to consider the specific ways in which street culture has been targeted by or butted up against social control mechanisms. There are particular implications in contemporary times where, as Harvey (2005) points out, neoliberal principles of economic management sit comfortably alongside neoconservative principles of punitive social control.

In contemporary terms, the notion of 'governing through crime' has been understood as a key means by which, for example, the US Government addresses the conditions of the urban poor (see Simon, 2007). As opposed to social welfare, expanded healthcare or accelerated public education, it has been the burgeoning criminal justice and prison systems which have become the signature American responses to urban poverty (see also Parenti, 2008). This 'culture of control' (Garland, 2001), for some scholars, can be viewed across much of the Anglophone world, albeit in more muted terms. Those street cultural crimes, examined in Chapter 5, thus become key targets in efforts to remedy the perceived ills of society. The potential of such strategies is open to question where they ultimately contribute to the same socio-economic and cultural exclusion which underpins such criminality in the first place.

Whereas this northern variant of oppression is achieved through symbolic violence, within the global south, there is far greater recourse to physical force to achieve a more extreme variant of a similar theme:

> ... In attempts to regain social order and power, the police may be involved in a form of vigilantism which extends to social cleansing, targeting groups of 'undesirables' such as suspected criminals, youth gang members, street children and homosexuals. Such police brutality is alarmingly common in many countries in the South, and while it is widely known that this violence exists, agents on the whole act with remarkable impunity (Winton, 2004: 173).

Without wishing to dismiss for one moment the behaviours of those sections of the urban poor that cause harm to members of their community and indeed wider society, the argument here is that they are nevertheless disproportionately criminalized (i.e. subjected to the workings of the criminal justice system) or worse. An orthodox Marxist analysis of this situation would view the state as an instrument of the ruling class, using criminal justice to oppress the poor who could threaten this privilege by realizing their power. This, however, is arguably too simplistic a reading. More contemporary radical perspectives on state power conceptualize the state as comprising numerous different bodies acting relatively independently: collectively an arena within which different interests compete but where money and influence grant a significant advantage (see e.g. Coleman et al., 2009).

This kind of nuanced view becomes particularly helpful, allowing for an understanding of the fact that different branches of the state (let alone individual agents) can pull in different directions, and furthermore recognizing that the contemporary state is often responding to stimuli, obligations and interests that lie beyond it, that is multinationally. Questions of inclusion and exclusion are particularly salient in how this complex assemblage operates. At various levels and in different ways, the behaviour and culture of the urban poor are held up to criticism and often punishment. Various different institutions, whether formally of the state or not, are involved in this process where often welfarist interventions are steeped in the logic of 'liberal other-ing' (Young, 2007: the treatment of the excluded as 'different' from those of a 'mainstream' disposition); at the level of political rhetoric where the poor are demonized as defective workers; through spatial controls from public order laws to urban planning; through economic policies and where policing and the coercive practices of the state fall hardest on socio-economically excluded street cultural practitioners.

The more 'welfarist' arms of the state, which regret and seek to ameliorate the conditions of the marginalized, often seem to operate under the assump-tion that their clients lack 'decent' values. For example, John Clarke's work (2002) examining the historic origins of British youth policy roots it within Victorian reform movements which saw the working-class family and commu-nity as poor socializing influences on the young (see also O'Sullivan, 1997). Welfarist interventions were thus initially a means of attempting to incul-cate what were seen as healthier, more middle-class orientations amongst marginalized youth. I argued that this principle continues to underpin youth justice interventions in much of the Anglophone world, where notions of 'punishing' young people for their criminal lifestyles is replaced by a sense that they should be instead inculcated into mainstream behavioural norms to replace their existing street cultural concerns (Ilan, 2010). Many youth justice systems thus, before incarcerating young people, work towards encour-aging what are seen as 'pro-social' principles: education, careerism, personal order etc. Tensions emerge, however, where street cultural principles exist in defiance of these imperatives (ibid.).

Where state interventions do not account for, or address, the structural underpinnings of street cultural behaviour; however, they risk becoming a liberal fig leaf, ostensibly signalling that the state is 'giving chances' to street cultural youth who nevertheless face increasing punishment if they continue offending. Such individuals can thus be treated as recalcitrant, dysfunctional and ultimately undeserving despite the evidence of the logic that underpins their practice of street culture in the first place. In other words, even progres-sive seeming interventions that seem concerned only with 'improvement' are often backed by the coercive forces of pure criminal justice.

Governments attempt to generate political capital through demonstrat-ing a willingness to combat what are viewed as moral failings within the socio-economic margins (see Simon, 2007; Pitts, 2003). In spatial terms, this approach has much in common with the 'zero tolerance' modes of policing which clamp down on low-level 'nuisance' crimes and incivilities. Andrew Millie (2008, 2011) rightly points out that the ability to define appropriate behaviour in many contexts is vested in those with existing economic and/or political power. Where moral, prudential, economic and aesthetic value judge-ments all determine the extent to which various behaviours will be permitted in particular spaces, it is the interpretation of these categories held by included and not marginalized groups which tend to abide. Thus class-cultural and commercial notions of what is right and sensible, economically beneficial (and to who) as well as aesthetically pleasing often determine who and what is permitted to be. Street cultural practitioners who are judged to possess deficient morals, untrustworthy judgement, deviant greed (as opposed to its legitimate variant) and a 'scruffy' or 'ghetto' aesthetic can thus become natural targets for legally backed clearance measures.

The regulation of space is undertaken variously by the state as well as pri-vate institutions (e.g. shopping malls, private security guards). Such practices often operate to segregate areas of consumption (including desirable gated residential communities) from the warehouses of urban poverty discussed in Chapter 4 (see Hayward, 2004; Davis, 1990). As Bannister et al. (2006: 923) note, the city is being 'cleansed of difference' where 'respectable' populations and activities are protected against the people and behaviours that have come to be understood as 'anti-social' (see also Ferrell, 2001). Again, in the global south where degrees of social inclusion and exclusion are more strongly pro-nounced these processes often operate to a more extreme degree. Whereas the slum clearances in the 1950s/1960s in northern Europe tended to facilitate large swathes of better quality public housing being built, the contemporary variant in the global south is frequently a means of 'spatially cleansing' signif-icant and potentially valuable land (see Davis, 2006). Recently, for example, there have been examples of this around infrastructure built for the soccer world cup in Brazil (Gibson and Watts, 2013).

The effect of such policies is often to manage out seemingly 'troublesome' populations and to 'regenerate' former slums as gentrified, high-value real estate. Indeed, policies akin to this operate also within the contemporary global north (see e.g. Ilan, 2011; Karn, 2007). Such 'property led regeneration' is an example of neoliberal principles which promote global investment into entrepreneurial cities (see Imrie and Raco, 2003; Jessop, 1997) over the fate of its disadvantaged residents. Indeed, this demonstrates the complex processes at play within contemporary governance and its treatment of the urban poor: financial opportunities for the wealthier sections of the included drive local municipal policy around planning and land use; this is supported by robust public order laws and urban regeneration agendas, and finally the police are deployed to coercively enforce such decisions where necessary.

Policing indeed represents a key process by which populations of urban disadvantage and street cultural practitioners are regulated. Here, particular policing cultures and everyday practices reinforce and magnify the tendency of legal regimes to target the crimes and lifestyles of the urban poor. Policing thus often represents the hard edge of socio-economic exclusion's realization within everyday experience and, as will be further explored, is often recognized by targeted communities as such. This unfolds through the ways in which police forces decide on operational priorities, and the ways in which individual officers exercise their judgement, discretion or indeed what captures their notice in the first place. For Waddington (1999):

> The exercise of police discretion is *intrinsically* discriminatory, because it imposes dominant social values upon subordinate sections of the population... police do not control the commission of crime, they contain criminality: that is they keep the excluded in their place (40–41, emphasis in original).

The particular factors which inform this wider principle within individual countries, regions and cities obviously vary, as there are distinctive characteristics to local varieties of exclusion. In many parts of the world and resonating with points made in Chapter 3, questions of race are tightly interwoven with debates over police practice and legitimacy. Thus, for example, in the UK, there has been a considerable amount of research and reflection around the presence of 'institutional racism' within the London Metropolitan Police Force, in particular since the racist murder of Steven Lawrence in 1994 and the botched investigation which followed (see e.g. Reiner, 2000; Bowling, 1999; Macpherson, 1999; Fitzgerald and Hale, 1996). Ultimately it is generally concluded that the police force in the UK is subject to the wider processes of prejudice and structural exclusion that exist within its wider society, a finding that could quite probably be applied universally.

Young men of colour are thus more likely to be stopped and 'searched' (or 'frisked' if they are American) than their white counterparts. Indeed, and as earlier noted, black Americans are disproportionately policed and criminalized to a very pronounced degree (see Roberts, 2004). The American concept of 'police property' (Lee, 1981) is particularly instructive in understanding how some of the most excluded populations experience their treatment by the police. This idea suggests that those who possess particular concentrations of disadvantage (e.g. that they are young, poor, from a disadvantaged area, uneducated and of colour) can be treated with a particular amount of impunity: as if they 'belong' to officers to do with as they please. Whilst processes operate to limit the practice of this tendency within most liberal democracies, it nevertheless significantly impacts on the characteristics of the interactions that officers often have with those of such demographic characteristics.

Choongh (1998) argues that, in policing those lower down the socio-economic spectrum, a concern with 'social discipline' often trumps formal operational procedures. The priority becomes aggressively asserting the authority of the police against individuals who are viewed as insufficiently deferent and chronically troublesome. It could be argued here that the police are directly responding to the behavioural imperatives that are associated with strong variants of street culture. Here, a visual grammar can serve as a manner of policing shorthand which can suggest to agents of the state the target-value of those they encounter:

> Legal authorities read and respond to the styles of lower-class and ethnic minority kids (and adults), to their collective presentation of self and construction of identity, and in doing so push them into downwards cycles of criminalization... Discriminatory policing or differential enforcement become meaningful... as interactive dynamics through which authorities pay more attention to one group than another and read (and misread) the stylistic patterns that construct group identity (Ferrell, 2004: 62).

Given the resonance of street style within wider, general pop and youth cultures, this phenomenon is further problematic still. There are clearly institutions operating within the state that patrol aspects of 'being' as much as behaviour. In other words, social control processes target particular identities as much as particular identified harms (whilst arguably virtually ignoring a range of other identities and harms). Moving beyond an orthodox Marxist reading of this scenario (which would rightly note the operation of economic structure here) it is useful to highlight a number of cultural processes at play. In particular, it would seem clear that forces of governance place stock in the distinction between the 'rough' and 'respectable', where the former are symbolically targeted and the latter ostensibly protected. It is perhaps tempting to interpret this as a clash of cultures, whereby the state's resources are deployed to champion 'mainstream' values against street cultural concerns that place notions of 'fast money' before more worthwhile virtues such as hard work and prudence.

The irony here is that, as noted earlier, street culture has much in common with the 'mainstream' in terms of fundamental values. It is thus no surprise that American correctional officers attempting to rehabilitate young offenders through particular programmes appeal to notions of consumerism as a reward for legitimate work and enterprise (Kramer et al., 2014). Of course, there is a tension here where consumerism was cited by these same young people as a significant factor motivating their offending in the first place. The real culture clash thus occurs within mainstream values themselves where traditional capitalist values derived from the Protestant work ethic (hard work, prudence, saving, deferred gratification) meet those of a materialist consumer culture (leisure, impulsivity, debt, instant gratification). Indeed, those American correctional officers sought instead to inculcate the combination of these value sets, despite their inherent contradictions.

Crusading against those of a street cultural orientation in a sense serves to vent an amount of the social discontent that emerges from this clear tension. If the ideal values of traditional capitalism do not hold true (where pay should follow performance; hard work should translate into financial rewards and social inclusion; and where destruction should not yield a greater profit than manufacturing), there is a significant threat to personal feelings of security and a more collective sense of social stability (Young, 1999, 2007). Young's argument is that these feelings of insecurity become channelled into processes of essentialism and blame whereby the perceived moral failings of the poor and excluded are scapegoated for a range of social ills. Here, conservative sentiments locate the cause of the increasingly unequal economic settlement in the behaviour of those who have least. They are variously viewed as unfairly taking from the public purse, disrupting the social order through engaging in criminality or indeed impeding economic development through projecting an image of 'backwardness'. A cultural practice of persecuting such groups obscures the inequities of the new economic settlements which are veritably at the heart of contemporary mass insecurities.

Effectively, thus, the signs and signifiers of street culture are read as indicating the flourishing of a 'rough' culture and come to indicate a greater existential threat to the 'law abiding majority' than they actually represent. Its associations both with feared street criminality (real and imagined) and the reviled 'lower' states of socio-economic existence render it an ideal symbolic target. Items that become linked to street culture in the public imaginary (e.g. crack cocaine; see Box 8.1) can thus attract particular legal sanctions. Moreover, conceptual blurring occurs whereby clear distinctions between behaviour and being are lost. Street cultural identities risk becoming targeted beyond street cultural behaviours, which as noted, if free of crime are readily commodifiable. The tendency to criminalize the marginalized does not necessarily interfere with the fascination with their forms of expressivity which can nevertheless persist.

Box 8.1 The powder/rock sentencing disparity

Shouldn't drug laws treat the same drug in the same way? This question has been asked extensively of US Federal Sentencing Guidelines. Although legislative/judicial reforms have now removed the sentencing disparity that used to apply to different forms of cocaine, it was a notable feature of American criminal justice for over two decades.

With high rates of drug-related violence being linked to crack cocaine in the 1980s and public outcry ensuing, the guidelines issued to American judges were amended. Those who trafficked crack cocaine were to be sentenced more severely than those who traded in its powder variant (see Shein, 1993). Specifically, a rule that came to be known as the '100 to 1' ratio essentially meant that those sentenced for possession of cocaine with intent to supply would face a sentence 100 times greater if the drug was in base (rock or crack) as opposed to powder form. Leaving aside the chemical nuances that these rules apparently glossed over, they were accused of specifically targeting poor, black cocaine users, who were considerably more likely to use crack than their wealthier white counterparts.

Indeed, the rules have been considered particularly controversial and have been the subject of numerous attempted reforms. One reason for this is because of the extent to which they create a regime of disparate sentences (essentially for possession of the same drug) between different races and/or social classes (see Sklansky, 1994). This has contributed, furthermore, to the massively disproportionate criminalization of poor, black men in the USA over any other demographic group. Examples such as this illustrate the way in which the social control of populations of disadvantage is achieved.

The criminalizing gaze's backwards reflection

Thus far the chapter has characterized the defiant nature of street culture, located it within the apolitical nature of contemporary deprivation and accounted for the ways in which it is often criminalized. Drawing once again on Jock Young's (1999) work, the interrelationship between the first and last of these issues can be understood as significant. He makes the case that crime and crime control in late-modernity operate in a 'dyadic' manner, where pressures apply both on the marginalized to commit crime and on the general public to view this criminality as existentially threatening. This insight can be stretched to apply to street culture more generally. To add to this, it might be argued that the arms of the dyad interact with each other to cyclically reproduce and augment exclusion.

Street cultural attitudes and concerns, as illustrated earlier in the book, can underpin a range of criminal behaviours. They can also call for adopting an outwardly hostile attitude to the forces of law and order. As noted above, seeming to belong to a more delinquent group can tend to draw the attention of police officers. This can be further exacerbated then by the exhibition of what would be perceived as an uncooperative attitude, which can ultimately affect the extent to which officers might exercise their discretion and ultimately the outcome of particular interactions (see e.g. Brown et al., 2009;

Terril and Mastrofski, 2002). In other words, not only does street culture operate to invite interaction with the forces of criminal justice, but it can prompt behaviours which are likely to sour the outcome. The accumulation of arrests and convictions serves to further an individual's socio-economic exclusion in most cases. Thus the street cultures born of socio-economic exclusion can promote crime, police attention and negative police interactions, ultimately reinforcing and exacerbating this exclusion.

This repeated defiance of behavioural expectations is not a form of resistance; as much like the mechanisms described by Paul Willis (1977) in relation to misbehaviour within the school system, such actions are central to the reproduction of the socio-economic status quo. The roles played by everyday behaviours and cultural norms in this process should be further considered. A street cultural orientation, as noted earlier, prompts a world view which tends to cast defiant or indeed criminal behaviours in a more positive light. Meanwhile, it simultaneously prompts a view of police interventions as generally heavy handed, malicious, discriminatory, unjust and illegitimate overall. This can be supported by negative interactions with police officers whether directly experienced or discussed as part of local knowledge/lore. Street culture, thus, draws clear lines around who is to be considered an enemy and what manner of relationship is permitted with them.

Anyone familiar with either the expressive products of street culture or indeed the normativity of many disadvantaged communities will have heard multiple slang words to describe those who speak to the police (beyond empty civilities, blanket denials or repeated refusals to provide any meaningful information): 'informers', 'snitches', 'rats', 'grasses', etc. Research, for example, in the USA (Carr et al., 2007) and the UK (Yates, 2006) demonstrates the extent to which the imperatives 'don't snitch' and 'don't grass' respectively have become firmly embedded as local taboos. This is essentially the legacy of many disadvantaged communities feeling that they are 'over-policed and under protected' – a belief that police forces have the goal of socially disciplining their members as opposed to listening to their concerns and ensuring that they are met. There is abundant evidence of this occurring across the world, where again issues of ethnicity and class weigh particularly heavily (see e.g. Sharp and Atherton, 2007; Brunson and Miller, 2006; Goldstein, 2003; Poynting, 1999). The result tends to be a perception that makes the job of policing more difficult and adversarial, itself contributing to greater degrees of over-policing and under-protection.

As demonstrated by a range of recent studies, people tend to cooperate with and trust in the police where they believe the police to be 'procedurally fair' (that they 'play by the rules') and identify with the same norms held by the community (Jackson and Bradford, 2009; Jackson and Sunshine, 2007; Tyler, 2004; Sunshine and Tyler, 2003). By contrast, the perception within disadvantaged communities tends to be opposite:

> Just as the police represent for many order, stability and cohesion, to people from these social groups they may represent the unfair priorities of the dominant social order, an interfering state or even oppression (Jackson and Bradford, 2009: 499).

This reduces the capacity for consent-based policing to operate and thus often precipitates a more robust policing approach. To give a concrete example and to return full circle to the vignette at the beginning of the book, it is worth imagining an interaction between a police officer and young male street cultural practitioners.

Fictionalizing for the purposes of explanation the motives that might prompt a police officer to stop and question a group of young black men standing beside a bicycle, one might assume that everything from the pos-tures, clothing, skin colour, accents and seeming 'lack of purpose' exhibited might have led to pause for thought. Any suspicions around the possibility of the bicycle being stolen might be inflamed by a quick double-take, observing the body language of the young men as they react to being noticed. Here the young people as street cultural practitioners might rehearse their antipathy to law and order by non-verbally exhibiting hostility. They might well feel that they are constantly and unfairly the target of police stops and resent this viscerally. They may feel simultaneously afraid that, for example, the bicycle, which one of their members might have cheaply purchased from a neighbour, could have been ultimately stolen and that if its serial number is checked then there could be a charge for handling stolen property. Equally, they may not be able to quite check the sense of anger that this pressure conjures. They may have received advice from a parent to be polite to officers, but in an effort to cull excess communication, which could either lead them into a more hostile reaction or, worse, be construed by onlookers as cooperation with the police, their responses to questions become terse and clipped. To the officers, this may be taken as confirmation of their street cultural status, prompting them perhaps to wonder whether they are guilty of some other criminal offence, even if not relating to the bicycle. This could thus prompt sterner treatment, a search or questions which to the young men only confirm that they are unduly targeted.

Whilst firmly rooted in the speculative, this reflection on the interactive dynamics between street cultural practitioners and agents of the state raises

important issues. The ways in which these young behave might tempt some to see 'resistance', but given the lack of political intent they are probably better understood if anything as 'defiance'. That said, the young men are operating under multiple pressures, from various state and private agents that treat them as suspicious or in need of reform, to street cultural practitioners who may react violently if it is felt that there has been excessive consultation with the police – indeed, it could significantly reduce one's street capital (see Chapter 3). The police, operating under their everyday cultural practices, may feel that they are acting logically by pursuing their trained and patterned instincts. In doing so, they are participating in an iterative process of reproducing and exacerbating both the social exclusion of the young men and the difficulties in policing their neighbourhood.

Public health practitioners arguably point to ways forward in dealing more effectively with street cultures from a welfarist perspective. Less adversarially orientated than criminal justice and it might be assumed, emanating from a tradition more concerned with positive outcomes than particular models of normativity, certain nursing perspectives have called for a provision of services that operates through an understanding of street cultural realities (see Pavis and Cunningham-Burley, 1999). This manner of approach provokes reflection around the possibilities of tackling urban poverty and its associated issues differently (Figure 8.1). This might mean addressing street cultural groups more so than individuals and jettisoning an approach that is concerned primarily with individual criminality as opposed to collective experiences of exclusion. It might mean tapping into rich veins of street entrepreneurialism, offering support and guidance through official bureaucracies, as opposed to attempting to stuff autonomy-orientated people into the heavily regulated and monotonous spaces of low-wage labour. It might ultimately mean working with rather than against street cultural institutions which might be tempted to trade criminal incomes for a variant that is accompanied by a more widely recognized form of respectability.

Where young people are concerned, international human rights discourses from the UN Declaration on the Rights of the Child to the Beijing Rules state that they should be at the heart of decisions that affect them, dealt with as far as possible outside of the criminal justice system, and that their welfare and development should be prioritized. Given what has been said about the conflation of street cultures and youth cultures within the criminalizing gaze, and indeed the generally youthful nature of street culture itself, these human rights positions give further pause for thought. Mainstream relationships to street culture need not be a case of criminalization on the one hand and (purely stylistic) emulation on the other. There is arguably scope for utilizing an understanding and appreciation of street culture

Figure 8.1 Understandings of ghetto youth are often dismissive of the talent, energy and hard work which animates the life of those who sit at various points on the street cultural spectrum. For many, the rewards of 'mainstream' life cannot compete with the seductions of street life just outside the window. Photo by Simon Wheatley

to promote less harmful modes of engaging with the socio-economically excluded.

Conclusion

This chapter has demonstrated the fact that street culture is not so much a form of resistance, but a form of defiantly embodying mainstream values through practices that are at times counter-normative and emotionally fulfilling. Notions of resistance can be better understood as occurring within political movements, which due to neoliberal dominance now exist to a far lesser extent within areas of urban disadvantage. The extent to which street culture has been associated with defiance, however, gives some indication as to why it is valued within youth markets by appealing to wider youth cultures that are inherently concerned with the negotiation of authority.

Concentrations of poverty and the operation of normative judgements by the included and powerful (again affected by the operation of the current socio-economic settlement) tend to result in the condemnation and/or punishment of street cultural practitioners and at times their communities. In the end, such sentiments are sensed by the excluded whose defiant attitudes serve often to exacerbate their situation. Meanwhile, state responses to the urban poor also often achieve this outcome. There is, however, the possibility of dealing differently with the problems caused by strong street cultural practices. These, however, will be very difficult to realize as long as current configurations of money, power and ideology continue to exist in their present form.

CHAPTER 9

Conclusion

The concept of street culture presented in this book has been shown to manifest across a broad range of human experiences. Nevertheless, its associations with urban poverty, its related criminality and the commodified 'cool' that is so much a part of youth lifestyles justify the approach that has been adopted here. The goal has been to present an overarching theoretical frame that can account for street culture's various manifestations within different parts of the world, located within an analysis that can operate simultaneously at multiple levels. At the macro level of social structure, the political economy of the globalized neoliberal world has resulted in deepening inequalities: deindustrialization in the global north reducing the scope for decently paid stable employment and desperate urbanization in the global south where cities swell with people but starve for economic opportunity. At the meso level of culture and the media, consumerist values reign supreme, ensuring that the relatively poor remain stigmatized whilst their street culture remains open to be opportunistically harvested by the cultural industries. At the micro or individual level, structural disadvantages are written onto personal dispositions. Choices are made not only on the basis of rational calculations universal in all people, but a through the lens of social position and through the tempest of various emotional and existential concerns.

It is possible to speak of a 'street culture': the values, dispositions, practices and styles associated with particular sections of disadvantaged urban populations. Whilst these values have much in common with the profit-above-all-else ethics of neoliberal capitalism, there are distinct systems of normativity and expressivity that have ultimately stemmed from the exclusion experienced by the most disadvantaged of the urban poor. Underpinned by a range of concerns from toughness and autonomy to survival and the visceral, street culture has been associated with a range of criminal lifestyles and expressive practices. Whilst there is much in street culture that accords with common, law-abiding norms, certain key areas such as questions of property, deploying violence and using the police tend to be very different. In street culture, informal relationships are important, whilst formal laws mean little.

The criminalizing gaze of the precariously included, moreover, does much to conflate being with behaviour, viewing entire sections of the population in a negative light. This same tendency to 'devalue' the urban poor makes the expressive and aesthetic practices associated with them particularly valuable to youth marketeers, keen to capitalize on the suggestion of transgression. Street culture is inherently 'cool', where both phenomena place a premium on an ability to shield emotions, defy orthodox conventions and display appropriate taste.

Street culture thus manifests as a spectrum: at the weakest point, the purchasing of decontextualized, commercial products or a part of the youthful search for autonomy; at the strongest, a willingness to deploy violence at the merest provocation, or to deal drugs and steal in order to generate funds for street consumer practices. Scholars, and indeed the public, have been fascinated with life within the disadvantaged areas of western cities for several decades. Studies over time also tended to identify different points on a spectrum of 'rough' beliefs and behaviours associated with the most marginalized within such communities of poverty. Although not always articulated as such, these scholars had identified the fact that groups and individuals responded in different ways to their perceived opportunities for greater socio-economic inclusion. Many of these works were completed in an era of democratic economic expansion in the west, where rises in the standard of living were widespread. Street culture would arguably become increasingly dominant in such areas during the deindustrialization of the late 20th century, where such opportunities were closing off.

Debates continue to exist around the best way to study such dispositions, whether they are the product of a distinctive, destructive underclass culture, or indeed a parallel system of aggressive wealth acquisition to that which orders many established businesses and states. Widening its scope beyond the boundaries of the global north in which so much social science is produced, this book has actively engaged with such debates, reiterating the need to move beyond the stock problematizing of 'usual suspect' populations and phenomena (such as 'gangs'). It has instead sought to draw on literature that is attentive to the realities of lived lives in a range of contexts. It demonstrated the extent to which social structures and demography impacts on the nature of street cultures. It noted, for example, how changing economies altered northern working-class cultures, cutting away traditional routes to livelihood and dignity, and creating particular pressures on men to adopt stronger variants of street culture. The complexity of gender relations in street worlds was furthermore examined, demonstrating the complex stresses faced by women in areas regulated by interpersonal violence.

Questions of race/ethnicity were considered, where street culture is often incorrectly conflated with 'black culture'. Instead, it was suggested that the prodigious street cultural expressivity of many black populations might have cemented this sense in the public imaginary, but that it is the exclusion fuelled by racism (and its intersections with poverty) which is the more salient factor to consider. Indeed, street cultures exist within various ethnic populations. By examining theory relating to the value of the self, it was concluded that there are particular difficulties for the urban poor to capitalize on their personas within the legitimate workplace, but that this might prove to be more straightforward-seeming within the illegitimate economy. The cultural industries can nevertheless squeeze the exchange value that exists within the disadvantaged self, using the wider public's fascination with such states of being to generate capital within the mainstream economy. Drawing on a Bourdieuian perspective (see Chapter 3), it was argued that the particularly marginalized do, however, have the capacity to generate capital within illicit street worlds, where their embodied capacities and orientations can be advantageous. In response to the emotional dynamics of specific contexts, individuals apply this 'natural' seeming (but socially structured) sense of appropriateness to behave in ways that can ultimately lead to their further exclusion.

It was furthermore demonstrated that it is important to consider the spatial qualities of socio-economic exclusion, where street culture tends to be associated with particular impoverished sections of the city. Variously inner-city and suburban, whether market-led, municipally planned or informally squatted, systems of housing have tended to collect and concentrate disadvantaged populations within areas that themselves become markers of exclusion. Of course, there are numerous nuances that nevertheless exist in this situation. The residents of 'slum' areas may indeed experience them as safe and familiar spaces of pride. Forms of street cultural practice, both criminal and expressive, can draw heavily on this sense of space. On the one hand, areas of concentrated disadvantage can harbour criminal institutions, shielding them from the interventions of state and security actors. On the other hand, street cultural institutions, such as drug trading gangs, can provide proto welfare and security services in those spaces that the state totally neglects.

In the realms of street cultural expressivity, from urban music to street art and dance, identifying with street culturally potent spaces can be a particularly important process. This can be constituted by the invocation of more abstract/discursive notions of 'ghettoness', or by representing one's own neighbourhood proudly. The connections between people and place have, however, been rendered more complex by the conditions of late-modernity.

Contemporary property markets have disrupted traditional patterns of settlement, variously pushing out the poor into new and different spaces, forcing them to cling more firmly to shrinking familiar territories or indeed rendering them increasingly nomadic across urban spaces. There are also smaller-scale consequences to the great swirls of migration occurring in late-modernity, whereby some people live lives of precarious residence straddled between disadvantaged spaces in the developed and developing worlds. The increasing prevalence of digital culture, moreover, has specific street spatial consequences, where online spaces can become the sites for interpersonal disputes and expressive practices that bleed into 'real-world' practices.

Whilst there have been spatial changes that have effected matters of street culture, this is not always the case. There continue to be disputes around 'territories' that are informally and symbolically claimed and disputed. It is important, however, to recognize that there are a diversity of ways in which street cultural practitioners (indeed at various levels of dedication) relate to their surrounding spaces. There has been less variety and nuance, unfortunately, in many academic and governmental understandings of street cultural groupings, which tend to imagine them as operating according to quite outmoded and unsuitable notions of 'the gang'. This book has argued for an end to the use of the term as a serious component of academic discourse and instead offers the more versatile and robust notion of street culture (subject to appropriate supplementary explanation) as a more suitable alternative.

A range of street cultural practices were described and analysed. On the one hand, these tend to be most associated with street crime and, on the other, more frequently identified within questions of lifestyle, leisure, cultural expressivity and media production. It was argued that clear distinctions between these categories are not always apparent, particularly between crimes that have a strong expressive element or practices that involve matters of trespass or criminal damage, as well as those with ambiguous connections to those who profess a criminal lifestyle. Indeed, a range of concerns around public behaviour can serve to criminalize weaker street cultural practices that may not otherwise be considered as crime. At the weaker end of the street cultural spectrum, a number of practices such as 'hanging around' and petty 'delinquency' feature frequently within general western youth cultures. Both street and youth cultures value the assertion of autonomy and independent activity. The young (even those who belong to more included groups) can be understood as experiencing a temporary form of socio-economic exclusion to some extent, which may partially explain this resonance.

Stronger, more harmful street cultural practices can be more or less instrumental and/or expressive. Acts such as dedicated theft or drug dealing are part and parcel of economic strategies judged by those ensconced in street culture to be appropriate, but more than this, provide at times a range of emotionally and existentially satisfying sensations. Similarly, whilst embodied violent potential and actualized violent behaviour perform significant regulatory functions in street life, they operate not just according to street norms, but also occur due to the emotional dynamics of particular moments. There is a street cultural logic which describes how and why violence takes place in street worlds, but this should be treated with caution because unpredictability and the less calculable effects of emotions also have their role.

The more expressive forms of street cultural practice from urban music and streetwear fashion, to its expression in bodily forms and modes of speech, not only can be explained through principles set out in this book, but are significant repertoires informing contemporary cultural-commercial practice and youth marketing. Those modes of being and behaviour which have stemmed from conditions of urban poverty are valuable commodities to those who realize their resonance with notions of cool and the desire of young consumers for decontextualized symbols of transgression. Street cultural expression from hip-hop music and dance to wearing low-slung trousers and baseball caps has greatly influenced the range of products made available to youth markets, but it also has informed the production and marketing architectures that secure their availability and popularity. In this sense, there is a contradiction in society's reception of street culture: fear and exclusion on the one hand and fascination and desire on the other.

Of course, this phenomenon does not create vast opportunities for the urban disadvantaged within the cultural industries (except for a minute number of exceptions). Rather, it vests those skilled in plumbing the vast online repositories of obscure practices and styles with the tools to carve out careers, provided they have the requisite business acumen and ability to capitalize on contacts. The harsh socio-economic exclusions that produce street culture are not ultimately upset by this symbolic, surface-level inclusion of street style within mainstream cultures. Indeed, overall it can simply be understood as an additional form of exploitation. Ironically, the stylistic expression of marginalized populations is often criticized for its gaucheness and lack of taste. It is usually only the styles and modes of being associated with particular demographic categories of the urban poor that have wider resonance (see Chapter 3) and when these are processed through branding exercises which distil out the commodifiable cool (see Chapter 6).

Such forms of intense consumerist commerce are one feature of late-capitalist economics. Another defining trait of this period in socio-economic history is the dominance and prevalence of neoliberal modes of global trade and governance. It was argued that these ideological and now ubiquitous principles have driven the inequalities in wealth that have resulted in particularly pronounced forms of economic marginalization which exist in very different ways between the developed and developing worlds. Moreover, such principles have seen states open up economic activity, remove regulation and privatize/remove state provision to the extent that their capacities to govern have diminished, and thus they resort to more coercive forms of crime and immigration control to shore up their falling power. The net effect of these broad structural arrangements is to increase the kinds of exclusion which give rise to street cultures in the first place.

Globalization is linked to street culture in other significant ways, where movements of people, goods and services (legal or otherwise) and ideas have helped shape the character of different local variations. Such differences are particularly relevant, where the extreme forms of material deprivation and violent oppression suffered by many in the developing world give rise to what are arguably particularly strong and institutionalized forms of street culture. Public fascination in the developed world towards the street expressivity found in spaces of southern deprivation exists to the extent that these too are harvested for the production of cool. The traffic is, however, significantly denser in the other direction where western modes of consumerism exert strong cultural pressures on the poor in the developing world. Here goods branded through street culturally informed tactics find favour amongst street cultural practitioners, despite their particularly deprived circumstances. Moreover, forms of street cultural expressivity such as rap music incongruously feature as part of the iconography of militias fighting in bloody conflicts.

It is that dangerous and transgressive character of street culture that establishes it as the powerful cultural trope that it is. It should not, however, be confused with 'resistance', a word which given its legacy in critical analysis should probably be reserved for phenomena more overtly political in nature. Of course, whilst there is a politics to it, street culture generally channels the defiance of exclusion as opposed to practical action towards altering configurations of power. Whilst street cultural populations and practices have been widely critiqued in public debate, labelled as destructive and morally deficient, the irony lies in the fact that their values share much with the profit-before-all-else mores of the contemporary neoliberal establishment. Street culture is defiant and aggressive, perhaps even oppositional in the normative stances it champions (e.g. against cooperating with police forces), but it runs parallel with, not counter to, dominant ideologies. It operates according to behavioural expectations that once did not exclude people in the same way as they do now.

Significantly, these street behavioural expectations are not just the product of socio-economic exclusion, they perpetuate and exacerbate it, prompting individuals to reject the particular routes to inclusion that are held out as appropriate. Unfortunately, questions hang over the extent to which following such behavioural codes around avoiding 'mischief', crime and drugs whilst engaging earnestly with education and the world of work will yield full socio-economic inclusion for all, particularly the young.

Ultimately, the issues raised and the analyses offered by this book are presented with a number of implications in mind. Firstly, it is clear that there is something to be gained by considering issues of street crime and the less-pressing seeming matters of lifestyle side-by-side. In particular contexts, these matters are inseparable. There is arguably scope for more research which adopts this approach, particularly in an interdisciplinary manner. In terms of research methodologies, ethnography with its attentiveness to lived experience and subjectivities has proved itself an invaluable tool to better understand the presence of social structures in everyday life. It captures the immediacy, pressures and visceral satisfactions of street life in a manner that allows for a broader range of theoretical interpretations and popular understandings. Other methodologies, of course, play their roles in the generation of knowledge, but exist at times at a greater level of abstracted removal from their subjects. The challenge is to retain a sense of subjective appreciation and participant orientation. For those of us who share an interest in many of the matters discussed in the book, would it be worth speaking about 'street cultural studies'?

Secondly, I have arguably made a case for understanding the place of street cultural practice within the lives of particular sections of the urban poor. Given the ways in which it can give purpose and determination to many who society would mislabel as lazy and ill-disciplined, there is vast potential here to develop forms of crime prevention that are more attuned to the world views of those they are aimed at. Providing individuals with tools to achieve economic and personal realization in a manner that sits comfortably with their norms and concerns is not necessarily within the gift of any kind of intervention – state, voluntary or otherwise. With that said, however, programmes which are seeking to 'make a difference' can perhaps adopt their strategies to these sensitivities.

There is also perhaps scope to recognize the role that street cultural institutions play in the social and economic life of those living in spaces of pronounced marginalization. Are these always an absolute enemy of popular welfare and the common good, or at times is their relationship to these abstract ideals somewhat more complex? When examining the role that certain street cultural institutions play within certain developing world slums, it is clear that with all the harm that they inflict, this is not the full extent of their interactions with local populations. Indeed, it can be within conflicts with such groups, or in attempting to mitigate the worst effects of conflicts between such groups, that states might open up to more innovative ways of responding to the needs of their most disadvantaged populations. Overall, social policy could be more open to ways of working with, as opposed to against, street life.

Of course, in order to respond to the existence of street culture in a less adversarial manner and indeed to stem its existence and potency, what is arguably ultimately required is the reduction of levels of socio-economic exclusion. Such matters are particularly complex, with legacies of material poverty, cultural and often ethnic marginalization, to tackle. The kinds of vast investments of resources and political will that are required to begin denting these malign tendencies are most likely the interventions that will have sustainable success in the long term. Although there might be an ideological tendency to seek the salvation of the urban poor through market mechanisms, the current state of the global economy, as experienced in popular, everyday life, would arguably suggest that this has not thus far succeeded. What can and should be done to address the human problems underpinning and indeed caused by street culture are questions, however, for research of their own.

Bibliography

Aas, K. F. (2007), *Globalization and Crime*, London: Sage.

Abrams, D. and Hogg, M. (2002), *Social Identifications: A Social Psychology of Intergroup Relations and Group Processes*, London: Routledge.

Adler, P. and Adler, P. (1993), *Wheeling and Dealing: An Ethnography of an Upper-Level Drug Dealing and Smuggling Community*, New York: Columbia University Press.

Agnew, R. (1992), 'Foundation for a General Strain Theory', *Criminology*, 30(1), 47–87.

Aldridge, J., Medina-Ariz, J. and Ralphs, R. (2012), 'Counting Gangs: Conceptual and Validity Problems with the Eurogang Definition', in Esbensen, F. and Maxson, C. (eds.), *Youth Gangs in International Perspective: Results from the Eurogang Program of Research*, Berlin: Springer, 35–51.

Alvelos, H. (2004), 'The Desert of Imagination in the City of Signs: Cultural Implications of Sponsored Transgression and Branded Graffiti', in Ferrell, J., Hayward, K., Morrison, W. and Presdee, M. (eds.), *Cultural Criminology Unleashed*, London: Psychology Press, 181–192.

Anderson, E. (1999), *Code of the Street: Decency, Violence and the Moral Life of the Inner City*, New York: Norton & Co.

Anderson, G. (2008), *Cityboy: Beer and Loathing in the Square Mile*, London: Hachette.

Anderson, N. (1927), *The Hobo: The Sociology of the Homeless Man*, Chicago: The University of Chicago Press.

Appadurai, A. (1996), *Modernity at Large: Cultural Dimensions of Globalization*, Minneapolis: University of Minnesota Press.

Arana, A. (2005), 'How the Street Gangs Took Central America', *Foreign Affairs*, 84(3), 98–110.

Ash, J. (2009), *Dress Behind Bars: Prison Clothing as Criminality*, London: IB Tauris & Company Limited.

Atkinson, M. (2009), 'Parkour, Anarcho-Environmentalism, and Poiesis', *Journal of Sport & Social Issues*, 33(2), 169–194.

Back, L. (1996), *New Ethnicities and Urban Culture*, London: Routledge.

Back, L. (1997), 'Nazism and the Call of the Jitterbug', in Thomas, H. (ed.), *Dance in the City*, New York: St. Martin's Press, 175–197.

Bahadur, J. (2011), *The Pirates of Somalia: Inside Their Hidden World*, London: Random House LLC.

Baker, S. (2012), 'Policing the Riots', in Briggs, D. (ed.), *The English Riots of 2011: A Summer of Discontent*, Hampshire: Waterside Press, 169–192.

Bakrania, F. (2013), *Bhangra and Asian Underground: South Asian Music and the Politics of Belonging in Britain*, Durham: Duke University Press.

Ball, R. and Curry, G. (1995), 'The Logic of Definition in Criminology: Purposes and Methods for Defining "gangs"', *Criminology*, 33(2), 225–245.

Bannister, J., Fyfe, N. and Kearns, A. (2006), 'Respectable or Respectful? (In) Civility and the City', *Urban Studies*, 43(5–6), 919–937.

Barry, M. (2006), *Youth Offending in Transition: The Search for Social Recognition*, London: Routledge.

Baudrillard, J. (1983), *Simulations*, New York: Semiotext(e).

Baudrillard, J. (1994), *Simulacra*, Ann Arbor: University of Michigan Press.

Baugh, J. (1983), *Black Street Speech*, Austin: University of Texas Press.

Bauman, Z. (1998), *Globalization: The Human Consequences*, New York: Columbia University Press.

Bauman, Z. (2000), *Liquid Modernity*, Cambridge: Polity Press.

Bauman, Z. (2004), *Work, Consumerism and the New Poor*, Buckingham: Open University Press.

Beck, U. (1992), *Risk Society: Towards a New Modernity*, London: Sage.

Becker, H. (1963), *Outsiders: Studies in the Sociology of Deviance*, New York: Free Press.

Bengtsson, T. (2012), 'Learning to Become a "gangster"?', *Journal of Youth Studies*, 15(6), 677–692.

Blackman, S. (2004) *'Chilling Out': The Cultural Politics of Substance Consumption, Youth and Drug Policy*, Maidenhead: McGrawHill-Open University Press

Blackman, S. (2005), 'Youth Subcultural Theory: A Critical Engagement with the Concept, Its Origins and Politics, from the Chicago School to Postmodernism', *Journal of Youth Studies*, 8(1), 1–20.

Blerk, L. (2005), 'Negotiating Spatial Identities: Mobile Perspectives on Street Life in Uganda', *Children's Geographies*, 3(1), 5–21.

Bluestone, B. and Harrison, B. (1982), *The Deindustrialization of America*, New York: Basic Books.

Bogazianos, D. (2012), *Five Grams: Crack Cocaine, Rap Music, and the War on Drugs*, New York: New York University Press.

Borja, J. and Castells, M. (1997), *Local and Global: Management of Cities in the Information Age*, London: Earthscan.

Bourdieu, P. (1977) *Outline of a Theory of Practice*, Cambridge: Cambridge University Press.

Bourdieu, P. (1984), *Distinction: A Social Critique of the Judgement of Taste*, Cambridge: Harvard University Press.

Bourdieu, P. (1986) 'The Forms of Capital', in Richardson, J. G. (ed.), *Handbook of Theory and Research for the Sociology of Education*, New York: Greenwood, 241–260.

Bourdieu, P. (1988) *Practical Reason: On the Theory of Action*: Cambridge: Polity Press.

Bourdieu, P. (1990) *The Logic of Practice*, Stanford: Stanford University Press.

Bourdieu, P. and Thompson, J. (1991), *Language and Symbolic Power*, Cambridge: Harvard University Press.

Bourgois, P. (1995/2003), *In Search of Respect: Selling Crack in El Barrio*, Cambridge: Cambridge University Press.

Bowling, B. (1999), *Violent Racism: Victimisation, Policing and Social Context*, Oxford: Oxford University Press.

Bowling, B. and Phillips, C. (2003), 'Policing Ethnic Minority Communities', in. Newburn, T. (ed.), *Handbook of Policing*, Collumption: Willan, 528–555.

Boyd, J. (2004), 'Dance, Culture, and Popular Film', *Feminist Media Studies*, 4(1), 67–83.

Bradley, L. (2001), *Bass Culture: When Reggae Was King*, London: Penguin.

Brezina, T., Agnew, R., Cullen, T. and Wright, J. P. (2004), 'A Quantitative Assessment of Elijah Anderson's Subculture of Violence Thesis and His Contribution to Youth Violence Research', *Youth Violence and Juvenile Justice*, 2(4), 303–328.

Brookman, F., Bennett, T., Hochstetler, A. and Copes, H. (2011), 'The "Code of the Street" and the Generation of Street Violence in the UK', *European Journal of Criminology*, 8(1), 17–31.

Brookman, F., Copes, H. and Hochstetler, A. (2011), 'Street Codes as Formula Stories: How Inmates Recount Violence', *Journal of Contemporary Ethnography*, 40(4), 397–424.

Brotherton, D. (2008), 'Beyond Social Reproduction: Bringing Resistance Back in Gang Theory', *Theoretical Criminology*, 12(1), 55–77.

Brotherton, D. and Barrios, L. (2004), *The Almighty Latin King and Queen Nation: Street Politics and the Transformation of a New York City Gang*, New York: Columbia University Press.

Brotherton, D. and Barrios, L. (2011). *Banished to the Homeland: Dominican Deportees and their Stories of Exile*, New York: Columbia University Press.

Brown, J. (2010), 'Buzz and Rumble: Global Pop Music and Utopian Impulse', *Social Text*, 28(1 & 2), 125–146.

Brown, R., Novak, K. and Frank, J. (2009), 'Identifying Variation in Police Officer Behavior Between Juveniles and Adults', *Journal of Criminal Justice*, 37(2), 200–208.

Brunson, R. and Miller, J. (2006), 'Young Black Men and Urban Policing in the United States', *British Journal of Criminology*, 46(4), 613–640.

Buccellato, J. (2014), 'Obscene Remainders: Neoliberalism and the Gang Crisis Narrative', *Journal of Theoretical & Philosophical Criminology*, 6(2), 129–144.

Bulmer, M. (1984), *The Chicago School of Sociology: Institutionalisation, Diversity and the Rise of Social Research*, Chicago: University of Chicago Press.

Butterfield, F. (1995), *All God's Children: The Bosket Family and the American Tradition of Violence*, New York: Avon.

Caputo-Levine, D. (2012), 'The Yard Face: The Contributions of Inmate Interpersonal Violence to the Carceral Habitus', *Ethnography*, 14(2), 165–185.

Carney, P. and Miller, V. (2009), 'Vague Spaces', in Jansson, A. and Lagerkvist, A. (eds.), *Strange Spaces: Explorations in Mediated Obscurity*, Farnham: Ashgate Publications, 33–56.

Carr, P., Napolitano, L. and Keating, J. (2007), 'We Never Call the Cops and Here Is Why: A Qualitative Examination of Legal Cynicism in Three Philadelphia Neighborhoods', *Criminology*, 45(2), 445–480.

Carver, T. (ed.) (1991), *The Cambridge Companion to Marx*, Cambridge: Cambridge University Press.

Castells, M. (1996), *The Rise of the Network Society. Vol. 1: The Information Age: Economy, Society and Culture*, Oxford: Blackwell.

Castells, M. (2010), *The Power of Identity. Vol. 2: The Information Age: Economy, Society, and Culture*, 2nd ed., London: John Wiley & Sons.

Chambliss, W. (1973), 'The Saints and the Roughnecks', *Society*, 11(1), 24–31.

Chang, J. (2005), *Can't Stop Won't Stop: A History of the Hip-Hop Generation*, New York: Picador.

Chappell, B. (2010), 'Custom Contestations: Lowriders and Urban Space', *City & Society*, 22(1), 25–47.

Charles, C. (2009), 'Violence, Musical Identity and the Celebrity of the Spanglers Crew in Jamaica', *Wadabagei: A Journal of the Caribbean and Its Diaspora*, 12(2), 52–79.

Charlesworth, S. (2000), *A Phenomenology of Working-class Experience*, Cambridge: Cambridge University Press.

Choongh, S. (1998), 'Policing the Dross: A Social Disciplinary Model of Policing', *The British Journal of Criminology*, 38, 623–634.

Clarke, J. (2002), 'The Three Rs: Repression, Rescue and Rehabilitation, Ideologies of Control for Working Class Youth', in Muncie, J., Hughes, G. and McLaughlin, E. (eds.), *Youth Justice: Critical Readings*, London: Open University Press, 123–137.

Cloward, R. and Ohlin L. (1960), *Delinquency and Opportunity: A Theory of Delinquent Gangs*, London: Routledge.

Cohen, A. (1955), *Delinquent Boys: The Culture of the Gang*, New York: Palgrave Macmillan.

Cohen, S. (1972), *Folk Devils and Moral Panic*, London: MacGibbon & Kee.

Cohen, S. (1973), 'Property Destruction: Motives and Meanings', in Ward, C. (ed.), *Vandalism*, London: Architectural Press, 23–53.

Cohen, S. (1985), *Visions of Social Control: Crime, Punishment and Classification*, Cambridge: Polity Press.

Coleman, L. (2007), 'The Gendered Violence of Development: Imaginative Geographies of Exclusion in the Imposition of Neo-liberal Capitalism', *The British Journal of Politics & International Relations*, 9(2), 204–219.

Coleman, R., Sim, J., Tombs, S. and Whyte, D. (2009), 'Introduction: State, Power, Crime', in Coleman, R., Sim, J., Tombs, S. and Whyte, D. (eds.), *State, Power, Crime*, London: Sage, 1–19.

Connell, R. (1995), *Masculinities*, Cambridge: Polity Press.

Connell, R. (2007), *Southern Theory: The Global Dynamics of Knowledge in Social Science*, Cambridge: Polity Press.

Connell, R. and Messerschmidt, J. (2005), 'Hegemonic Masculinity: Rethinking the Concept', *Gender & Society*, 19(6), 829–859.

Conquergood, D. (1994a), 'Homeboys and Hoods: Gang Communication and Cultural Space', in Frey, L. (ed.), *Group Communication in Context: Studies of Natural Groups*, Hillsdale: Lawrence Erlbaum Associates.

Conquergood, D. (1994b), 'How Street Gangs Problematize Patriotism', in Simons, H. and Billig, M. (eds.), *After Postmodernism: Reconstructing Ideology Critique*, Thousand Oaks: Sage.

Corrigan, P. (1979), *Schooling the Smash Street Kids*, London: Palgrave Macmillan.

Cottee, S. and Hayward, K. (2011), 'Terrorist (E) Motives: The Existential Attractions of Terrorism', *Studies in Conflict & Terrorism*, 34(12), 963–986.

Crawford, A. (2009), 'Criminalizing Sociability Through Anti-Social Behaviour Legislation: Dispersal Powers, Young People and the Police', *Youth Justice*, 9(1), 5–26.

Currie, E. (1997), 'Market, Crime and Community Toward a Mid-Range Theory of Post-Industrial Violence', *Theoretical Criminology*, 1(2), 147–172.

Curry, G. and Decker, S. (2003), *Confronting Gangs: Crime and Community*, Los Angeles: Roxbury Publishing Company.

Curtis, R. (1998), 'Improbable Transformation of Inner-City Neighborhoods: Crime, Violence, Drugs, and Youth in the 1990s', *Journal of Criminal Law and Criminology*, 88(4), 1233–1276.

Daniel, I. (2012), 'Poverty, Road Culture and Deviance Among Areaboys in Lagos Central Neighbourhood', *International Journal of Prevention and Treatment*, 1(1), 1–10.

Davis, M. (1990), *Cities of Quartz*, London: Verso.

Davis, M. (1992), 'The LA Inferno', *Socialist Review*, 22(1), 57–81.

Davis, M. (2006), *Planet of Slums*, London: Verso.

De Certeau, M. (1984), *The Practice of Everyday Life*, Berkeley: University of California Press.

De Jong, A. and Schuilenburg, M. (2006), *Mediapolis: Popular Culture and the City*, Rotterdam: 010 Publishers.

Decker, S. and Van Winkle, B. (1996), *Life in the Gang: Family, Friends and Violence*, Cambridge: Cambridge University Press.

DeMello, M. (1995), 'Not Just for Bikers Anymore: Popular Representations of American Tattooing', *Journal of Popular Culture*, 29, 37–52.

de Sousa Santos, B. (2002), *Toward a New Legal Common Sense: Law, Globalization, and Emancipation*, Cambridge: Cambridge University Press.

Densley, J. and Stevens, A. (2014), ' "We'll Show you Gang" ': The Subterranean Structuration of Gang Life in London, *Criminology and Criminal Justice*, online first doi:10.1177/1748895814522079.

Devereaux, A. (2007), ' "What Chew Know About Down the Hill?" Baltimore Club Music, Subgenre Crossover, and the New Subcultural Capital of Race and Space', *Journal of Popular Music Studies* 19, 311–341.

Dimou, E. (2013), *'Revolutionising' Subcultural Theory: The Cases of Cuban Underground Rap and Cuban Reggaeton*, Unpublished PhD Thesis, Canterbury: University of Kent.

Doran, M. (2004), 'Negotiating Between Bourge and Racaille: Verlan as Youth Identity Practice in Suburban Paris', in Pavlenko, A. and Blackledge, A. (eds.), *Negotiation of Identities in Multilingual Contexts*, Clevedon: Multilingual Matters.

Douglas, M. (1966/2003), *Purity and Danger: An Analysis of Concepts of Pollution and Taboo*, London: Routledge.

Dowdney, L. (2003), *Children of the Drug Trade: A Case Study of Children in Organised Armed Violence in Rio de Janeiro*, Rio de Janeiro: 7Letras.

Dowdney, L. (2005), *Neither War nor Peace: International Comparisons of Children and Youth in Organised Armed Violence*, Rio de Janeiro: 7Letras.

Downes, D. (1966), *The Delinquent Solution: A Study in Sub-cultural Theory*, London: Routledge & Kegan Paul.

Duneier, M. (1999), *Sidewalk*, New York: Farrar, Straus & Giroux.

Elias, N. (1969/1994), *The Civilizing Process*, Trans. Edmund Jephcott, Oxford: Blackwell.

Elias, N. and Scotson, J. (1994), *The Established and the Outsiders: A Social Enquiry into Community Problems*, London: Sage.

Engels, F. (1891/2009), The Condition of the Working Class in England, Oxford: Oxford University Press.

Esbensen, F. and Maxson, C. (eds.) (2012), '*Youth Gangs in International Perspective: Results from the Eurogang Program of Research*, Berlin: Springer.

Escobar, A. (2004), 'Development, Violence and the New Imperial Order', *Development*, 47(1), 15–21.

Felson, M. (2002), *Crime and Everyday Life*, 3rd ed., Thousand Oaks: Sage.

Fenwick, M. and Hayward, K. (2000), 'Youth Crime, Excitement and Consumer Culture: The Reconstruction of Aetiology in Contemporary Theoretical Criminology', in Pickford. J. (ed.), *Youth Justice: Theory and practice*, London: Cavendish.

Ferrell, J. (1996), *Crimes of Style: Urban Graffiti and the Politics of Criminality*, Boston: Northeastern University Press.

Ferrell, J. (2001), *Tearing Down the Streets: Adventures in Urban Anarchy*, New York: Palgrave Macmillan.

Ferrell, J. (2004), 'Style Matters', in Ferrell, J., Hayward, K., Morrison, W. and Presdee, M. (eds.), *Cultural Criminology Unleashed*, London: Glasshouse Press.

Ferrell, J., Hayward, K. and Young, J. (2008), *Cultural Criminology: An Invitation*, London: Sage.

Ferrell, J. and Ilan, J. (2013), 'Crime, Culture, and Everyday Life', in Hale, C., Hayward, K., Wahidin, A. and Wincup, E. (eds.), *Criminology*, 2nd ed., Oxford: Oxford University Press.

FitzGerald, M. and Hale, C. (1996), *Ethnic Minorities: Victimisation and Racial Harassment: Findings from the 1988 and 1992 British Crime Surveys*, Home Office Research Study 154, London: Home Office.

Fleetwood, J. (2014), 'Keeping Out of Trouble: Female Crack Cocaine Dealers in England', *European Journal of Criminology*, 11(1), 91–109.

Forman, M. (2002), *The 'Hood Comes First: Race, Space, and Place in Rap and Hip-Hop*, Middletown: Wesleyan University Press.

Foster, J. (1990), *Villains: Crime and Community in the Inner City*, London: Routledge.

France, A. (2007), *Understanding Youth in Late Modernity*, Maidenhead: McGraw-Hill International.

Frank, T. (1998), *The Conquest of Cool: Business Culture, Counterculture, and the Rise of Hip Consumerism*, Chicago: University of Chicago Press.

Fraser, A. (2013) 'Street Habitus: Gangs, Territorialism and Social Change in Glasgow', *Journal of Youth Studies*', 16(8), 970–985.

Gale, D. (1996), *Understanding Urban Unrest: From Reverend King to Rodney King*, Thousand Oaks: Sage.

Garbin, D. and Millington, G. (2012), 'Territorial Stigma and the Politics of Resistance in a Parisian Banlieue: La Courneuve and Beyond', *Urban Studies*, 49(10), 2067–2083.

Garcia, B. (2006), *Where'd You Get Those?: New York City's Sneaker Culture: 1960–1987*, New York: Testify Books.

Garland, D. (2001), *The Culture of Control: Crime and Social Order in Contemporary Society*, Oxford: Oxford University Press.

Garot, R. (2007), ' "Where You From!" Gang Identity as Performance', *Journal of Contemporary Ethnography*, 36(1), 50–84.

Gibson, O. and Watts, J. (2013), World Cup: Rio Favelas Being 'socially cleansed' in Runup to Sporting Events, *The Guardian*, Friday 6 December 2013, available at http://www.theguardian.com/world/2013/dec/05/world-cup-favelas-socially-cleansed-olympics, accessed 28/01/2015.

Giddens, A. (1991), *Modernity and Self-Identity: Self and Identity in the Late Modern Age*, Cambridge: Polity Press.

Gilfoyle, T. (2004), 'Street-Rats and Gutter-Snipes: Child Pickpockets and Street Culture in New York City, 1850–1900', *Journal of Social History*, 37(4), 853–862.

Gill, O. (1977), *Luke Street: Housing Policy, Conflict and the Creation of the Delinquent Area*, London: Macmillan.

Gillespie, N., Lovett, T. and Garner, W. (1992), *Youth Work and Working Class Youth Culture: Rules and Resistance in West Belfast*, Buckingham: Open University Press.

Gilman, N., Goldhammer, J. and Weber, S. (2011), 'Deviant Globalization', in Gilman, N., Goldhammer, J. and Weber, S. (eds.), *Deviant Globalization: Black Market Economy 'in the 21st Century*, New York: Bloomsbury Publishing.

Gilroy, P. (1993), *The Black Atlantic: Modernity and Double Consciousness*, Cambridge: Harvard University Press.

Giroux, H. (2012), Hoodie Politics: Trayvon Martin and Racist Violence in Post Racial America. *Truth-out.org*, available at http://www.smirkingchimp.com/thread/henry-giroux/42367/hoodie-politics-trayvon-martin-and-racist-violence-in-post-racial-america, accessed 22/10/2013.

Gladwell, M. (1997) 'The Coolhunt', *The New Yorker*, 17 March 1997, 78–88.

Goldstein, D. (2003), *Laughter Out of Place: Race, Class, Violence, and Sexuality in a Rio Shantytown*, Stanford: University of California Press.

Goodley, S. (2012) 'Goldman Sachs "Muppet" Trader Says Unsophisticated Clients Targeted', www.guardian.com, 22 October 2012, available at http://www.theguardian.com/business/2012/oct/22/goldman-sachs-muppets-greg-smith-clients, accessed 28/01/2015.

Grosfoguel, R. (2004), 'Race and Ethnicity or Racialized Ethnicities? Identities Within Global Coloniality', *Ethnicities*, 4(3), 315–336.

Grundetjern, H. and Sandberg, S. (2012), 'Dealing with a Gendered Economy: Female Drug Dealers and Street Capital', *European Journal of Criminology*, 9(6), 621–635.

Gunst, L. (2003), *Born Fi' Dead*, Edinburgh: Canongate Books.

Gunter, A. (2008), 'Growing up Bad: Black Youth, Road Culture and Badness in an East London Neighbourhood', *Crime, Media, Culture*, 4(3), 349–366.

Haddad, Y. and Balz, M. (2006), 'The October Riots in France: A Failed Immigration Policy or the Empire Strikes Back?', *International Migration*, 44(2), 23–34.

Hagedorn, J. (2007), 'Gangs in Late Modernity', in Hagedorn, J. (ed.), *Gangs in the Global City: Alternatives to Traditional Criminology*, Chicago: University of Illinois Press.

Hagedorn, J. (2008), *A World of Gangs: Armed Young Men and Gangsta Culture*, Minneapolis: University of Minnesota Press.

Hagedorn, J. and Macon, P. (1988), *People and Folks. Gangs, Crime and the Underclass in a Rustbelt City*, Chicago: Lake View Press.

Hall, S. and Jefferson, T. (eds.) (1976), *Resistance Through Rituals: Youth Subcultures in Post-war Britain*, London: Hutchinson.

Hall, S. and Winlow, S. (2007), 'Cultural Criminology and Primitive Accumulation: A Formal Introduction for Two Strangers who Should Really Become more Intimate', *Crime, Media, Culture*, 3(1), 82–90.

Hall, S., Winlow, S. and Ancrum, C. (2008), *Criminal Identities and Consumer Culture: Crime, Exclusion and the New Culture of Narcissism*, Collumpton: Willan.

Hallsworth, S. (2005), *Street Crime*, Collumpton: Willan.

Hallsworth, S. (2011), 'Gangland Britain', in Goldson, B. (ed.), *Youth in Crisis?:'gangs', Territoriality and Violence*, London: Routledge.

Hallsworth, S. (2013), *The Gang and Beyond: Interpreting Violent Street Worlds*, London: Palgrave Macmillan.

Hallsworth, S. and Silverstone, D. (2009), ' "That's Life Innit" A British Perspective on Guns, Crime and Social Order', *Criminology and Criminal Justice*, 9(3), 359–377.

Hallsworth, S. and Young, T. (2008), 'Gang Talk and Gang Talkers: A Critique', *Crime, Media, Culture*, 4(2), 175–195.

Hannerz, U. (1969), *Soulside: Inquiries into Ghetto Culture and Community*, Chicago: University of Chicago Press.

Harding, S. (2014), *The Street Casino: Survival in Violent Street Gangs*, Bristol: Policy Press.

Hartigan, J. (1997), 'Unpopular Culture: The Case of "white trash" ', *Cultural Studies*, 11(2), 316–343.

Harvey, D. (1973/2009), *Social Justice and the City*, Athens: University of Georgia Press.

Harvey, D. (1990), *The Condition of Postmodernity: An Enquiry into the Origins of Cultural Change*, Oxford: Blackwell.

Harvey, D. (2005), *A Brief History of Neoliberalism*, Oxford: Oxford University Press.

Haylett, C. (2003), 'Culture, Class and Urban Policy: Reconsidering Equality', *Antipode*, 35(1), 55–73.

Hayward, K. (2004), *City Limits: Crime, Consumer Culture and the Urban Experience*, London: Routledge.

Hayward, K. (2007), 'Situational Crime Prevention and its Discontents: Rational Choice Theory versus the "Culture of Now" ', *Social Policy & Administration*, 41(3), 232–250.

Hayward, K. (2012), 'Five Spaces of Cultural Criminology', *British Journal of Criminology*, 52(3), 441–462.

Hayward, K. and Ilan, J. (2011), 'Deviant Subcultures', in Bryant, C. (ed.), *Handbook of Deviant Behaviour*, London: Routledge, 233–239.

Hayward, K. and Yar, M. (2006), 'The "Chav" Phenomenon: Consumption, Media and the Construction of a New Underclass', *Crime Media Culture*, 2(1), 9–28.

Hearn, J. (1999), 'A Crisis in Masculinity, or New Agendas for Men?', in Walby, S. (ed.), *New Agendas for Women*, London: Palgrave Macmillan. pp. 148–168.

Hebdige, D. (1979/2005), *Subculture: The Meaning of Style*, London: Routledge.

Henry, W. (2006), *What the Deejay Said: A Critique from the Street!*, London: Learning By Choice Publications.

Hernandez, J. (2009), ' "Miss, You Look Like a Bratz Doll": On Chonga Girls and Sexual-Aesthetic Excess', *NWSA Journal*, 21(3), 63.

Hillyard, P. and Tombs, S. (2004), 'Beyond Criminology?', in Hillyard, P., Pantazis, C., Tombs, S. and Gordon, D. (eds.), *Beyond Criminology: Taking Harm Seriously*, London: Pluto Press, 2004.

Hobbs, D. (1988), *Doing the Business: Entrepreneurship, the Working Class and Detectives in the East End of London*, Oxford: Oxford University Press.

Hobbs, D. (1998), 'Going Down the Glocal: The Local Context of Organised Crime', *The Howard Journal of Criminal Justice*, 37(4), 407–442.

Hobbs, D. (2001), 'Ethnography and the Study of Deviance', in Atkinson, P., Coffey, A., Delamont, S., Lofland, J. and Lofland, L. (eds.), *Handbook of Ethnography*, Thousand Oaks: Sage.

Hobbs, D. (2013), *Lush Life: Constructing Organized Crime in the UK*, Oxford: Oxford University Press.

Hobbs, D., Lister, S., Hadfield, P. and Winlow, S. (2003), *Bouncers: Violence and Governance in the Night-Time Economy*, Oxford: Oxford University Press.

Hobsbawm, E. (1959/2010), *Bandits*, London: Hachette.

Hobsbawm, E. (1994), *The Age of Extremes: A History of the World, 1914–1991*, New York: Pantheon Books.

Hoffman, D. (2007), 'The City as Barracks: Freetown, Monrovia, and the Organization of Violence in Postcolonial African Cities', *Cultural Anthropology*, 22(3), 400–428.

Hollander, J. and Einwohner, R. (2004), 'Conceptualizing Resistance', *Sociological Forum*, 19(4), 533–554.

Holloway, S. and Valentine, G. (2000), 'Spatiality and the New Social Studies of Childhood', in Holloway, S. and Valentine, G. (eds.), *Children's Geographies: Playing, Living, Learning*, London: Routledge.

Horowitz, D. (2001), *The Deadly Ethnic Riot*, Berkeley: University of California Press.

Hujic, L. (2010), *The First to Know: How Hipsters and Mavericks Shape the Zeitgeist*, London: Bubble Publishing.

Hutnyk, J. (2000), *Critique of Exotica: Music, Politics and the Culture Industry*, London: Pluto Press.

Ilan, J. (2007) *Still Playing the Game: An Ethnography of Young People, Street Crime and Juvenile Justice in an inner-city Dublin community*, Unpublished PhD Thesis, Dublin: Dublin Institute of Technology.

Ilan, J. (2010), ' "If You Don't Let Us In, We'll Get Arrested": Class-Cultural Dynamics in the Provision of, and Resistance to, Youth Justice Work', *Youth Justice*, 10(1), 25–39.

Ilan, J. (2011), 'Reclaiming Respectability? The Class-Cultural Dynamics of Crime, Community and Governance in Inner-City Dublin', *Urban Studies*, 48(6), 1137–1155.

Ilan, J. (2012), ' "The Industry's the New Road": Crime, Commodification and Street Cultural Tropes in UK Urban Music', *Crime, Media, Culture*, 8(1), 39–55.

Ilan, J. (2013), 'Street Social Capital in the Liquid City', *Ethnography*, 14(1), 3–24.

Ilan, J. (2014), 'Commodifying Compliance? UK Urban Music and the New Mediascape', *Tijdscrift over Cultuur & Criminaliteit*, 4(1), 67–79.

Imrie, R. and Raco, M. (2003), 'Community and the Changing Nature of Urban Policy', in Imrie, R. and Raco, M. (eds.), *Urban Renaissance? New Labour, Community and Urban Policy*, Bristol: Policy Press, 3–36.

Innes, M. (2003), *Understanding Social Control: Crime and Social Order in Late Modernity*, New York: McGraw-Hill International.

Institut français de recherche en Afrique (1997), *Youth, Street Culture, and Urban Violence in Africa: Report of the International Symposium Held in Abidjan*, 5–7 May, Ibadan: IFRA/African Book Builders.

Irwin, J. and Cressey, D. (1962), 'Thieves, Convicts and the Inmate Culture', *Social Problems*, 10(2), 142–155.

Jackson, J. and Bradford, B. (2009), 'Crime, Policing and Social Order: On the Expressive Nature of Public Confidence in Policing', *British Journal of Sociology*, 60(3), 493–521.

Jackson, J. and Sunshine, J. (2007), 'Public Confidence in Policing: A Neo-Durkheimian Perspective', *British Journal of Criminology*, 47(2), 214–233.

Jacobs, J. (1961), *The Death and Life of Great American Cities*, New York: Random House.

Jacobs, B. (1999), *Dealing Crack: The Social World of Streetcorner Selling*, Boston: Northeastern University Press.

Jacobs, B. A. and Wright, R. (1999), 'Stick Up, Street Culture, and Offender Motivation', *Criminology*, 37(1), 149–174.

Jacobs, B. and Wright, R. (2006), *Street Justice: Retaliation in the Criminal Underworld*, Cambridge: Cambridge University Press.

Jaffe, R. (2012), 'Talkin' 'bout the Ghetto: Popular Culture and Urban Imaginaries of Immobility', *International Journal of Urban and Regional Research*, 36(4), 674–688.

Jeffries, M. (2011), *Thug Life: Race, Gender, and the Meaning of Hip-Hop*, Chicago: University of Chicago Press.

Jenkins, R. (1983), *Lads, Citizens and Ordinary Kids: Working-class Youth Life-Styles in Belfast*, London: Routledge and Paul.

Jenks, C. (2003), *Transgression*, London: Routledge.

Jessop, B. (1997), 'The Entrepreneurial City: Re-imaging Localities, Redesigning Economic Governance or Restructuring Capital?', in Jewson, N. and MacGregor, S. (eds.), *Transforming Cities: Contested Governance and New Spatial Divisions*, London: Routledge.

Jones, L. (2008), The Luxury Brand with a Chequered Past, Burberry's Shaken off Its Chav Image to Become the Fashionistas' Favourite Once More, Mail Online, 2 June 2008, http://www.dailymail.co.uk/femail/article-1023460/Burberrys-shaken-chav-image-fashionistas-favourite.html, accessed 15/10/13.

Karn, J. (2007), *Narratives of Neglect: Community, Regeneration and the Governance of Security*, Collumpton: Willan.

Katz, J. (1988), *Seductions of Crime: Moral and Sensual Attractions in Doing Evil*, New York: Basic Books.

Katz, J. and Jackson-Jacobs, C. (2003), 'The Criminologists' Gang', in Sumner, C. (ed.), *Blackwell Companion to Criminology*, Oxford: Blackwell, 91–124.

Keyes, C. (2002), *Rap Music and Street Consciousness*, Chicago: University of Illinois Press.

Kintrea, K., Bannister, J., Pickering, J., Reid, M. and Suzuki, N. (2008), *Young People and Territoriality in British Cities*, New York: Joseph Rowntree Foundation, available at http://www.jrf.org.uk/sites/files/jrf/2278-young-people-territoriality.pdf, accessed 28/01/2015.

Kitwana, B. (2005), *Why White Kids Love Hip-Hop: Wangstas, Wiggers, Wannabes, and the New Reality of Race in America*, New York: Basic Civitas Books.

Klein, M. and Maxson, C. (2006), *Street Gang Patterns and Policies*, Oxford: Oxford University Press.

Klein, M., Weerman, F. and Thornberry, T. (2006), 'Street Gang Violence in Europe', *European Journal of Criminology*, 3(4), 413–437.

Konkol, M., Janssesn, K. and Hortion, A. (2012), 'Lil Jojo Tweeted His Location Just Hours Before He was Slain', *Chicago Sun-Times*, 5 September 2012, available at http://www.suntimes.com/14964520-761/lil-jojo-murdered-in-chicago-police-now-looking-at-chief-keefs-tweets-source-says.html, accessed 27/09/2013.

Kramer, R., Rajah, V. and Sung, H. (2014), 'Entrapments of Consumerism: Adolescent Prisoners, Cognitive Treatment, and Consumption', *Journal of Consumer Culture*, online first doi: 10.1177/1469540514536196.

Kubrin, C. (2005), 'Gangstas, Thugs and Hustlas: Identity and the Code of the Street in Rap Music', *Social Problems*, 52(3), 360–378.

Lalor, K. (1999), 'Street Children: A Comparative Perspective', *Child Abuse and Neglect*, 23(8), 759–770.

Lea, J. and Stenson, K. (2007) 'Security, Sovereignty, and Non-State Governance "From Below"', *Canadian Journal of Law and Society*, 22(2), 9–27.

Leach, N. (2005), 'Belonging: Towards a Theory of Identification with Space', in Hillier, J. and Rooksby, E. (eds.), *Habitus: A Sense of Place*, 2nd ed., Aldershot: Ashgate.

Lee, J. (1981), 'Some Structural Aspects of Police Deviance in Relations with Minority Groups', in Shearing, C. (ed.), *Organisational Police Deviance*, Toronto: Butterworth.

Leeds, E. (1996), 'Cocaine and Parallel Polities in the Brazilian Urban Periphery: Constraints on Local-level Democratization', *Latin American Research Review*, 31(3), 47–83.

Lefebvre, H. (1991), *Critique of Everyday Life: Vol. 1*, Trans. John Moore, London: Verso.

Lewis, M. (1989), *Liar's Poker*, London: Hodder and Stoughton.

Liebow, E. (1967), *Tally's Corner – A Study of Negro Street Corner Men*, Boston: Little, Brow & Co.

Lim, W., Ting, D., Leo, E. and Jayanthy, C. (2013), 'Contemporary Perceptions of Body Modifications and Its Acceptability in the Asian Society: A Case of Tattoos and Body Piercings', *Asian Social Science*, 9(10), 37–42.

Lombard, K. (2007), 'Gen E (Generation Extremist): The Significance of Youth Culture and New Media in Youth Extremism', in Mendis, P., Lai, J., Dawson, E. and Abbass, H. (eds.), *Recent Advances in Security Technology, Proceedings of the 2007 RNSA Security Technology Conference*, Melbourne, 168.

López, V. (2014), 'Unaffordable Cities: Squatting in Caracas's Tower of Broken Dreams', *The Guardian*, 12 February 2014, available at http://www.theguardian.com/cities/2014/feb/12/unaffordable-cities-caracas-tower-squatting-families-bank, accessed 28/01/2015.

Lumsden, K. (2013), *Boy Racer Culture: Youth, Masculinity and Deviance*, London: Routledge.

Lury, C. (1998), *Prosthetic Culture: Photography, Memory and Identity*, London: Routledge.

Lyng, S. (1990), 'Edgework: A Social Psychological Analysis of Voluntary Risk Taking', *American Journal of Sociology*, 95(4), 851–886.

Lyng, S. (ed.) (2005), *Edgework: The Sociology of Risk-Taking*, New York: Psychology Press.

Macdonald, N. (2001), *The Graffiti Subculture*, New York: Palgrave Macmillan.

Macdonald, R. and Shildrick, T. (2007), 'Street Corner Society: Leisure Careers, Youth (Sub) Culture and Social Exclusion', *Leisure Studies*, 26(3), 339–355.

MacDonald, R., Shildrick, T., Webster, C. and Simpson, D. (2005), 'Growing up in Poor Neighbourhoods: The Significance of Class and Place in the Extended Transitions of "socially excluded"', *Young Adults' Sociology*, 39(5), 873–891.

Macpherson, W. (1999), *Inquiry into the Matters Arising from the Death of Stephen Lawrence: Final Report*, London: The Stationery Office.

Maher, L. (2000), *Sexed Work: Gender, Race, and Resistance in a Brooklyn Drug Market*, Oxford: Clarendon Press

Maher, L. and Curtis, R. (1992), 'Women on the Edge of Crime: Crack Cocaine and the Changing Contexts of Street-Level Sex Work in New York City', *Crime, Law and Social Change*, 18(3), 221–258.

Mailer, N. (1957), The White Negro, *Dissent Magazine*, Fall 1957, available at http://www.dissentmagazine.org/online_articles/the-white-negro-fall-1957, accessed 28/01/2015.

Majors, R. and Billson, J. (1992), *Cool Pose: The Dilemmas of African American Manhood in America*, New York: Lexington Books.

Malone, K. (2002), 'Street Life: Youth, Culture and Competing Uses of Public Space', *Environment and Urbanization*, 14(2), 157–168.

Manuel, P. and Marshall, W. (2006), 'The Riddim Method: Aesthetics, Practice, and Ownership in Jamaican Dancehall', *Popular Music*, 25(3), 447–470.

Marcuse, P. (1989), ' "Dual City": A Muddy Metaphor for a Quartered City,' *International Journal of Urban and Regional Research*, 13(4), 697–708.

Marsh, I. and Melville, G. (2011), 'Moral Panics and the British Media – A Look at Some Contemporary "Folk Devils"', *Internet Journal of Criminology*, 267–272.

Maruna, S. (2001), *Making Good*, Washington, DC: American Psychological Association Books.

Matthews, H., Limb, M. and Taylor, M. (2000), 'The "Street as Thirdspace"', in Holloway, S. and Valentine, G. (eds.), *Children's Geographies: Playing, Living, Learning*, London: Routledge, 63–79.

Matza, D. (1964), *Delinquency and Drift*, New York: John Wiley.

Matza, D. and Sykes, G. (1961), 'Juvenile Delinquency and Subterranean Values', *American Sociological Review*, 26(5), 712–719.

Mays, J. (1964), *Growing up in the City*, Liverpool: Liverpool University Press.

Mazelle, B. (2013), Solidarity Is for Miley Cyrus: The Racial Implications of Her VMA Performance, Blog Entry on *Jezebel.com* Posted 26 August 2013, available at http://groupthink.jezebel.com/solidarity-is-for-miley-cyrus-1203666732, accessed 03/12/13.

McBee, R. (2000), *Dance Hall Days: Intimacy and Leisure Among Working-Class Immigrants in the United States*, New York: New York University Press.

McRobbie, A. (1978/2006), 'Working Class Girls and the Culture of Femininity', in Centre for Contemporary Cultural Studies (ed.), *Women Take Issue*, London: Routledge, 96–108.

McRobbie, A. (1997), 'Dance Narratives and Fantasies of Achievement', in Desmond, J. (ed.), *Meaning in Motion*, Durham: Duke University Press, 207–231.

McVeigh, K. (2012), 'Chicago Hip-Hop Feud Deepens After Death of Joseph "Lil Jojo" Coleman', *guardian.co.uk*, Thursday 13 September 2012, available at http://www.guardian.co.uk/world/2012/sep/13/chicago-hip-hop-feud-joseph-lil-jojo-coleman, accessed 27/09/2013.

Measham, F. and Brain, K. (2005), '"Binge" Drinking, British Alcohol Policy and the New Culture of Intoxication', *Crime, Media, Culture*, 1(3), 262–283.

Merton, R. (1938), 'Social Structure and Anomie', *American Sociological Review*, 3(5), 672–682.

Messerschmidt, J. (1993), *Masculinities and Crime: Critique and Reconceptualization of Theory*, Lanham: Rowman & Littlefield Publishers.

Messerschmidt, J. (1997), *Crime as Structured Action: Gender, Race, Class and Crime in the Making*, Thousand Oaks: Sage.

Messner, S. and Rosenfeld, R. (1994), *Crime and the American Dream*, Belmont: Wadsworth.

Mignolo, W. (2012), *Local Histories/Global Designs: Coloniality, Subaltern Knowledges, and Border Thinking*, Princeton: Princeton University Press.

Miguel Cruz, J. (2010), 'Central American Maras: From Youth Street Gangs to Transnational Protection Rackets', *Global Crime*, 11(4), 379–398.

Miller, W. (1958), 'Lower Class Culture as a Generating Milieu of Gang Delinquency', *Journal of Social Issues*, 14(3), 5–19.

Miller, J. (2001a), 'Bringing the Individual Back In: A Commentary on Wacquant and Anderson', *Punishment & Society*, 3(1), 153–160.

Miller, J. (2001b), *One of the Guys: Girls, Gangs, and Gender*, New York: Oxford University Press, USA.

Miller, J. (2008), *Getting Played: African American Girls, Urban Inequality, and Gendered Violence*, New York: New York University Press.

Miller, V. (2011), *Understanding Digital Culture*, London: Sage.

Millie, A. (2008), 'Anti-social Behaviour, Behavioural Expectations and an Urban Aesthetic', *British Journal of Criminology*, 48(3), 379–394.

Millie, A. (2011), 'Value Judgments and Criminalization', *British Journal of Criminology*, 51(2), 278–295.

Mollenkopf, J. and Castells, M. (eds.) (1991), *Dual City: Restructuring New York*, New York: Russell Sage Foundation.

Mooney, G. and Danson, M. (1997), 'Beyond Culture City: Glasgow as a Dual City', in Jewson, N. and MacGregor, S. (eds.), *Transforming Cities*, London: Routledge.

Mooney, J. and Young, J. (2006), 'The Decline in Crime and the Rise of Anti-social Behaviour', *Probation Journal*, 53(4), 397–407.

Moore, J. (1978), *Homeboys: Gangs, Drugs and Prisons in the Barrios of Los Angeles*, Philadelphia: Temple University Press.

Moore, J., Vigil, D. and Garcia, R. (1983), 'Residence and Territoriality in Chicano Gangs', *Social Problems*, 31(2), 182–194.

Moore, N. (2013), Chicago's Gang Culture Remixed, JET Magazine, 13 March 2013, available at http://www.ebony.com/news-views/enough-chicagos-gang-culture-remixed-405#axzz2iROKS1uj, accessed 22/10/2013.

Morselli, C., Turcotte, M. and Tenti, V. (2010), *The Mobility of Criminal Groups*, Ottawa: Public Safety Canada.

Muggleton, D. (2000), *Inside Subculture: The Postmodern Meaning of Style*, Oxford: Berg.

Muggleton, D. and Weinzierl, R. (eds.) (2003), *The Post-Subcultures Reader*, Oxford: Berg.

Mullins, C. (2006), *Holding Your Square: Masculinities, Streetlife and Violence*, Collumpton: Willan.

Murray, C. (1990), *The Emerging British Underclass*, London: IEA Health and Welfare Unit.

Muzzatti, S. (2010), ' "Drive it like you stole it": A Cultural Criminology of Car Commercials', in Hayward, K. and Presdee, M. (eds.), *Framing Crime: Cultural Criminology and the Image*, London: Routledge, 138–155.

Naomi, K. (2000), *No Logo: Taking Aim at the Brand Bullies*, New York: Picador.

Nayak, A. (2006), 'Displaced Masculinities: Chavs, Youth and Class in the Post-Industrial City', *Sociology*, 40(5), 813–831.

Neate, P. (2003), *Where You're At: Notes from the Frontline of a Hip-hop Planet*, London: Bloomsbury.

Newman, K. (1999), *No Shame in My Game: The Working Poor in the Inner City*, New York: Random House.

Nightingale, C. (1993), *On the Edge*, New York: Basic Books.

Nowacki, J. (2012), 'Sugar, Spice, and Street Codes: The Influences of Gender and Family Attachment on Street Code Adoption', *Deviant Behavior*, 33(10), 831–844.

Nyamnjoh, F. (2000), ' "For Many are Called but Few are Chosen": Globalisation and Popular Disenchantment in Africa', *African Sociological Review/Revue Africaine de Sociologie*, 4(2), 1–45.

O'Brien, K. (forthcoming), *Dealing Tac: Young People, Gender and Neighbourhood Drug Markets*, London: Routledge.

O'Connell, S. (2006), 'From Toad of Toad Hall to the "Death Drivers" of Belfast: An Exploratory History of "Joyriding"', *British Journal of Criminology*, 46(3), 455–469.

O'Sullivan, E. (1997), 'Juvenile Justice and the Regulation of the Poor: "Restored to virtue, to society and to God"', *Irish Criminal Law Journal*, 7(2), 171–194.

Osumare, H. (2002), 'Global Breakdancing and the Intercultural Body', *Dance Research Journal*, 34(2), 30–45.

Padilla, F. (1992), *The Gang as an American Enterprise*, Piscataway Township: Rutgers University Press.

Parenti, C. (2008), *Lockdown America: Police and Prisons in the Age of Crisis*, New York: Verso.

Park, R., Burgess, E. and McKenzie, R. (1925), *The City: Suggestions for Investigation of Human Behaviour in the Urban Environment*, Chicago: University of Chicago Press.

Parker, H. (1974), *View from the Boys: A Sociology of Downtown Adolescents*, London: David & Charles.

Pavis, S. and Cunningham-Burley, S. (1999), 'Male Youth Street Culture: Understanding the Context of Health-Related Behaviours', *Health Education Research*, 14(5), 583–596.

Pearson, G. (1984), *Hooligan: A History of Respectable Fears*, London: Palgrave Macmillan.

Pearson, J. (2013), *The Profession of Violence: The Rise and Fall of the Kray Twins*, London: Bloomsbury Publishing.

Perkins, W. (ed.) (1996), *Droppin' Science: Critical Essays on Rap Music and Hip Hop Culture*, Philadelphia: Temple University Press.

Phillips, S. (2009), 'Crip Walk, Villain Dance, Pueblo Stroll: The Embodiment of Writing in African American Gang Dance', *Anthropological Quarterly*, 82(1), 69–97.

Pickering, J., Kintrea, K. and Bannister, J. (2012), 'Invisible Walls and Visible Youth Territoriality Among Young People in British Cities', *Urban Studies*, 49(5), 945–960.

Pieslak, J. (2009), *Sound Targets: American Soldiers and Music in the Iraq War*, Bloomington: Indiana University Press.

Pitts, J. (2003), *The New Politics of Youth Crime*, Lyme Regis: Russell House.

Pitts, J. (2008), *Reluctant Gangsters: The Changing Face of Youth Crime*, Abington: Taylor & Francis.

Polhemus, T. (1994), *Streetstyle: From Sidewalk to Catwalk*, London: Thames and Hudson.

Polsky, N. (1967), *Hustlers Beats and Others*, Chicago: Aldine.

Pountain, D. and Robins, D. (2000), *Cool Rules: Anatomy of an Attitude*, London: Reaktion Books.

Poynting, S. (1999), 'When Zero Tolerance Looks Like Racial Intolerance: Lebanese Youth Gangs, Discrimination and Resistance', *Current Issues in Criminal Justice*, 11(1), 74.

Presdee, M. (2000), *Cultural Criminology and the Carnival of Crime*, London: Routledge.

Presser, L. (2009), 'The Narratives of Offenders', *Theoretical Criminology*, 13(2), 177–200.

Pryce, K. (1986), *Endless Pressure: A Study of West Indian Lifestyles in Britain*, 2nd ed., Bristol: Bristol Classical Press.

Quinn, E. (2000), '"Who's The Mack?": The Performativity and Politics of the Pimp Figure in Gangsta Rap', *Journal of American Studies*, 34(1), 115–136.

Quinn, E. (2005), *Nuthin' but a 'G' Thang: The Culture and Commerce of Gangsta Rap*, New York: Columbia University Press.

Qurashi, F. (2013), *British Muslim Radicalism*, Unpublished PhD Dissertation, Canterbury: University of Kent.

Ramsey, G. (2003), *Race Music: Black Cultures from Bebop to Hip-Hop*, Berkley: University of California Press.

Raz, J. (1992), 'Self-Presentation and Performance in the Yakuza Way of Life', in Goodman, R. and Refsing, K. (eds.), *Ideology and Practice in Modern Japan*, London: Routledge.

Reiner, R. (2000), *The Politics of the Police*, Oxford: Oxford University Press.

Reynolds, T. (2013), ' "Them and Us": "Black neighbourhoods" as a Social Capital Resource Among Black Youths Living in Inner-City London', *Urban Studies*, 50(3), 484–498.

Rinehart, R. (2008), 'ESPN's X Games, Contests of Opposition, Resistance, Co-option, and Negotiation', in Atkinson, M. and Young, K. (eds.), *Tribal Play: Subcultural Journeys Through Sport*, Vol. 4, Bingley: Emerald Group Publishing, 175–195.

Rivera, R., Marshall, W. and Hernandez, D. (eds.) (2009), *Reggaeton*, Durham: Duke University Press.

Roberts, D. (2004), 'The Social and Moral Cost of Mass Incarceration in African American Communities', *Stanford Law Review*, 89(3), 1271–1305.

Roberts, S. (2013) 'Boys will be boys...won't they? Change and continuities in contemporary young working-class masculinities', *Sociology*, 47(4), 671–686.

Robins, D. and Cohen, P. (1978), *Knuckle Sandwich. Growing up in the Working-Class City*, Harmondsworth: Penguin.

Rose, T. (1994), *Black Noise: Rap Music and Black Culture in Contemporary America*, Middletown: Wesleyan University Press.

Rushkoff, D. (2001), *The Merchants of Cool* (Frontline Documentary Film), New York: PBS, available at http://www.pbs.org/wgbh/pages/frontline/shows/cool/, accessed 28/01/2015.

Sampson, R., Raudenbush S. and Earls, F. (1997), 'Neighborhoods and Violent Crime: A Multilevel Study of Collective Efficacy', *Science*, 277(5328), 918–924.

Sampson, R. and Wilson, W. (1995), 'Toward a Theory of Race, Crime, and Urban Inequality', in Gabbidon, S. and Taylor Greene, H. (eds.), *Race, Crime, and Justice: A Reader*, New York: Routledge, 177–190.

Sanchez, M. (2006), 'Insecurity and Violence as a New Power Relation in Latin America', *The Annals of the American Academy of Political and Social Science*, 606(1), 178–195.

Sanchez-Jankowski, M. (1991), *Islands in the Street: Gangs and American Urban Society*, Berkley: University of California Press.

Sanchez-Jankowski, M. (2003), 'Gangs and Social Change', *Theoretical Criminology*, 7(2), 191–216.

Sandberg, S. (2008a), 'Black Drug Dealers in a White Welfare State: Cannabis Dealing and Street Capital in Norway', *British Journal of Criminology*, 48(5), 604–619.

Sandberg, S. (2008b), 'Street Capital: Ethnicity and Violence on the Streets of Oslo', *Theoretical Criminology*, 12(2), 153–171.

Sandberg, S. (2010), 'What Can "lies" Tell us About Life? Notes Towards a Framework of Narrative Criminology', *Journal of Criminal Justice Education*, 21(4), 447–465.

Sandberg, S. and Pedersen, W. (2009), *Street Capital: Black Cannabis Dealers in a White Welfare State*, Bristol: The Policy Press.

Sanders, B. (2005), *Youth Crime and Youth Culture in the Inner City*, Oxon: Routledge.

Sassen, S. (1999), *Globalization and its Discontents: Essays on the new Mobility of People and Money*, New York: New Press.

Sassen, S. (2007), 'Introduction: Deciphering the Global', in Sassen, S. (ed.), *Deciphering the Global: Its Scales, Spaces and Subjects*, London: Routledge.

Sassen, S. (2010), 'A Savage Sorting of Winners and Losers: Contemporary Versions of Primitive Accumulation', *Globalizations*, 7(1–2), 23–50.

Savage, M. (2000), *Class Analysis and Social Transformation*, Buckingham: Open University Press.

Schuilenburg, M. and Hayward, K. (2014), 'To Resist – To Create? Some Thoughts on the Concept of Resistance in Cultural Criminology', *Tijdschrift over Cultuur & Criminaliteit*, 4(1), 22–36.

Scott, G. (2004), ' "It's a Sucker's Outfit": How Urban Gangs Enable and Impede the Integration of Ex-convicts', *Ethnography*, 5(1), 107–140.

Scott, J. C. (2008), *Weapons of the Weak: Everyday Forms of Peasant Resistance*, New Haven: Yale University Press.

Seabourne, M. (2011), Essay in Seaborne, M. and Sparham, A. (eds.), *London Street Photography*, London: Dewi Lewis Publishing.

Sellin, T. (1938), 'Culture Conflict and Crime', *American Journal of Sociology*, 44(1), 97–103.

Sharp, D. and Atherton, S. (2007), 'To Serve and Protect?: The Experiences of Policing in the Community of Young People from Black and Other Ethnic Minority Groups', *British Journal of Criminology*, 47(5), 746–763.

Shaw, C. and McKay, H. (1942), *Juvenile Delinquency and Urban Areas*, Chicago: University of Chicago Press.

Shein, M. (1993), 'Racial Disparity in Crack Cocaine Sentencing', *Criminal Justice Magazine*, 8, 28.

Sherman, L. (2010), What Will Happen to Tommy Hilfiger, Fashionista, 5 March 2010, available at http://fashionista.com/2010/03/what-will-happen-to-tommy-hilfiger/, accessed 15/10/13.

Shilling, C. (2012), *The Body and Social Theory*, London: Sage.

Shover, N. and Honaker, D. (1992), 'The Socially Bounded Decision Making of Persistent Property Offenders', *The Howard Journal of Criminal Justice*, 31(4), 276–293.

Sibley, D. (1995), *Geographies of Exclusion: Society and Difference in the West*, London: Routledge.

Silver, T. and Chalfant, H. (1983), *Style Wars* (PBS Broadcast Documentary Film), New York: PBS.

Silverman, D. (2004), 'Street Crime and Street Culture', *International Economic Review*, 45(3), 761–786.

Silverstone, D. and Savage, S. (2010). Farmers, Factories and Funds: Organised Crime and Illicit Drugs Cultivation within the British Vietnamese Community, *Global Crime, 11*(1), 16–33.

Silverstone, D. (2011), 'A Response to: Morselli, C., Turcotte, M. and Tenti, V. (2010) The Mobility of Criminal Groups', *Global Crime*, 12(3), 189–206.

Simon, J. (2007), *Governing Through Crime: How the War on Crime Transformed American Democracy and Created a Culture of Fear*, Oxford: Oxford University Press.

Skeggs, B. (1997), *Formations of Class & Gender: Becoming Respectable*, London: Sage.

Skeggs, B. (2004), *Class, Self, Culture*, London: Routledge.

Skeggs, B. (2011), 'Imagining Personhood Differently: Person Value and Autonomist Working-class Value Practices', *The Sociological Review*, 59(3), 496–513.

Skelton, T. and Gough, K. (2013), 'Introduction: Young People's im/mobile Urban Geographies', *Urban Studies*, 50(3), 455–466.

Sklansky, D. (1994), 'Cocaine, Race, and Equal Protection', *Stanford Law Review*, 47, 1283.

Slim, I. (2009), *Pimp*, Edinburgh: Canongate Books.

Smith, N. (1996), *The New Urban Frontier: Gentrification and the Revanchist City*, London: Routledge.

Smith, N. (2002), 'New Globalism, New Urbanism: Gentrification as Global Urban Strategy', *Antipode*, 34(3), 427–450.

Sneed, P. (2008), 'Favela Utopias: The Bailes Funk in Rio's Crisis of Social Exclusion and Violence', *Latin American Research Review*, 43(2), 57–79.

Snyder, G. (2006), 'Graffiti Media and the Perpetuation of an Illegal Subculture', *Crime Media Culture*, 2(1), 93–101.

Snyder, G. (2009), *Graffiti Lives: Beyond the Tag in New York's Urban Underground*, New York: New York University Press.

Snyder, G. (2012), 'The City and the Subculture Career: Professional Street Skateboarding in LA', *Ethnography*, 13(3), 306–329.

Sommers, M. (2003), *Urbanization, War, and Africa's Youth at Risk: Towards Understanding and Addressing Future Challenges*, Atlanta: CARE.

Spatial Information Design Lab (2009), *Justice Reinvestment New Orleans*, New York: Columbia University Graduate School of Architecture, Planning and Preservation, available at http://www.spatialinformationdesignlab.org/MEDIA/JR_NewOrleans.pdf, accessed 22/04/13.

Spergel, I. (2007) *Reducing Youth Gang Violence: The Little Village Gang Project in Chicago*, Lanham: Rowman Altamira.

Spiegler, M. (1996), 'Marketing Street Culture', *American Demographics*, 18(11), 28–34.

Springhall, J. (1998), *Youth, Popular Culture and Moral Panics: Penny Gaffs to Gangsta-Rap, 1830–1996*, Basingstoke: Palgrave Macmillan.

Squires, P. and Stephen, D. (2005), *Rougher Justice: Young People and Antisocial Behaviour*, Cullompton: Willan Publishing.

Stallybrass, P. and White, A. (1986), *The Poetics and Politics of Transgression*, London: Methuen.

Staples, R. (1975), 'Black Crime, White Racism and American Justice: An Application of the Colonial Model to Explain Crime and Race', *Phylon*, 36(1), 14–22.

Stehlik, L. (2012), 'Chief Keef Takes Chicago's Drill Sound Overground', *The Guardian*, Friday 16 November 2012, available at http://www.guardian.co.uk/music/2012/nov/16/chief-keef-chicago-drill-rap.

Stephens, D. and Phillips, L. (2003), 'Freaks, Gold Diggers, Divas and Dykes: The Socio-Historical Development of African American Female Adolescent Scripts', *Sexuality and Culture*, 7, 3–47.

Stephenson, S. (2001), 'Street Children in Moscow: Using and Creating Social Capital', *The Sociological Review*, 49(4), 530–547.

Stewart, E. and Simons, R. (2010), 'Race, Code of the Street and Violent Delinquency: A Multilevel Investigation of Neighbourhood Street Culture and Individual Norms of Violence', *Criminology*, 48(2), 569–605.

Stewart, E., Schreck, C. and Simons, R. (2006) 'I Ain't Gonna Let no One Disrespect Me: Does the Code of the Street Reduce or Increase Violent Victimization Amongst African-American Adolescents', *Journal of Research in Crime and Delinquency*, 43, 427–458.

Stolzoff, N. (2000), *Wake the Town and Tell the People: Dancehall Culture in Jamaica*, Washington, DC: Duke University Press Books.

Sullivan, J. (2011), 'Future Conflict: Criminal Insurgencies, Gangs and Intelligence', in Gilman, N., Goldhammer, J. and Weber, S. (eds.), *Deviant Globalization: Black Market Economy in the 21st Century*, New York: Bloomsbury Publishing.

Sumner, C. (1994), *The Sociology of Deviance: An Obituary*, New York: Continuum.

Sunshine, J. and Tyler, T. (2003), 'The Role of Procedural Justice and Legitimacy in Public Support for Policing', *Law and Society Review*, 37(3), 513–548.

Suttles, G. (1968), *The Social Order of the Slum*, Chicago: University of Chicago Press.

Sweney, M. (2013), YouTube Video Channel SB.TV Wins Private Equity Backing, *theguardian.com*, 21 October 2013, available at http://www.theguardian.com/media/2013/oct/21/youtube-video-channel-sbtv, accessed on 06/01/14.

Terrill, W. and Mastrofski, S. (2002), 'Situational and Officer-based Determinates of Police Coercion', *Justice Quarterly*, 19, 215–248.

Thompson, E. P. (1963), *The Making of the English Working Class*, London: Victor Gollancz Ltd.

Thompson, R. (1973), 'An Aesthetic of the Cool', *African Arts*, 7(1), 41–91.

Thornberry, T. (ed.) (2003), *Gangs and Delinquency in a Developmental Perspective*, Cambridge: Cambridge University Press.

Thornton, S. (1995), *Club Cultures: Music, Media and Subcultural Capital*, Cambridge: Polity Press.

Thorsten, S. (1938), *Culture Conflict and Crime*, New Jersey: Social Science Research Council.

Thrasher, F. (1927/1963), *The Gang*, Abridged ed., Chicago: University of Chicago Press.

Tonry, M. (1996), *Malign Neglect: Race, Crime, and Punishment in America*, New York: Oxford University Press.

Tonry, M. (1997), 'Ethnicity, Crime, and Immigration', *Crime and Justice*, 21, 1–29.

Treadwell, J., Briggs, D., Winlow, S. and Hall, S. (2013), 'Shopocalypse Now Consumer Culture and the English Riots of 2011', *British Journal of Criminology*, 53(1), 1–17.

Turk, A. (1969), *Criminality and Legal Order*, Chicago: Rand McNally.

Tyler, T. (2004), 'Enhancing Police Legitimacy', *Annals of the American Academy of Political & Social Science*, 593, 84–89.

Tyler, T. and Wakslak, C. (2004), 'Profiling and Police Legitimacy: Procedural Justice, Attributions of Motive, and Acceptance of Police Authority', *Criminology*, 42(2), 253–282.

Vaidyanathan, R. (2011), *Big Buttocks: Where Does Our Obsession Come from?* BBC News 11 February 2011, available at http://www.bbc.co.uk/news/world-us-canada-12411274, accessed 15/10/13.

Valentine, G. (1996), 'Children Should Be Seen and Not Heard: The Production and Transgression of Adults' Public Space', *Urban Geography*, 17(3), 205–220.

Van Blerk, L. (2005), 'Negotiating Spatial Identities: Mobile Perspectives on Street Life in Uganda', *Children's Geographies*, 3(1), 5–21.

Van Hellemont, E. (2012), 'Gangland Online: Performing the Real Imaginary World of Gangstas and Ghettos in Brussels', *European Journal of Crime, Criminal Law and Criminal Justice*, 20, 165–180.

Venkatesh, S. (1997), 'The Social Organization of Street Gang Activity in an Urban Ghetto,' *American Journal of Sociology*, 103(1), 82–111.

Venkatesh, S. (2008), *Off the Books: The Underground Economy of the Urban Poor*, Cambridge: Harvard University Press.

Verán, C. (1999), 'The Rise and Fall and Rise of the B-Boy Kingdom', in Light, A. (ed.), *The Vibe History of Hip Hop*, New Jersey: Rutgers University Press.

Vidino, L. (2010), *The New Muslim Brotherhood in the West*, New York: Columbia University Press.

Vigil, J. (1988), *Barrio Gangs: Street life and identity in Southern California*, Austin: University of Texas Press.

Wacquant, L. (1999), 'Suitable Enemies', *Punishment and Society*, 1(2), 215–222.

Wacquant, L. (2002), 'Scrutinizing the Street: Poverty, Morality, and the Pitfalls of Urban Ethnography', *American Journal of Sociology*, 107(6), 1468–1532.

Wacquant, L. (2008), *Urban Outcasts: A Comparative Sociology of Advanced Marginality*, Cambridge: Polity Press.

Waddington, P. (1999), *Policing Citizens: Authority and rights*, London: University College Press.

Waldron, L. and Chambers, C. (2012), 'Macho Cops, Corner Boys and Soldiers: The Construction of Race and Masculinity on HBO's the Wire', in Bissler, D. and Conners, J. (eds.), *The Harms of Crime Media: Essays on the Perpetuation of Racism, Sexism and Class Stereotypes*, Jefferson: McFarland, 171–189.

Watson, R. (2011), ' "Daggering" and the Regulation of Questionable Broadcast Media Content in Jamaica', *Communication Law and Policy*, 16(3), 255–315.

Weber, M. (1962/2002), *The Protestant Ethic and the Spirit of Capitalism: And Other Writings*, London: Penguin.

West, C. (1993), *Race Matters*, London: Random House LLC.

West, C. and Zimmerman, D. (1987), 'Doing Gender', *Gender & Society*, 1(2), 125–151.

White, R. (2008), 'Disputed Definitions and Fluid Identities: The Limitations of Social Profiling in Relation to Ethnic Youth Gangs', *Youth Justice*, 8(2), 149–161.

White, R. (2009), 'Indigenous Youth and Gangs as Family', *Youth Studies Australia*, 28(3), 47–56.

White, R. and Mason, R. (2006), 'Youth Gangs and Youth Violence: Charting the Key Dimensions', *The Australia and New Zealand Journal of Criminology*, 39(1), 54–70.

Whyte, W. (1943), *Street Corner Society*, Chicago: University of Chicago Press.

Wild, M. (2004) 'Members of many Gangs: Childhood and Ethno-racial Identity on the Streets of Twentieth-century Urban America', in Gabaccia, D. and Leach, C. (eds.), *Immigrant Life in the US: Multi-disciplinary Perspectives*, New York: Routledge, 99–112.

Williams, C. (2013) *The Birth of Hip-Hop Fashion*, Wax Poetics Blog, 22 August 2013, available at http://www.waxpoetics.com/features/articles/the-birth-of-hip-hop-fashion, accessed 15/10/13.

Williams, R. (1986), *Keywords: A Vocabulary of Culture and Society*, 2nd ed., London: Fontana Press.

Williams, T. (1990), *The Cocaine Kids: The Inside Story of a Teenage Drug Ring*, New York: Da Capo Press.

Willis, P. (1977), *Learning to Labour: How Working Class Kids Get Working Class Jobs*, Westmead: Saxonhouse.

Wilson, J. and Kelling, G. (1982), 'Broken Windows', *Atlantic Monthly*, 249(3), 29–38.

Wilson, W. (1996), *The Truly Disadvantaged: The Inner City, the Underclass, and Public Policy*, Chicago: University of Chicago Press.

Winlow, S. (2001), *Badfellas: Crime, Tradition and New Masculinities*, Oxford: Berg Publishers.

Winlow, S. and Hall, S. (2006), *Violent Night: Urban Leisure and Contemporary Culture*, Oxford: Berg.

Winlow, S. and Hall, S. (2009), 'Retaliate First: Memory, Humiliation and Male Violence', *Crime, Media, Culture*, 5(3), 285–304.

Winton, A. (2004), 'Urban Violence: A Guide to the Literature', *Environment and Urbanization*, 16(2), 165–183.

Wright, R., Brookman F. and Bennett T. (2006), 'The Foreground Dynamics of Street Robbery in Britain', *British Journal of Criminology* 46(1), 1–16.

Yar, M. (2012), 'Crime, Media and the Will-to-Representation: Reconsidering Relationships in the New Media Age', *Crime, Media, Culture*, 8(3), 245–260.

Yates, J. (2006), '"You Just Don't Grass": Youth, Crime and "Grassing" in a Working Class Community', *Youth Justice*, 6(3), 195–210.

Young, J. (1999), *The Exclusive Society, Social Exclusion, Crime and Difference in Late Modernity*, London: Sage.

Young, J. (2003), 'Merton with Energy, Katz with Structure: The Sociology of Vindictiveness and the Criminology of Transgression', *Theoretical Criminology, 7*(3) 388–414.

Young, J. (2007), *The Vertigo of Late Modernity*, London: Sage.

Young, J. (2011), *The Criminological Imagination*, Cambridge: Polity Press.

Young, M. and Wilmott, P. (1957/2012), *Family and Kinship in East London*, London: Routledge.

Young, T. (2009), 'Girls and Gangs: "Shemale" Gangsters in the UK?', *Youth Justice*, 9(3), 224–238.

Youth Justice Board, (2012), Young People and the August 2011 Disturbances, London: Youth Justice Board, available at: http://yjbpublications.justice.gov.uk/en-gb/Scripts/prodView.asp?idproduct=503&eP= , accessed 05/12/2014.

Zorbaugh, H. (1925), *The Gold Coast and the Slum*, Chicago: University of Chicago Press.

Media References

80 Blocks from Tiffany's (1979), Dir. Gary Weis, Above Average Productions.

A Clockwork Orange (1971), Dir. Stanley Kubrick, Warner Bros. Pictures.

Baby Got Back (1992), Sir Mix-a-lot, Def American Records.

Boyz n the Hood (1991), Dir. John Singleton, Columbia Pictures.

Casino Royale (2006), Dir. Martin Campbell, Columbia Pictures.

City of God (2002), Dirs. Fernando Meirelles and Katia Lund, 02 Filmes.

District 13 (2004), Dir. Pierre Morel, Europacorp.

Dogtown and Z-Boys (2001), Dir. Stacy Peralta, Sony Picture Classics.

Doin it in the Park (2012), Dir. Bobbito Garcia, Goldcrest Films.

Ghosts of Cite de Soleil (2006), Dirs. Asger Leth and Milos Loncarevic, Sony BMG Pictures.

Grand Theft Auto: San Andreas (2004), Rockstar Games.

Little Ghetto Boy (1972), Donny Hathaway, Atco Records.

New Jack City (1991), Dir. Mario Van Peebles, Warner Bros. Pictures.

Original Pirate Material (2002), The Streets, Warner Music.

Rebel Without a Cause (1955), Dir. Nicholas Rey, Warner Bros. Pictures.

Something from Nothing: The Art of Rap (2012), Dirs. Ice-T and Andy Baybutt, Indomina Releasing.

Straight Outta Compton (1988), NWA, Ruthless Records.

The Message (1982), Grandmaster Flash and the Furious Five, Sugar Hill Records.

The Wire (2002–2008), Creator David Simon, HBO.

The Warriors (1979), Dir. Walter Hill, Paramount Pictures.

Index